✦ ✦ ✦

"This is the definitive book on the Malcolm Baldrige National Quality Award. No other author has so thoroughly researched the field; visited so many companies; interviewed so many key players; and read so extensively in the literature. The resulting database has been transformed into a book which resounds with the ring of reality. The title, *The Baldrige Quality System: The Do-It-Yourself Way to Transform Your Business* correctly describes what the book can do for operating organizations."

> —Dr. J.M. Jurann
> Founder, Juran Institute
> Malcolm Baldrige National Quality Award
> Board of Overseers

"*The Baldrige Quality System* unleashes the power of the Baldrige criteria as a business management model. With comprehensive research and insightful articulation, the author provides a roadmap to world class quality and superior competitive position. If you only have time to read one book on quality, read this one."

> —Arnold Weimerskirch
> Member, Panel of Judges, Malcolm
> Baldrige National
> Quality Award
> Corporate Quality Director
> Honeywell, Inc

"This book is a landmark effort and will be useful to any service or manufacturing organization that is seriously pursuing a goal of customer satisfaction through total quality management."

> —Debra A. Owens
> Director, Corporate Quality
> Strategy and Planning
> The Baxter Healthcare Corporation

The Baldrige Quality System

The Do-It-Yourself Way to Transform Your Business

— ✦ ✦ ✦ —

Stephen George

John Wiley & Sons, Inc.

New York • Chichester • Brisbane • Toronto • Singapore

To Ellen

Copyright ©1992 by Stephen George

Library of Congress Cataloging-in-Publication Data

George, Stephen, 1948-
  The Baldrige Quality System: The do-it-yourself way to transform your business / by Stephen George.
    p.   cm.
    Includes index.
    ISBN 0-471-55798-6
    1. Malcolm Baldrige National Quality Award. 2. Total quality management–United States. I. Title.
HD62 15.G46 1992
658, 5′62–dc20   92-8636 CIP

Printed in the United States of America.
10 9 8 7 6 5 4 3 2 1

CONTENTS

———————————— ✦ ✦ ✦ ————————————

ACKNOWLEDGMENTS

✦ ✦ ✦

I have carried the dream of writing a book since I was a child in the small town of Pomeroy, Iowa. In my mind, I have composed these acknowledgments time and again. It is a relief to have the book written; it is a pleasure to have the opportunity to acknowledge people who are important in my life:

My parents, Bob and Wanda George, for instilling in me a belief in my abilities and a tenacity to do what it takes to get the job done.

My brother and friend, Dave, and my sisters, Paula Sawlidi and Monica Teuscher, for their unwavering support.

Bob and Nancy Bevan, high school teachers I have long wanted to thank in print for the staying power of their encouragement.

Howard DeMotts, who took a "leap of faith" when he gave me my first writing job and all the assignments that followed.

My friends, Jeff and Juli Rasmussen, who prove you do not need a good fence to have good neighbors.

My in-laws, Ed and Laura Carroll, for their generosity and kindness.

Dr. J. M. Juran, for his interest in this project and his encouragement.

My four "readers" who critiqued the first draft of this book and shared their reactions: Curt Reimann at NIST, Bill Lesner at Cadillac, Debra Owens at Baxter Healthcare, and Mike Horsman at St. Paul Fire and Marine Insurance Company.

Julia Peterson and Mary Louise Lose at the Cargill Information Center, who found valuable Baldrige-related articles in more publications and in less time than I ever could have.

The many others who contributed to this book, including Chuck Aubrey, Jim Buckman, Liz Swanson, John Cooney, Sam Malone, Gary Floss, Robert Galvin, Paul Noakes, Roger Kane, Hope Scamehorn, Lori Kirkland, Ron Kubinski, Kathy Leedy, Ann Rothgeb, Bob Lea, Jane McAuliffe,

Mary Lo Sardo, Frank McCabe, Bob McGrath, David Mitchell, Cliff Moore, Paul Noakes, Jean Otte, Scott Pfotenhauer, Jeff Rendall, Ron Schmidt, John Steel, Maureen Steinwall, Kent Sterett, John Vinyard, Arnie Weimerskirch, John West, Dan Whelan, and D. Otis Wolkins.

My children, Dan, Kate, Allie, and Zack, who contribute precious perspective to the book and enormous joy to my life.

My wife, Ellen Carroll George, who shared the dream and more: she worked overtime, many times, to make this book possible. Her ability to give unselfishly is a gift I am very lucky to receive.

PREFACE

◆ ◆ ◆

I was first introduced to the notion of "do-it-yourself quality" by Curt Reimann, director of the Baldrige program. During a conversation at his offices in Gaithersburg, he referred to the Baldrige criteria as "more of a do-it-yourself kit than has previously been on the market."

I like the idea of do-it-yourself quality. It puts the responsibility for quality improvement in the hands of the people who want to improve—and *can* improve—their organizations. It is the opposite of "delegate-to-someone-else quality," a common response when people do not understand what quality improvement means, or where to start, or what to do. Anxious to do *something* to improve quality, they delegate it to someone in their department, to the company's quality professional, or to outside quality consultants. They delegate *quality,* not just improvement, because the whole business seems too complex.

Well, it *is* complex, but it cannot be delegated. Each individual must take personal responsibility for quality, or efforts to improve it will flounder and fail. The Baldrige criteria stress driving an organization's quality values from senior executives to all managers and supervisors, and then to all employees. When every member of the organizations takes responsibility for quality, quality improves.

"Do-it-yourself quality" implies that quality improvement is a do-it-yourself effort. *Of course it is.* Study any quality leader anywhere in the world and you will discover that it made its own decisions about pursuing quality improvement, charted its own course, improved its own processes, trained and recognized its own people, identified and served its customers, and managed all the other tasks necessary to improve. The company, which is to say the people who *are* the company, did it themselves. You can, too.

But you can't do it alone. An essential part of the Baldrige "kit" is the desire and ability to learn from others, whether through benchmarking, making competitive comparisons, studying quality leaders, taking quality training, or hiring quality consultants.

Do-it-yourself quality does not mean do-it-*all-by*-yourself. If you decided to redecorate a bedroom, your list of tools and materials might range from measuring tapes and putty knives to paint and wallpaper, from "how-to" books to professional advice from your neighborhood hardware store manager. It is still a do-it-yourself project, however, because *you* decided to do it, *you* took responsibility for doing it, *you* determined a course of action, and *you* performed or supervised the steps in the process.

The same is true for do-it-yourself quality. Pick any Baldrige Award winner and you will find that it practices a distinct "house brand" of quality that is constantly challenged and improved by "stealing shamelessly" from every possible source. An innovate way of measuring? We can use that. A new problem-solving tool? We'll try it. A creative approach to planning? We'll borrow it. Ideas on benchmarking? We'll take them.

Neither the Baldrige criteria nor the do-it-yourself quality concept precludes popular quality philosophies, programs, solutions, or the teachings of our country's best-known quality gurus. Zytec, which won a Baldrige Award in 1991, was founded on and continues to be guided by W. Edward Demings' principles. J.M. Juran, who has been an advocate of the Baldrige program, is a member of the program's guiding body, the Board of Overseers. Milliken, which won a Baldrige Award in 1989, took advice and guidance from Philip Crosby in the early 1980s.

The Baldrige program is a do-it-yourself kit for transforming your organization. How you use the kit and the other quality resources available is up to you.

"For companies that have not invested in quality," Reimann said, "the Baldrige criteria represent a big bite, but instead of taking it piece by piece, some feel they need help. My judgment is that that's part of the mistake they're making. Chances are that 99.9 percent of these companies have within their ranks the people who could pick this apart and say, 'Here's what it means, boss. Let's go through it. Here are some things we can do now. Here are some things we can do six months from now. Here are some things we can do a year from now. Let's get on with it.'"

That is a do-it-yourself's attitude: "Let's get on with it." I believe that *The Baldrige Quality System: The Do-It-Yourself Way to Transform Your Business* is a good place to start.

Let's get on with it.

Stephen George
June 3, 1992

PART ONE

---✦ ✦ ✦---

The Baldrige System

CHAPTER 1

The Baldrige Do-It-Yourself Kit

Through 1991, the Malcolm Baldrige National Quality Award had been given to 12 companies. Each has its own unique quality philosophy, objectives, and system, but together they proclaim a single compelling truth: *You can do it, too—and you can do it yourself.*

You can understand the scope and operation of your organization's total quality system, no matter what type of organization it is: service company, manufacturing company, nonprofit organization, educational institution, or government agency.

You can deepen senior management's commitment to quality and spread it throughout your organization, creating a unified team working together to achieve the same goals.

You can construct a systematic approach to managing the information you need to ensure and improve your competitive performance.

You can plan for quality leadership: in five years, in one year, next month, this week.

You can develop a trained, empowered, and enthusiastic workforce dedicated to continuous improvement.

You can initiate improvements that address the most serious deficiencies—and the most promising opportunities—in all of your processes.

You can gain, retain, and delight customers by focusing every part of your quality system—every person, every task, every goal, every decision—on meeting your customers' needs and expectations.

You can become a quality leader. All you need is the confidence of a do-it-yourselfer and the right tools for the job.

Confidence comes from knowing what to expect and how to respond. It begins with a basic understanding of the system, whether that system is plumbing, electrical, mechanical, or quality. Like any system, a quality system can seem mysterious, complex, and forbidding. But like any system, it can be understood with a little assistance and a lot of tenacity.

As one CEO said, "It's not part of some Japanese samurai tradition. Quality is tangible, measurable, and achievable by any organization." The Baldrige Award winners prove this point. Throughout this book you will read how they and other quality leaders have achieved success in different areas of their quality systems. These areas are called "categories" by the Baldrige criteria. In this book you will learn what the categories are and what they include, and you will see them come to life through America's quality role models.

As you become familiar with the nature of a quality system, you will want to begin working on your own. To do that you will need tools, and one of the best tools on the market is the Baldrige criteria.

In fact, *the Baldrige Award program is a do-it-yourself kit for transforming your organization.* Companies that have discovered the kit have used it to learn about and improve their quality systems. This book describes how they have used the Baldrige criteria, the application process, the feedback to their applications, the site visit experience, and other aspects of the Baldrige program to dramatically improve quality.

THE BALDRIGE PATH TO QUALITY

The Baldrige Award program "was designed as a value system, an education/communications tool, a vehicle for cooperation and a device to help evaluate quality standards," says Curt Reimann, director of the Baldrige program. "It's adaptable to the needs of any organization, and is being used throughout the United States in four basic areas: assessment, setting up a quality system, communications, and education and training."

The Baldrige Award program is run by the National Institute of Standards and Technology (NIST), which led the development of the criteria and the award process. Companies can apply in the manufacturing, service, or small business (500 full-time employees or less) categories. To apply, they complete a report responding to the Baldrige criteria, which address key requirements for achieving quality excellence. (The 1992 Baldrige criteria are presented in Appendix A.)

Members of the Board of Examiners evaluate the applications and recommend up to two award winners per category per year. In the first four years of the program, eight manufacturing companies, one service company, and three small businesses have won the Baldrige Award.

You will find details of the Baldrige Award program—how it was created, how it is organized, and what the criteria address—in Chapter 3. Chapters 4 through 9 walk you through the criteria category by category, presenting each dimension of a total quality system through the processes, systems, and experiences of our country's quality leaders.

Of all the Baldrige Award program elements, the most valuable is the Baldrige criteria, which organizations use to assess their quality systems. The criteria define the key requirements an organization must focus on to achieve quality excellence. The fact that such an all-encompassing definition never existed before is one reason American managers have had so much trouble getting their arms around quality.

"It's really a genius document, as far as I'm concerned, because it allows you to go back to the basics and see the common thread that exists in everything you do," says Joe Rocca, one of the leaders of IBM Rochester's 1990 Baldrige Award–winning application effort. "Things net down to some very basic fundamentals that you know are at work. If you can put your finger on them, you look at life with a clearer vision of what it's about and why things are happening."

Clearer vision is a major benefit of the Baldrige criteria. The bits and pieces you have collected about what it takes to instill and improve quality can be found in the criteria. It is a systematic guide to any organization's quality system. "I think of it as a Dewey Decimal System," says Cliff Moore, a quality consultant and Baldrige Award judge. "The companies I work with have lots of good things in place but they haven't marshaled their forces. It's like a thousand ships in the water that haven't yet formed an armada."

When she talks about quality and the Baldrige criteria, Debra Owens, director of corporate quality strategy and planning for Baxter Healthcare and a Baldrige examiner for four years, begins with a slide showing sailboats adrift in a sea and the sun, labeled "World Class," distant on the horizon. Each sail is identified by a quality acronym: SPC, EI, JIT, and others. Her next slide shows the sailboats lined up and heading toward the "World Class" sun (see Figure 1.1). On both sides of the armada are buoys marked "BQA criteria." "The Baldrige criteria are tools to diagnose the health of your organization," Owens says. "They're not a standard but a model you use to create your own standard."

The criteria are intentionally and fiercely nonprescriptive. They can help you figure out where your quality system needs to be fixed, but they cannot tell you how to fix it. They do, however, present quality truths, such as management-led and customer-driven, and suggest ways you can find

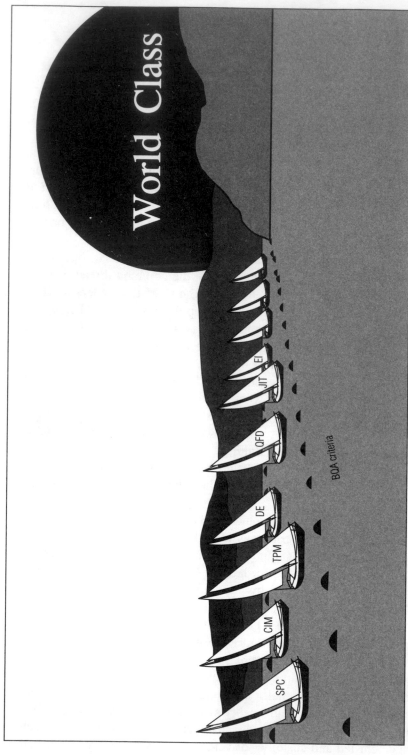

Figure 1.1 An illustration of sailboats aligned and heading toward a sun labeled "World Class." (Courtesy of Debra Owens, Baxter Healthcare)

the answers, such as benchmarking and competitive comparisons. They indicate the kinds of data you should be gathering for your planning and decision making. They suggest what you should be measuring. And they also force you to examine your relationship with your customers, suppliers, and employees: who they are, what they expect from you, and how well you are meeting their expectations.

"Until the Baldrige criteria came along, I didn't have a good, firm way of evaluating a division's quality, of measuring it and encouraging the division to improve," says Arnold Weimerskirch, director of corporate quality for Honeywell. "With the advent of the criteria, suddenly we can measure quality. We can take an abstract notion and quantify it. Now we can go to a division and say, 'Tailor quality to your business; then we'll measure how you're doing using the criteria.' "

The criteria lay the road map to quality improvement before you, then put you on the right path to reach it. You will notice at several points in this book that people refer to the criteria as a road map, whereas others use the terms "framework," "model," and "blueprint." *Organizations across the country (and around the world) are using the Baldrige criteria as their primary means of assessing and improving quality.*

In 1991, NIST distributed 250,000 copies of the Baldrige Application Guidelines, the booklet that explains the Baldrige Award application process and presents the criteria. More than one-half were sent out *after* the deadline for application reports passed. Many companies and states reprint the guidelines for their own quality programs or awards, significantly increasing the number of copies in circulation.

Requests for the guidelines are not limited to those that can apply for the award. Nonprofit organizations, educational institutions, and government agencies are discovering that the criteria can be adapted to their own needs. The requests are not even limited to organizations in the United States. Foreign companies use the criteria in the same way that many American companies use them: as a self-assessment tool. Baldrige self-assessment courses regularly include people from non-U.S. companies who are eager to learn how to use the criteria to improve quality.

The criteria's popularity has surprised even those closest to the program. Kent Sterett, executive vice-president of quality for Southern Pacific Transportation Company, was active in lobbying for the legislation that created the Baldrige Award and in studying what the award program should look like. He was a Baldrige judge for four years.

"The number of companies that have applied isn't too surprising," Sterett says. "In Japan, you get maybe 10 applications for the Deming

Prize. Here, the idea was to encourage applications even though, when you get a hundred applications, it requires much more labor."

"What we didn't anticipate was cascading the use of the criteria beyond applying for the award," he says. "Two hundred thousand guidelines? I don't think any of us would have believed that. One thousand maybe. Twenty thousand in our wildest dreams. We favored the idea of using the criteria as a self-assessment, but we couldn't have imagined 250,000 copies."

Companies are hungry for a guide through the maze of quality programs, techniques, ideas, and personalities. They are using the criteria to assess their quality systems, to measure progress, to evaluate applicants for their own internal quality awards, to measure performance, and to improve quality. Their stories in Chapters 10 and 11 provide practical advice for companies curious about how they can use the criteria.

"The Baldrige criteria are an excellent, tough set of guidelines. If you apply them to your company, you can't help but improve," says Robert McGrath, quality consultant and Baldrige examiner who managed the preparation of Westinghouse Commercial Nuclear Fuel Division's Baldrige Award-winning application in 1988.

Many companies improve by completing application reports that explain how their quality systems compare to the Baldrige criteria. Some use their applications only as an assessment tool, learning from the process and from the finished report what areas need to be improved. Others actually apply for something—a company, city, regional, or state quality award, or the Baldrige Award.

To learn about the benefits of going through the application process, read Chapter 12. It outlines the effort involved in producing an application, including the time and money required, and describes the lessons companies have learned in the process. To find out how to proceed through the application process—how to organize, collect information, write the application, create graphics, and assess the report—read through the 14 steps explained in Chapters 13 and 14.

Chapter 15 tells how companies communicate their applications throughout their organizations and what happens when their applications earn them a Baldrige site visit. Chapter 16 profiles the dozen Baldrige Award winners from 1988 to 1991 and describes the benefits of winning and the demands placed on the winners.

You will come across these companies repeatedly throughout the book. They are America's quality leaders, role models for the shape world-class quality systems can take.

"I believe Americans learn by role modeling," Weimerskirch says. "I remember attending a regional quality conference where there were Baldrige examiners and Baldrige Award winners. When participants were given a choice of talking to either group, they gravitated toward the winners. The examiners could tell them what their companies needed to do to improve quality. The winners could tell them what *they* did to improve quality. The participants sought out the role models, not the experts."

Americans like stories. Examiners can give you theories and methods and programs. Winners tell stories about what they tried, what worked, and what they learned. To give you an idea of whose stories you are reading, I would like to briefly introduce the Baldrige Award winners. As I mentioned, you can learn more about why they won in Chapter 16. If you want to contact them, see the list of contacts in Appendix B.

THE BALDRIGE AWARD WINNERS

Globe Metallurgical Inc. (1988)

Globe manufactures silicon metal and ferrosilicon products. It has over 200 employees at two plants, one in Selma, Alabama, and the other at its headquarters in Beverly, Ohio. Its primary market is the automotive industry.

Westinghouse Commercial Nuclear Fuel Division (1988)

The Commercial Nuclear Fuel Division (CNFD) employs approximately 2,000 people at three sites in Pennsylvania and South Carolina. CNFD supplies about 40 percent of the U.S. market and 20 percent of the world market for fuel-rod assemblies used in nuclear power plants.

Motorola Inc. (1988)

Motorola, headquartered in Schaumburg, Illinois, has more than 100,000 employees. It produces a variety of products and is the world leader in two-way radio communications, radio paging communications systems and pagers, car telephone systems and telephones, modems, and many parts of the semiconductor industry.

Milliken & Company (1989)

Headquartered in Spartanburg, South Carolina, Milliken has 13,000 "associates" employed at 47 plants in the United States. It produces more than 45,000 textile and chemical products ranging from apparel fabrics and automotive fabrics to specialty chemicals and floor coverings.

Xerox Business Products and Systems (1989)

One of two Xerox Corporation businesses, Business Products and Systems (BP&S) employs more than 50,000 people at 83 U.S. locations. BP&S makes more than 250 types of document-processing equipment, with copiers and other duplicating equipment accounting for nearly 70 percent of its revenues.

Wallace Co., Inc. (1990)

Wallace is a family-owned distributor, primarily of pipe, valves, and fittings, to the chemical and petrochemical industries. Its 10 offices in Texas, Louisiana, and Alabama distribute directly in the Gulf Coast area and also serve international markets. The company, headquartered in Houston, has nearly 300 "associates."

IBM Rochester (1990)

IBM Rochester manufactures intermediate computer systems for the Application Business Systems line of products and hard disk drives for the Enterprise Systems line of products. More than 8,000 employees work at the 3.6 million-square-foot Rochester site.

Cadillac Motor Car Company (1990)

Cadillac employs about 10,000 people at its Detroit-area headquarters, four Michigan-based manufacturing plants, and 10 sales and service zone offices in the United States. In the domestic market, cars are sold through a network of 1,600 franchised dealerships.

Federal Express (1990)

Federal Express has over 84,000 employees at more than 1,650 sites tracking 1.5 million shipments daily, sorting at facilities in Memphis, Indianapolis, Newark, Oakland, Los Angeles, Anchorage, and Brussels, and shipping by land and through the largest air cargo fleet in the world. In 1989, Federal Express had 43 percent of the domestic delivery market.

Marlow Industries (1991)

Marlow makes small thermoelectric coolers that cool, heat, or stabilize the temperatures of electronic components in products ranging from medical diagnostic equipment to missile-guidance systems. It has 160 employees at its plant in Dallas.

Zytec Corporation (1991)

Zytec's 750+ employees design and manufacture electronic power supplies for domestic manufacturers who integrate Zytec's products into their systems, which range from computers to peripheral, medical, and office products, and test equipment. The company also repairs power supplies and CRT monitors. Zytec has two facilities in Minnesota: its headquarters in Eden Prairie and its manufacturing plant in Redwood Falls.

Solectron Corporation (1991)

Solectron has 2,300 employees in eight manufacturing plants in San José and one in Malaysia. The company does not design its own products but manufactures and assembles electronic equipment and systems designed by its customers, including complex printed circuit boards for telecommunications equipment, medical equipment, and computers.

This exemplary group offers something for almost everyone, from manufacturing companies to service companies, from quality systems that work for 160 people to quality systems that work for 100,000, from quality processes that produce electronics to quality processes that produce textiles, metal castings, cars, and nuclear fuel rods. And they are willing to share what they know. As the Baldrige Criteria state, "[award] recipients are expected to share information about their successful quality strategies with other U.S. organizations."

CRITICISM OF THE AWARD

As the most visible part of the Baldrige program, the award contest has drawn national attention to the Baldrige criteria and application process. "I don't particularly like contests myself," Reimann says, "but if we had the best quality standard in the universe handed down by the hand of God without a contest attached to it, I don't think we'd have been this far along. The contest adds spice."

It also adds controversy. The visibility of the Baldrige Award has made it a new target for business publications and consultants. "We were told early on that the media would be interested in the contest aspect and controversy but the good news aspect will not be covered very well," says Reimann, "and it's followed that path."

Articles in major publications, most notably *The Wall Street Journal* and *Fortune,* have focused the most attention on what companies have gone through to apply for the award. Spending large sums of money and/or hiring Baldrige experts to help with the application draw the most criticism. I will discuss both of these issues more fully in Chapter 12, but because these and other issues have influenced people's perception of the Baldrige Award, I think it is important to address them now.

For many people, the negative publicity is all they remember about the Baldrige Award. Instead of exploring whether the criteria can help their companies, they write the award program off as costing too much, being too difficult, creating too much work, adding unnecessary bureaucracy, being biased against small business and service companies, or setting quality back instead of moving it forward. Senior executives use these excuses to avoid using the criteria. Even those who value the criteria, including Baldrige Award winners and administrators, feel it is necessary to respond to the criticism.

Most of the charges, however, are groundless, misinformed, or extremely short-sighted, beginning with the most common complaint: It costs too much. In 1989, Xerox spent $800,000 during its application process. Critics justifiably cringe at the thought of spending nearly a million dollars for a quality award, but what the critics choose to ignore is what that money really bought. The primary goal of Xerox's application process was a total assessment of its quality system. When it finished that assessment, it had identified 500 problem areas that needed to be improved. The Xerox National Quality Award team condensed those areas into 51 problem sets, which it presented in a report to senior management.

Based on this report, management initiated a five-year effort to improve quality in six key areas:

1. Voice of the customer

2. Employee motivation and empowerment

3. Quality leadership by line management

4. Deployment of clear direction and objectives

5. Quality challenges—identified and met

6. Management by fact

David Kearns, Xerox's CEO at the time, said the assessment report was worth millions to his company. His estimate of its value puts the amount spent on the assessment into perspective.

Critics have taken Xerox's experience and assumed that every company must spend hundreds of thousands of dollars to apply for the Baldrige Award. That's baloney. At a news conference after the 1991 Baldrige Award ceremony, Ronald Schmidt, CEO of award-winning Zytec, said his company spent $8,900 on its application. Solectron estimates it spent $20,000. You can apply without spending a fortune.

The issue of consultants troubles critics who believe that no company should need consultants to apply for the Baldrige Award. Well, they don't. Throughout its entire 1990 application process, Cadillac did not use a single consultant. The fact that others chose to use consultants means only that they wanted expert assistance with the criteria or the process, much as one would hire an ad agency for expert help with advertising or an accounting firm for expert advice on financial matters. To imply that companies hire quality consultants to "buy the Baldrige" shows a complete ignorance of the evaluation process.

Much of the criticism directed at the Baldrige Award seems to be knee-jerk reaction to the critics' own prejudices. They believe the process should be free of outside influence and cost nothing. To them, that is the ideal. Any company falling short of their ideal gets blasted.

The criticism flies from all quarters. David Mason, an analyst at a "think tank" called the Heritage Foundation, admitted to *Incentive* magazine that he doesn't know a lot about corporate quality, but that a lot of the application process "depends on gamesmanship—fulfilling the application requirements, which are staggering—and what your political connections are." It requires a particularly warped lens, however, to see gamesmanship and political connections in the Baldrige Award process, as you will notice when you read Chapter 12.

Misguided criticism of the Baldrige Award has not been limited to quality neophytes. Some leading business and quality authorities have rebuked the award, most notably W. Edwards Deming, Tom Peters, and Philip Crosby.

In an article in the *Harvard Business Review,* Deming wrote that the Baldrige Award "contains nothing about management of quality. The award is focused purely on results." In fact, roughly two-thirds of the criteria are *not* focused on results, but are instead focused on how an organization approaches and deploys quality excellence in the areas of leadership, information and data, planning, human resources, processes, and customer satisfaction. And the other third measures the results of the organization's management of quality.

Peters has publicly expressed three major problems with the Baldrige program: (1) the criteria are "strangely silent on the topic of bureaucracy"; (2) they "celebrate a lifeless form of quality"; and (3) the lack of service company winners is perplexing because, according to Peters, "the top manufacturing companies in the United States can't hold a candle to the top service companies in the United States when it comes to understanding this [quality] stuff."

Curt Reimann, director of the Baldrige program, has read Peters's concerns. "I can understand where the concern about creating a bureaucracy comes from, but I don't think Mr. Peters has read the criteria line by line," Reimann says. "We were born nonprescriptive and that means nonprescriptive in every sense of the word. You don't have to have a customer service department. You don't have to have a quality department. You don't even have to be organized in a particular way."

The Baldrige criteria do not address bureaucracy because bureaucracy per se is not an issue. The issue is whether a company's quality system enables that company to understand and meet or exceed customer expectations. If a bureaucracy gets in the way of achieving this, then the bureaucracy becomes a quality issue. If it does not, the bureaucracy becomes an issue for management consultants to address.

Peters's second concern is easily refuted. The Baldrige Award winners are passionate about quality. They make thousands of presentations about their quality systems to groups across the country every year. They organize regular tours of their facilities and write articles. They work even harder to live up to their reputations as quality role models than they did to get them. You will hear their passion in the stories in this book, especially when they talk about their Baldrige site visits.

The dearth of service company winners is a problem only if you measure quality by anecdotal evidence. When you measure quality *systems,* the reverse of Peters's statement is closer to the truth: the top service companies cannot hold a candle to the top manufacturing companies.

Charles Aubrey has been a quality professional in the service industry for 17 years. He is vice-president and senior quality officer for Banc One Corporation, a senior Baldrige examiner, and president-elect of the American Society for Quality Control, the largest organization of quality professionals in the country. He disagrees with Peters's assessment. "It's not in my experience that the great majority of service companies have quality systems in place," Aubrey says. "Companies like American Express and MBNA America [the fourth largest bank credit card issuer in the United States] have a great customer focus, but they don't have pervasive quality systems. The lack of such systems could be the reason not many service companies have applied for or won the Baldrige Award."

Manufacturing companies were the first to feel the heat of global competition, and they were the first to learn how to compete with quality. Service companies are late to the quality bandwagon.

In an article in "The Quality Imperative," a special edition of *BusinessWeek,* a quality consulting company called Gunneson Group International reported that only "10 percent of American service companies today have any kind of quality program." According to Lakewood Research in Minneapolis, the average manufacturing company spends 20 to 40 percent more on employee training than business, health, and educational service companies, and it spends 80 percent more than the retail and wholesale trade. Manufacturers are about twice as likely as service companies to try self-managed work teams. Manufacturing still accounts for 75 percent of ASQC's membership.

In fact, when the criteria were first created in 1987, they had a strong manufacturing bias because most of the quality experts were in manufacturing. Reimann and others have worked hard to correct that. "I don't believe the criteria are slanted," Aubrey says. "Early on the language was slanted toward manufacturing jargon, but we've worked over four years to make it much more generic."

Crosby has expressed disappointment that the criteria are more concerned with the quality of processes than with customer satisfaction.

Customer satisfaction is actually the largest category in the criteria. Crosby also claims that the criteria do not reflect a modern system. "It's a 1960s system," he has said. The thousands of hours devoted by quality, marketing, and management professionals to improving the Baldrige criteria would suggest that the criteria accurately reflect current thinking about quality systems.

Having taken issue with their criticism, I also believe the Baldrige program can benefit from the counsel of these respected authorities. W. Edwards Deming's relentless pursuit of profound knowledge, reflected in his 14 Points for Management, sets high standards for the American quality movement. Deming is also a strong proponent of continuous innovation as the only way to retain customers.

Tom Peters recognizes the need for change, thrives on change, seeks companies that are innovative, and challenges our dearest assumptions. The more established the Baldrige program becomes, the more it will be threatened by complacency. The challenge will be to improve it at least as fast as the companies it measures.

Philip Crosby knows how to sell quality. The company he founded, Philip Crosby Associates, had $84 million in revenues from quality-related business in 1990. Crosby understands where companies are coming from, where they want to go, and how to get them to follow his lead. Such marketing savvy applied to the Baldrige program would help make it accessible to more companies.

One quality leader who has embraced the Baldrige program is Dr. J. M. Juran. Along with Deming and others, he helped the Japanese learn and implement total quality control after World War II. In 1951 he wrote the *Quality Control Handbook,* a complete reference guide to quality control. He has written several books and training courses since then, earning him international awards and honors. In 1979 he founded Juran Institute, which has become a respected quality consultant to companies worldwide.

Juran served for four years on the Baldrige Board of Overseers, the group responsible for ensuring that the award program fulfills its legislative mandate. He believes much of the attention given the Baldrige program has been misplaced. "*The Wall Street Journal* and *Fortune* have fallen into the trap of believing that filling out the application is the most important story," Juran says. "It's not. Meeting the criteria is the heroic effort."

The ways companies meet the criteria are revealed through the telling of their stories in this book. They are heroic for their clear vision, their single-minded determination, their willingness to fail, their ability to excel, and their eagerness to share. They are leading a national effort to compete globally on the strength of American quality.

"For a decade or more, a lot of people have beaten on the government, business leaders, trade associations, and professional associations," says Reimann. "They've asked, 'Why don't you do something about this mess? Why do you sit there and let other nations eat our lunch?' Well, here we are, making companies more competitive, working with them to define the elements of competitiveness, and alerting a lot of organizations to what they need to do to help the national effort."

What every company must do first is understand the scope of its own quality system. The next chapter offers a do-it-yourself guide to identifying the elements in *your* quality system.

CHAPTER 2

Improving Your Quality System

L ife does not lend itself to systems thinking. Busy chopping down trees, we know we are working in a forest, but so what? After this tree, another demands our attention, and then another, and if we stop to catch our breath, we may notice our fellow lumberjacks, the blue sky, even the other trees in the area. But who considers the forest, the larger system within which we function?

We live and work within systems. The family is a system. Schools, churches, health clubs, and restaurants are systems. Our community, city, state, region, and country are systems. A business is a fairly well-defined system, which contains many more systems defined by common goals, products, services, processes, or other dimensions.

One of those systems is the quality system. Depending on where you are on the quality improvement scale, your quality system may be pervasive, or it may be barely visible. But even if you are not sure where to find it, you have a quality system.

In *Kaizen,* Masaaki Imai's excellent book on managing quality improvement, Imai describes a quality system as a sphere that "extends vertically from top management to middle management, from middle management to supervisors, from supervisors to workers, and from workers to part-time workers. This is also why it extends horizontally from vendors on one end to customers on the other."

A quality system touches every part of an organization. Every decision made, every action taken, every customer served reflects that system. Here are two examples:

1. Intent on satisfying its customers (the shareholders), senior management decides to boost productivity by implementing a "hot" quality program (just-in-time manufacturing, or JIT), by laying off some middle managers, and by exhorting the remaining employees to do a better job. Banners and posters appear saying "Quality Is Everyone's Job" and "Think Quality." After learning the basics of JIT, supervisors are told to "hit the ground running."

Meanwhile, production workers grumble about having more work to do and customers complain because delivery has slowed. The effect on the bottom line is negligible or worse.

2. Customer needs and expectations drive the company's actions. In this case, the customer is defined as the end user of the company's products and services. Senior management leads the quality improvement process by studying the company's quality system and developing a quality vision and plan. Employees are given the training, responsibility, and resources they need to serve customers. Processes are measured, analyzed, and improved. Suppliers are involved in quality improvement. Customers are happy, which increases customer retention and improves profitability—and that pleases shareholders.

You can choose one of these quality systems or another option or have it chosen for you, but you cannot choose not to have a quality system. I have a seven-year-old daughter who, when asked whether she wants apple juice or milk with her dinner, will invariably say, "Pop." (That's soda for the East Coast reader.) We repeat her options until she chooses from our menu—or we choose for her.

The same is true for your quality system. The title of the menu is "Quality Systems." You can choose one, or have one chosen for you, but you cannot ask for a different menu or for something not on the menu.

The "Quality Systems" menu presents a do-it-yourself checklist of areas that determine quality excellence. Every quality system in every organization—manufacturing, service, non-profit, government, or education—includes six areas—six of the seven categories in the Baldrige criteria:

1.0   Leadership

2.0   Information and Analysis

3.0   Strategic Quality Planning

4.0   Human Resource Development and Management

5.0   Management of Process Quality

7.0   Customer Focus and Satisfaction

The final category in the Baldrige criteria is 6.0, Quality and Operational Results, the focus and purpose of all quality system actions.

When quality experts describe quality systems, their descriptions can be categorized by these seven areas. Specific elements of a quality system can be placed within these categories. For example, many quality experts believe benchmarking—the process of improving quality by making comparisons with the best companies in your industry or in the world—is an essential element in a quality system. Benchmarking is part of several Baldrige categories. The benchmarking process is assessed in the "Information and Analysis" category. The processes to be benchmarked and improved are described in the "Management of Process Quality" category. The "Customer Focus and Satisfaction" category looks at how customers help determine what should be benchmarked, and the benchmark data are used in the "Strategic Quality Planning" category.

Quality training is frequently mentioned as an essential part of any quality system. It is covered in the "Human Resource Development and Management" and "Leadership" categories. Innovation is part of "Management of Process Quality, as is improving speed (reducing cycle times) and the quality of suppliers.

Every element of a quality system can fit into one of the Baldrige categories. Some debate that contention, but we will save the debate for later. Right now, it is important to recognize the existence of a quality system in your organization and to know where to find it, because you cannot improve quality unless you improve your quality system.

Until recently, many U.S. businesses addressed quality improvement with a "Quality Program of the Month" mentality. Quality circles were a symptom. Zero defects can also be a symptom, as can just-in-time manufacturing, statistical process control, cross-functional teams, management by objectives, and Computer-Aided Design /Computer-Aided Manufacturing (CAD/CAM). These may be *parts* of a quality system. However, if you change one part but the rest of the system is wretched, the system remains wretched. *If you do not change the system, nothing changes.*

There is the rub. Telling someone else to change one process is easier than participating in changing an entire system. We resist change as individuals and as companies. We may not like where we are, but at least we know what it looks and feels like. Change pushes us into unknown territory. We fear that it could make things worse.

CHANGING QUALITY SYSTEMS

Changing a quality system requires intelligence and courage—the intelligence to know that change is absolutely necessary and the courage to initiate it. Those of us who need a mountain of support before we act do

21

not have to look far. Books, magazines, and trade publications document the impact of global competition in a global marketplace. Even companies that market their products and services domestically, without foreign competitors, feel the pressure of stiffer competition and higher customer expectations.

No industry has been more besieged than the electronics industry. Since 1970, the U.S. market share of electronic products manufactured in the United States has plummeted. For example, American-made telephones accounted for 99 percent of the market in 1970, but only 25 percent in 1988. The percent of audiotape recorders manufactured in the United States dropped from 40 percent to 1 percent. Semiconductors dropped from 89 percent to 64 percent. Color televisions made by U.S. companies accounted for 98 percent of all color televisions sold in this country in 1970. In 1988, their share was 10 percent.

To find out where that market share went, look to the Rising Sun. Japan rose from the ashes of World War II to become the world quality leader in the 1980s. How they did it has been the focus of several books, countless magazine articles, and endless executive trips to the Far East. Japanese success—and America's decline—has been attributed most often to *business leadership*.

Japan's focus on quality can be traced to 1940, when Matsushita launched a quality improvement campaign with a customer-focused statement that could have been proposed as a mission statement by any U.S. corporate executive today:

> It is important not merely to produce and sell products, but to produce and sell quality products, without fail. Not only from the production side, but also from the distribution side, we must constantly review whether customers are satisfied with our products and whether customers are satisfied with our service. We must be perfect in satisfying.

After the war, the Japanese wanted to rebuild by learning America's secret to winning the war, which they believed was statistical process control (SPC). What they got instead was a quality system, courtesy of Homer M. Sarasohn, an American systems and electronics engineer.

General Douglas MacArthur, head of the occupational forces, asked Sarasohn to help Japan with its communications problems. To do that, they needed to get their factories running first. The Japanese wanted the part of the quality system they believed would solve their problems: SPC. Sarasohn gave them the system.

Eight hours a day, four days a week, for eight weeks, Sarasohn taught the fundamentals. Why are you in business? Who are your customers? What do they expect and need from you? How are you going to deliver it? He taught his management seminar to senior executives, whose attendance was required. Their involvement is considered the primary reason Japan ranks as the world quality leader today.

"Japan created its own quality revolution," says Dr. J. M. Juran, one of a few Americans, along with Dr. W. Edwards Deming, credited with helping the Japanese become a world leader. "If Ed Deming and I hadn't gone there, they'd still be right where they are now, because the chief contributors to the revolution have been the Japanese managers. I learned a lot more from Japanese managers than they learned from us."

This is not necessarily what we want to hear. It is much easier to believe that the Japanese are kicking our butts because they have an unfair trade advantage or their culture makes it possible. Armed with excuses, we can rationalize away the need to change. We can rant about the unfairness of it all rather than working at competing.

The excuses are wearing thin.

In *Managing Quality*, David Garvin points out that "Bridgestone Tire's radial truck tire plant in LaVergne, Tennessee . . . now claims scrap and defect rates comparable to its Japanese plant. Nissan's factory in Smyrna, Tennessee appears to have reached the same goal. Both Matsushita and Sanyo have reduced defect and service call rates by as much as 90 percent at the color television plants they purchased in Illinois and Arkansas, while keeping work forces intact." No unfair trade or cultural advantages, just a continuously improving quality system.

"Japan is proof positive that quality is revolutionary, with a revolutionary impact," says Congressman Donald Ritter (R-PA), a member of the House committee that legislated the Baldrige program. "The success of Japanese quality is based on their pursuit of quality and their ability to organize their efforts. I'm encouraged by the U.S. companies that have organized to pursue quality, but I'm alarmed by the far greater number that haven't."

We have no more time for excuses. In 1966, Juran told a European quality control group that "the Japanese are headed for world quality leadership and will attain it in the next two decades because no one else is moving there at the same pace." It didn't take two decades for the Japanese and, fortunately for U.S. companies, it doesn't have to take two decades to catch up.

Juran sees positive signs. Speaking at a Quest for Excellence conference in February 1990, he said:

> I have become optimistic for the first time since the quality crisis descended on the United States. I now believe that, during the 1990s, the number of U.S. companies that have achieved stunning results will increase by orders of magnitude. I also believe that, during the 1990s, the United States will make great strides toward making "Made in the USA" a symbol of world-class quality.

The reason for such optimism is growing evidence that U.S. companies *can* compete. Faced with a costly gap between the quality of their products and those of their Japanese competitors, companies such as Motorola and Xerox dramatically improved the quality of their products. Not by a little and certainly not haphazardly, but systematically and comprehensively.

They changed their paradigms, their models of how to function as a business. Knowing that small improvements were not enough, they set ambitious goals that demanded a new way of thinking, "stretch goals" such as improving defect rates to 99.999975 percent (commonly referred to as Six Sigma quality) and reducing cycle times from months to minutes. Because they could not achieve these goals through existing processes, they were forced to abandon existing methods and search for new solutions. It became a companywide quest, fueled by an aggressive, companywide commitment to a total quality system.

THE BENEFITS OF AN IMPROVED QUALITY SYSTEM

Companies have found that they can lower costs, retain customers and employees, and improve profitability by dramatically improving their quality systems. Let's look at each of these benefits.

Lower Costs

The cost of quality (COQ; sometimes referred to as the cost of poor quality) is usually expressed as a percent of sales. Quality costs can come from any part of a quality system, usually falling into four categories:

1. Internal failures. The cost of failures or poor processes while producing the product or service. Scrap, rework, and process losses are examples. Federal Express has a 1–10–100 Rule: It costs $1 or

one hour to resolve a problem immediately, 10 times more to fix a mistake caught downstream in another department or location, and 100 times more if an error reaches a customer.

2. External failures. The cost to fix or replace a defective product or service, or to refund its cost. Warranty and product liability claims are examples.

3. Appraisal costs. The cost of meeting the company's quality standards. Inspection, testing, and product audits are examples.

4. Prevention costs. The cost of acting to prevent defects. Training and process control are examples.

Most American executives believe their cost of poor quality is around 5 percent of their revenues. Wrong! In December of 1980, early in his company's quality journey, Roger Milliken brought together 267 of his managers to hear Philip Crosby speak. Crosby told them a lot they did not want to hear, such as "management is the problem," but the statement that really got people riled was "the cost of quality at your company, if it's like most, is 18 to 22 percent of your revenues." One senior manager got up and shook his finger at Crosby as he asserted that there was no way his division's COQ was that high.

After the meeting, Milliken formed a task force to nail down the company's cost of quality and sure enough, Crosby was wrong. It was not 18 to 22 percent; it was 26 percent. In other words, one-fourth of Milliken's sales revenues were being spent on fixing internal and external failures, inspecting, testing, auditing, and preventing defects. Apply that rate to your company. How much is one-fourth of your annual sales revenues? How much is poor quality costing you?

Motorola tracks its cost of quality quarterly in manufacturing. The company estimates that it had $750 million in COQ savings in 1990 and $1.5 billion from 1986 to 1990. According to Paul Noakes, a Motorola vice-president and director of external quality programs, "the non-manufacturing environment is not as far along, but we estimate we can achieve one billion dollars a year in COQ savings in this area."

Retain Customers and Employees

The reason for such optimism is that poor service quality, far more than poor manufacturing quality, costs a company customers. In one survey, almost 70 percent of the customers surveyed said their reasons for leaving a company had nothing to do with the product. A 1986 survey by the Technical Assistance Research Programs (TARP) Institute noted that "at any time 25 percent of your customers are dissatisfied enough with your service to stop doing business with you. Only 4 percent will complain."

Charles Aubrey is chief quality officer for Banc One Corporation and president-elect of the American Society for Quality Control. In 1989, Banc One began using TARP for market damage analysis. "We found we're probably losing one-sixth of all accounts because of poor service quality," says Aubrey, "and it could be twice that."

Retaining customers is important, Aubrey says, "because it costs more to get a customer than to keep one, and because you can build existing accounts from the normal one-and-a-half products per customer to three or four products per customer."

In "The Quality Imperative," a special issue of *BusinessWeek* magazine, Frederick F. Reichheld of Bain & Co. says a 20-year customer is worth 85 percent more than a 10-year one, and boosting customer retention 2 percent can have the same effect on profits as cutting costs by 10 percent.

One reason is the revenue lost every time a customer leaves. Here is an example: Let's say Company MNO has revenues of $24 million from 600 customers. Using the "25 percent are dissatisfied enough to leave" figure, that translates into 150 customers who are thinking of switching. If three-fourths of them do, Company MNO has lost 113 customers. Company MNO's revenue per customer is $40,000. The number of lost customers (113) times the revenue per customer ($40,000) means that Company MNO will lose $4.5 million because of poor service.

Improve Profitability

If you improve service, you improve profitability.

Banc One reduced its COQ by $12 million in 1990. Paul Revere Insurance Group has saved almost $18 million in eight years because of its quality improvement process.

Dr. Gary Ballman, director of research for Lakewood Research, studied the relationship between quality and profitability and found a direct correlation. "The higher the quality standards, the higher [the company's] profitability. And profitability here is measured in profits as a percentage of revenue, which factors out the big-company or small-company effect."

Profit Impact of Marketing Strategies (PIMS) studies of nearly 3,000 business units showed that "those businesses in the top 20th percentile ranking for perceived quality had an average return on investment of over 30 percent, nearly double that of companies in the bottom 20th percentile. Return on sales followed a similar pattern." Another PIMS study showed that, whether the companies' market shares were high, middle, or low, those companies with superior quality always realized a greater return on investment (ROI) than those companies with average or inferior quality.

Superior quality is profitable. Just how profitable is still being debated, but studies underway at the corporate and national levels should provide quality professionals with numbers that will get the attention of bottom-line senior executives.

If that does not work, losing customers and revenue to competitors with superior quality systems should eventually snap them to attention. Companies can no longer expect average quality to impress prospective customers. Quality is merely the ticket into the game. Superior quality—delighting customers enough to attract and retain them—will be required to succeed in every industry.

Frank Burge, the publisher of *Electronic News,* described a speech he heard by Chris Galvin, a Motorola executive and son of the company's chairman, Robert Galvin. Chris Galvin talked about using Six Sigma quality as a competitive weapon, an idea new to Burge:

> I have been in the electronics business 35 years, and this is the first time I have ever heard an American executive talk about using quality as a competitive advantage and then tying numbers to the quality program. No slogans. No empty, arm-waving quality claims. Numbers. Think about it. The new paradigm suggests one search for major market segments where your technology gets you in the door and your quality changes the rules of the game.

Motorola changes the rules because of its strong and pervasive quality system. As early as 1981, Motorola committed to improving quality by 10 times by 1986. It achieved its objective. In January 1987, Motorola restated its corporate quality goal to be the following:

- Improve 10 times by 1989

- Improve 100 times by 1991

- Achieve Six Sigma capability by 1992

These "stretch goals" forced the company to analyze and improve every aspect of its quality system, a system recognized for its excellence in 1988 when Motorola became one of the first companies to win the Malcolm Baldrige National Quality Award.

QUALITY PIONEERS

While many of today's competitors for the award use the Baldrige criteria to assess and improve their quality systems with the hope of winning in the future, the first year's winners—Motorola, Westinghouse Commercial Nuclear Fuel Division, and Globe Metallurgical—were recognized for their existing quality systems.

"I read about the Baldrige Award in the *Chicago Tribune* the day it was announced," Robert Galvin remembers. He was the CEO at Motorola in 1988. "I asked my staff if this was something we should pursue. Turned out it was."

Motorola won the Baldrige Award on the strength of its quality system. Its 1988 Baldrige application reflected the scope of that system. The following summary of that application introduces one of the best total quality systems in the country and provides a sampling of the issues addressed in the seven Baldrige categories. The names of the categories have changed slightly since Motorola applied, but their responses remain relevant.

Leadership (Baldrige category 1.0) sets the company's objectives, beliefs, goals, and key initiatives with quality as a central theme. Twice quarterly operating and policy committees always begin with an update of the quality program, including the results of management visits to customers, the results of quality system reviews of major parts of the company, cost of poor quality reports, supplier-Motorola activity, and a review of quality breakthroughs and shortfalls. A major business manager then reports on the current status of his or her particular quality initiative.

Information and Analysis (2.0) is driven by Motorola's Six Sigma Quality program. The principles of Six Sigma Quality are applied to manufacturing and nonmanufacturing activities, giving Motorola a way of benchmarking the quality of its products and services. The company changed its data systems to record defects, opportunities, and the means, variations, and limits of both product and process.

Strategic Quality Planning (3.0) grew out of the company's commitment to total customer satisfaction. Quality improvement goals of 10 times in two years, 100 times in four years, and achievement of Six Sigma capability in five years accelerate Motorola's quality improvement process. Each business incorporates these goals into its long range and annual plans.

Human Resource Utilization (4.0) at Motorola begins with training. The Motorola Training and Education Center (now called Motorola University) provides training on quality at all levels, with specific emphasis on providing all employees with the knowledge and skills necessary to achieve the company's quality goals. In 1987, Motorola spent $44 million on training.

Quality Assurance of Products and Services (5.0) depends on listening to the "voice of the customer." Motorola and its customers work together to bring new solutions to the customer's requirements and to the marketplace.

Quality Results (6.0) reflect the across-the-board quality of Motorola's processes, products, and services. For example, Motorola was the only non-Japanese supplier of pagers to Nippon Telegraph and Telephone because Motorola's pagers were released at a proven reliability level 40 percent higher than existing standards in Japan.

Customer Satisfaction (7.0), the company's fundamental objective, drives quality at Motorola. The CEO and all top executives regularly visit key customers. In addition, a senior manager in each sector and group is a "customer champion." In 1986–1987, Motorola received nearly 50 quality awards and certified supplier citations, proof that the company's customers recognize Motorola as the leader in quality.

This very general summary hints at the scope of Motorola's quality system. Motorola and the other Baldrige Award winners excel because they do not see quality as a department or a program or a goal. Quality defines the steps they take to serve their customers. It is part of every decision, every task, and every process. Its pursuit is systematic and comprehensive. Its achievement is integrated across all departments and functions.

Quality leaders excel because of their quality systems, because they are great at some things and good at everything. The Malcolm Baldrige National Quality Award (MBNQA) recognizes those companies that have improved their quality systems.

In July 1991, *Fortune* magazine noted that "the award has established a national standard for quality, and hundreds of major corporations use the criteria in its application form as a basic management guide."

"Prior to the Baldrige Award," says Juran, "any company that didn't have a quality revolution was confused. Quality consultants were tugging them in different directions. We lost a decade that way. The criteria can become the focal point around which the renaissance can be built."

The seven categories in the Baldrige criteria represent the major components of a quality management system. Companies across the country—small and large, service and manufacturing, even non-profit organizations, government agencies, and schools—are using the criteria to assess the state of their quality systems, to identify strengths and weaknesses, and to improve.

"My six-year-old and I like to put together those puzzles with the big pieces," says Debra Owens, director of corporate quality strategy and planning for Baxter Healthcare and a Baldrige examiner. "One time, we put the pieces in a bag because we lost the box. When we took it out again a few months later, we had trouble putting it together because we didn't have the big picture. The Baldrige criteria are like the picture on the box. They help you see how the big quality pieces fit together."

Seeing "the big picture" is one of senior management's major responsibilities. Until the Baldrige criteria came along, the big quality picture was a fuzzy area for most managers. Does quality mean quality products? Does it mean quality circles? Does it mean zero defects? Does it mean quality slogans? Do we have it? Where can we get it?

Without a clear sense of what quality means, a company flounders. The first step to industry leadership and world-class status must be taken by top management, the "driver" of the quality improvement process. Every quality expert, every book about quality stresses what the Baldrige criteria declare: senior executives lead the quality revolution in their companies.

Zytec Corporation won the Baldrige Award in 1991. The company was only seven years old. One of the first decisions Zytec's senior management made in 1984 was to focus on quality, and to improve quality by implementing Dr. W. Edwards Deming's 14 Points for Management. "When we started, we went on a leap of faith," says Ron Schmidt, Zytec's chief executive officer.

At some point, all of America's quality leaders have taken that leap of faith because they have "witnessed the miracles." Some went to Japan to witness the miracles. Others saw little miracles where they were and imagined what would happen to a whole company. Robert Galvin, Fred Smith, Roger Milliken, David Kearns, John Grettenberger, Winston Chen, Ron Schmidt, Ray Marlow, and other leaders of Baldrige Award-winning companies believed in their souls that total quality management was the best way to run their companies. They implemented a quality system that empowered them to assess and improve quality.

And thanks to the Baldrige program, they are sharing their systems with anyone who asks.

CHAPTER 3

An American Quality System

Americans love competition. Tell us to do something because it is the right thing to do and many of us will ignore you. Tell us to do it because we can win national recognition and we're ready to rock and roll. The evolution of the Malcolm Baldrige National Quality Award program began with a burning need to improve quality across the country, a need which continues to attract people to the Baldrige criteria. But it was the contest, the award, that grabbed the media's eye and many a CEO's heart and established the Baldrige criteria as a framework for quality and quality improvement in the United States.

In the early 1980s, U.S. business and government leaders worried about the nation's ability to compete. They formed councils to study the problem. They participated in conferences and sat on committees whose sole aim was to figure out how to improve the quality of U.S. products and services on a national level.

In 1983, the final report on seven computer networking conferences sponsored by the American Productivity and Quality Center (APQC), in which about 175 corporate executives, business leaders, and academicians participated, recommended the creation of a National Quality Award.

Later that same year, the National Productivity Advisory Committee, a group of corporate executives, academicians, labor leaders, and government officials, recommended creating a national medal for productivity achievement.

In April 1984, a report by the White House Conference on Productivity called for a national medal for productivity. Other groups, both public and private, debated solutions to American competitiveness. Many called for a national award.

In September 1985, corporate quality business leaders formed the Committee to Establish a National Quality Award. Over the next year, the committee developed a structure for administering a national quality award and funding to support it.

At the same time, parallel efforts were underway to legislate a national quality award, spearheaded by Florida Power & Light (FPL). FPL was working closely with the Union of Japanese Scientists & Engineers as it prepared to apply for Japan's highest quality award, the Deming Prize.

In August 1986, Congressman Don Fuqua (D-FL) introduced House Bill 5321 "to establish a National Quality Improvement Award, with the objective of encouraging American business and industrial enterprises to practice effective quality control in the provision of their goods and services." Congress never acted on it.

The next year, with Fuqua no longer in the House, Congressman Doug Walgren (D-PA) reintroduced the legislation. Senator Bob Graham (D-FL) sponsored a Senate version of the bill. On June 8, 1987, the measure passed the House and was sent to the Senate, where nothing happened for six weeks.

"What slowed the process down was the question of the right approach to implementing a national quality award," says Kent Sterett, who headed quality at FPL at the time. "There was a great deal of discussion about whether it should be a private initiative or a government approach or some combination of the two. The prognosis for pushing it through wasn't good."

Part of the problem was the lukewarm response of the Reagan administration, including the government's most notable business leader, Secretary of Commerce Malcolm Baldrige. The bill called for government involvement in administering the award program. That was anathema to Reagan's "hands-off" philosophy. Ironically, Malcolm Baldrige ended up providing the final push that created a national quality award.

The son of a Nebraska congressman, Baldrige earned his reputation as an excellent manager when he was the chief executive officer of Scovill, Inc., a Connecticut-based brass mill. He was credited with transforming the financially troubled company into a multimillion dollar success.

Baldrige was also an avid horseman. A professional rider who won many awards on the rodeo circuit, he was inducted into the National Cowboy Hall of Fame in 1984. On July 25, 1987, on a private ranch near San Francisco, Malcolm Baldrige was killed in a riding accident.

"The Monday after the weekend Baldrige died," Sterett recalls, "I went to dinner with a small group of staffers for Senators and Representatives. The idea had surfaced to name the national quality award after Malcolm Baldrige." That idea appealed to the president, who wanted to honor the friend he had lost.

Three days after Baldrige's death, the Senate Committee on Commerce, Science, and Transportation renamed the legislation in his honor. The Senate passed the bill, the House agreed to the name change, and on August 20, 1987, President Reagan signed the Malcolm Baldrige National Quality Improvement Act of 1987 into law.

BALDRIGE AWARD LEGISLATION

Responsibility for the award was assigned to the Department of Commerce, which gave it to one of its agencies, the National Bureau of Standards, since renamed the National Institute of Standards and Technology (NIST). Much of NIST's work relates to quality and quality-related requirements in developing and utilizing technology.

A look at the legislation hints at how the award program and criteria were created and how they have evolved. The legislation depicts the state of quality in the United States in 1987 and identifies how a national quality award can help improve it. The Findings and Purposes section of the legislation, Public Law 100–107, states the following:

1. The leadership of the United States in product and process quality has been challenged strongly (and sometimes successfully) by foreign competition, and our nation's productivity growth has improved less than our competitors' over the last two decades.

2. American business and industry are beginning to understand that poor quality costs companies as much as 20 percent of sales revenues nationally, and that improved quality of goods and services goes hand in hand with improved productivity, lower costs, and increased profitability.

3. Strategic planning for quality and quality improvement programs, through a commitment to excellence in manufacturing and services, is becoming more and more essential to the well-being of our Nation's economy and our ability to compete effectively in the global marketplace.

4. Improved management understanding of the factory floor, worker involvement in quality, and greater emphasis on statistical process control can lead to dramatic improvements in the cost and quality of manufactured products.

5. The concept of quality improvement is directly applicable to small companies as well as large, to service industries as well as manufacturing, and to the public sector as well as private enterprise.

6. In order to be successful, quality improvement programs must be management-led and customer-oriented, and this may

require fundamental changes in the way companies and agencies do business.

7. Several major industrial nations have successfully coupled rigorous private-sector quality audits with national awards giving special recognition to those enterprises the audits identify as the very best.

8. A national quality award program of this kind in the United States would help improve quality and productivity by:
   A. Helping to stimulate American companies to improve quality and productivity for the pride of recognition while obtaining a competitive edge through increased profits;
   B. Recognizing the achievements of those companies that improve the quality of their goods and services and providing an example to others;
   C. Establishing guidelines and criteria that can be used by business, industrial, governmental, and other organizations in evaluating their own quality improvement efforts; and
   D. Providing specific guidance for other American organizations that wish to learn how to manage for high quality by making available detailed information on how winning organizations were able to change their cultures and achieve eminence.

The Findings and Purposes Section defines the Malcolm Baldrige National Quality Award program. The Baldrige criteria reflect the wording of this section by emphasizing that "quality improvement programs must be management-led and customer-oriented." "Strategic planning for quality and quality improvement programs" is a category in the Baldrige criteria. Another category, Human Resources Utilization, values "worker involvement in quality, and greater emphasis on statistical process control."

The program's objectives, listed in point #8, guided the development of the program and remain the goals that direct the evolution of the criteria and the choice of award winners. The judges who choose the Baldrige Award winners refer to these objectives in cases where more than two companies are being considered in a particular category. All things being equal, the company that will be the best role model for other U.S. companies is given the nod.

According to the Baldrige criteria, the award promotes:

- awareness of quality as an increasingly important element in competitiveness

- understanding of the requirements for quality excellence

- sharing of information on successful quality strategies and the benefits derived from implementation of these strategies

Award winners are expected to willingly share information about their successful quality strategies with other U.S. organizations. This requirement is one reason that awareness of the Baldrige Award and criteria has grown so rapidly in just four years. The dozen Baldrige Award winners have been besieged by requests for information. All have carried out their responsibilities diligently, spreading the quality gospel across the land. Stories describing the demands placed on Baldrige winners are presented in Chapter 16.

To respond to the legislation and successfully promote its goals, the Baldrige program relied on new and existing business and government organizations (see Figure 3.1): American Society for Quality Control (ASQC), Board of Overseers, Foundation for the MBNQA, Board of Examiners, and National Institute of Standards and Technology (NIST).

Companies submit their applications to ASQC, which administers the award under NIST's management. Formed in 1946, ASQC is the largest organization of quality professionals in the country, offering programs, publications, and courses in quality to more than 100,000 members.

"We aren't decision makers in the award process," says Jeff Rendall, manager of ASQC's Baldrige administrative function. "We support the Board of Examiners by publishing the Criteria and Application Forms and Instructions, collecting all the applications, circulating them to the appropriate examiners, collecting and tabulating scores, and publishing the examiners' feedback for the applicants."

ASQC also creates promotional materials for the Baldrige Award program, writes the winners' briefs, works with NIST to organize the awards ceremony each year, and produces the award ceremony videotape.

The Baldrige program's broad direction comes from the Board of Overseers. By legislation, the Board must consist of at least five people selected by the Secretary of Commerce, in consultation with the director of NIST, for their preeminence in the field of quality management. In 1991, the Board was chaired by Robert Galvin of Motorola, and included

National Institute of Standards and Technology (NIST)
- agency of the Department of Commerce's Technology Administration
- manages the award program
- helps winners communicate their quality systems
- develops and improves policies and criteria
- selects members of the Board of Examiners and develops examiner training
- monitors consensus meetings and site visits
- helps organize awards ceremony

Board of Examiners
- includes judges, senior examiners, and examiners
- evaluates applications
- prepares feedback reports
- makes award recommendations
- help improve criteria and process
- promote awareness of Baldrige program and quality

Baldrige Award Program

Foundation for the MBNQA
- raises funds to support the program

Board of Overseers
- chosen by Secretary of Commerce
- oversees design and execution of, conformance to, and integrity of award process
- monitors funding
- oversees performance of other components
- recommends improvements
- suggests legislative changes

American Society for Quality Control (ASQC)
- publishes Criteria and Application Forms and Instructions
- collects applications, circulates them to examiners, collects and tabulates scores
- publishes examiner feedback
- creates promotional materials
- writes award winners' briefs
- helps organize awards ceremony
- produces award ceremony videotape

Figure 3.1 A diagram of the groups involved in the Baldrige Award program.

William Eggleston, IBM; Dr. Armand Feigenbaum, General Systems Co.; John Hudiberg, Florida Power & Light; William Golomski, W.A. Golomski & Associates; Dr. J. M. Juran, Juran Institute; and Nancy Steorts, Nancy Harvey Steorts, International.

Although the Board's specific responsibilities are not strictly defined, their attention has been focused on the following areas:

- oversee the design and execution of the award process

- review conformance to the award process

- assure the integrity of the award process

- assess the adequacy of funding

- oversee the performance of examiners, judges, NIST, and ASQC

- oversee the improvement process

- recommend changes and improvements to the Secretary of Commerce

- suggest legislative changes

The Board meets formally once a year to review reports from NIST and ASQC and to discuss policy, standards, and financial issues. Board members also work on committees, including joint committees with Baldrige judges, to explore important issues.

"We're the conscience of the Baldrige process," says Galvin. "We take a broad look at the whole award program to see if it is filling the legislative mandate to the highest standards." Two issues the Board of Overseers has been debating involve expanding the program to hand out more awards, and including more types of organizations.

EXPANDING THE AWARD

Unlike the Deming Prize, which is awarded to every company that passes muster, the Baldrige Award can only be given to two companies in each of three categories per year. The Board's consensus seems to be that the number of awards needs to be expanded, perhaps at first to three or four awards per category. Increasing the number—or getting rid of the limit altogether—would help to make the competition a more cooperative effort.

The second issue is not as easily resolved. People in the nonprofit, health care, education, and government sectors have been lobbying the Board to create award categories for them. They cite precedence in state programs (New York's quality award, the Excelsior Award, is given to winners in the public, private, and education sectors) and in the experiences of noneligible organizations that are using the Baldrige criteria to improve quality.

The Board of Overseers faces two problems with opening the program to other sectors. First, the focus of the legislation and of the program is on business. The quality processes of nonprofit and health care organizations can be captured in the criteria, but adapting the criteria to schools and government agencies is more difficult.

The second problem is financial. Adding new sectors would increase the financial burden on NIST. Although volunteer examiners, subsidized by their own companies, ease the strain, the program may not be able to handle an influx of applications or the cost of training and supporting the examiners needed to evaluate educational institutions and government agencies.

The best guess is that, once the financial obstacles are overcome, a nonprofit category will be added. Government agencies and educational institutions will likely have to wait awhile.

Financial support for the Baldrige program comes from three sources: companies that donate examiners' time and travel expenses; application fees; and the Foundation for the Malcolm Baldrige National Quality Award. No funding comes from the government. The Foundation is run by trustees who are leaders of major U.S. companies. When the award was legislated, the Foundation raised money by asking companies for donations. More than 800 companies donated $10.4 million. The interest on that endowment pays the program's operating costs.

The Foundation has no part in the criteria design or judging process. Special care is taken so that information about contributors cannot influence the examiners' or judges' decisions. It is ludicrous to believe that the judges, weighing the relative merits of finalists, refer to a list of contributors to the program to help them make their choice. In fact, while many of 1991's site visit companies were members of the Foundation, none of the winners appear on its roster.

The evaluation branch of the Baldrige program is the Board of Examiners, which consists of judges, senior examiners, and examiners. They are chosen for their quality knowledge and experience and come from industry, professional and trade associations, universities, health care organizations, and government agencies. Their role in evaluating applications and choosing winners is explained in Chapter 12.

The Panel of Judges has responsibilities in addition to judging applications. Together with NIST, they recommend the members of the Board of Examiners. They speak to groups about the Baldrige Award program. They also participate in subcommittees focused on some aspect of the Baldrige program, such as information transfer or small business evaluation. Major policy recommendations are passed along to the Board of Overseers; decisions about less policy-oriented issues are made by the judges.

"If we decided that additional emphasis was needed on how to best evaluate a small business," says Kent Sterett, a Baldrige judge for four years, "that decision is made without review by the overseers. But if we decided to embark on a plan to lobby Congress to change the law in some manner or decide to install an additional category, those are policy issues that would be taken to the Board of Overseers."

MANAGING THE PROGRAM

The final cog in the Baldrige Award program "machine" is the group within NIST that manages the program. Its responsibilities include information transfer; policy development and improvement; communicating the Baldrige quality system to states, industries, and other groups; running the Baldrige Award contest, including monitoring the consensus meetings, site visits, and feedback system, and selecting and developing training for examiners; organizing the award ceremony; and improving the criteria.

Each of these responsibilities is a major job. Information transfer involves working with award winners to help them communicate their quality systems accurately and effectively. Policies affecting the application process are continually reviewed and improved. Communicating the Baldrige quality system is the fastest growing responsibility because of the growing interest in the Baldrige Award. Running the contest includes choosing and training examiners, assigning them to applications, assembling site visit teams, coordinating and monitoring site visits, collecting data for judging, and producing feedback reports.

The criteria are the handiwork of Curt Reimann, director of the Baldrige program. He orchestrated the effort that created them and he remains actively involved in their continuous improvement.

In the mid-1980s, as director of a chemical center for the National Bureau of Standards, Reimann studied the quality community to find out the direction quality measurements were taking and to alert the community to the services his group offered.

"I became the house agent linked to the quality community," says Reimann. "When the Baldrige legislation gave responsibilities to this agency, my head was sticking conspicuously higher than anyone else's, so I got the job. And I'm glad I did, because it is without a doubt the most challenging assignment I've ever had."

Reimann stepped from one field, chemistry, where the structure for knowledge is well-defined and constantly being debated by scholars, to another field, quality, where neither was the case. "I was struck by the absence of a structure for the knowledge in quality," says Reimann. "Here was a field that is supposedly very important to our nation's survival in the world economy and all you get are little vignettes and anecdotes. This group formed a quality circle and everything's great. No, JIT is the way. All these things come at you like a blitz in what seems like an infinite checklist. How do they all fit together?"

The legislation and the U.S. quality movement needed a quality system, and the National Bureau of Standards (which later became NIST) and Reimann were uniquely positioned to provide it. As a standards organization, they thought in terms of broad structures and generic concepts across industry and sector boundaries. The National Bureau of Standards had a long history of helping industry improve the quality of its products and services by developing and supplying measurement services. It was seen as a catalyst for the exchange of information, which was an objective of the Baldrige program. And it was a neutral third party.

"We weren't identified with any camp," says Reimann. "We're a highly respected agency. We're apolitical. And we didn't carry any baggage into a charged atmosphere."

The field of quality did not agree on a well-defined system, but it wasn't for lack of discussion. Quality leaders such as Dr. W. Edwards Deming, Dr. J. M. Juran, Philip Crosby, and Armand Feigenbaum helped shape the debate. Organizations such as ASQC and the American Productivity and Quality Center provided forums for an ongoing dialogue. These individuals and groups had done much to identify and communicate the elements in a quality system, but they had not agreed on the basic structure of that system.

Reimann started where the criteria ask others to start: with the customer. An assessment of the needs of American companies revealed that most organizations did not have systematic quality improvement processes, and those that did lacked a total quality focus. It found that many organizations were only beginning to focus on quality improvement, and that quality improvement was not a priority among trade, business, and professional associations, or business schools.

At the same time, Reimann's group collected everything they could from every available source that would help them develop a quality system. "We made every effort to find out what was going on in the quality community and to see the intellectual frameworks others had developed," says Reimann, "but if you look at the criteria that emerged, they formed a new quality system. Quality was no longer a philosophy based on a particular clique or community."

"Not surprisingly, we took a standards orientation and set out to develop a nonprescriptive framework that addressed the quality requirements," says Reimann. "We took it in that direction because we are a standards organization, because we feel that quality is not one thing you can write a prescription for and say that prescription fits your organization and mine and his and hers. It's a set of requirements that gives you considerable latitude in fashioning your own quality system."

The framework took a structure/substructure approach. The structure, the seven Baldrige categories, represented the basic requirements of total quality management and were applicable to any business of any size (see Table 3.1).

"What I found was that, after I had the set of seven, I could explain anything else in terms of the seven," Reimann says. "If I tried to throw away one of the seven I was throwing away something really valuable. If I tried to add something I found it was already there or could be incorporated in one of the seven. Each of these seven categories represents a great, significant purpose that relates to the functioning of an organization."

Within the seven categories, examination items address key requirements for excellence. A company's response to these items, which are further defined by "areas to address," projects its value system for total quality management. Each item, like each category, is assigned a point value. The contest demands points, but point values are not intended to suggest that one item is more important than another. All 28 items are important to a total quality system.

Reading through the list of items gives you some sense of the structure and scope of the Baldrige quality system. The complete 1992 Examination, with categories, items, and areas to address, is included in Appendix A.

Scanning the point values, two areas of emphasis are obvious: customer satisfaction is worth nearly one-third of the possible points, and measurable results are valued.

HOW APPLICATIONS ARE EVALUATED

"Results" is one of three dimensions used to evaluate an application. The other two are "approach" and "deployment." When you respond to an item, you are asked to frame your response according to one, two, or all three of these dimensions.

"Approach" refers to how your company achieves the purposes addressed in the item. Thought of in terms of basic questions, an approach would include the following: How did you determine a course of action?

Table 3.1 1992 Baldrige Criteria

Categories and items	Maximum points
1.0 Leadership	**90**
1.1 Senior Executive Leadership	45
1.2 Management for Quality	25
1.3 Public Responsibility	20
2.0 Information and Analysis	**80**
2.1 Scope and Management of Quality and Performance Data and Information	15
2.2 Competitive Comparisons and Benchmarks	25
2.3 Analysis of Uses of Company-Level Data	40
3.0 Strategic Quality Planning	**60**
3.1 Strategic Quality and Company Performance Planning Process	35
3.2 Quality and Performance Plans	25
4.0 Human Resource Development and Management	**150**
4.1 Human Resource Management	20
4.2 Employee Involvement	40
4.3 Employee Education and Training	40
4.4 Employee Performance and Recognition	25
4.5 Employee Well-Being and Morale	25
5.0 Management of Process Quality	**140**
5.1 Design and Introduction of Quality Products and Services	40
5.2 Process Management—Product and Service Production and Delivery Processes	35
5.3 Process Management—Business Processes and Support Services	30
5.4 Supplier Quality	20
5.5 Quality Assessment	15
6.0 Quality and Operational Results	**180**
6.1 Product and Service Quality Results	75
6.2 Company Operational Results	45
6.3 Business Process and Support Service Results	25
6.4 Supplier Quality Results	35
7.0 Customer Focus and Satisfaction	**300**
7.1 Customer Relationship Management	65
7.2 Commitment to Customers	15
7.3 Customer Satisfaction Determination	35
7.4 Customer Satisfaction Results	75
7.5 Customer Satisfaction Comparisons	75
7.6 Future Requirements and Expectations of Customers	35

Who did you involve, and how did you involve them? What processes did you follow? How did you evaluate the effectiveness of your approach?

When an examiner scores your application, he or she evaluates the approach you took based on the following:

- how appropriate were the methods, tools, and techniques to the requirements, and how effective were they

- how systematic, integrated, and consistently applied is the approach

- how well does the approach include effective evaluation and improvement cycles

- how well is the approach based on objective and reliable information

- how well is the approach prevention-based

- what are the indicators of unique and innovative approaches

Based on these judging criteria, if your company does a terrific job of responding to problems but does not correct the cause of those problems so they do not recur, or act to prevent problems before they occur, you will not score very high. If groups and departments have great approaches, but they do not speak the same language or work together to streamline processes and reduce cycle times, you will not score well. If your company has never heard of an evaluation/improvement cycle, forget it.

"Deployment," the second dimension used to evaluate an application, refers to how extensively your approaches have been implemented. Have you used the same approach for all relevant areas and activities, have you used it sporadically, or are you just beginning to use it? How widely is the approach spread across the organization? How well are lower-level activities tied to strategic goals?

When an examiner scores your application, he or she evaluates your deployment based on the following:

- has the approach been applied to all appropriate product and service characteristics

- has the approach been applied to all appropriate transactions and interactions with customers, suppliers, and the public

- has the approach been applied to all appropriate internal processes, activities, facilities, and employees

Most items ask for your company's approach and deployment. For example, under item 2.2, "Competitive Comparisons and Benchmarks," the fourth area to address asks "how the company evaluates and improves the scope, sources, and uses of competitive and benchmark data." The best response would explain a systematic approach used by all functions to improve their competitive comparisons and benchmarking activities.

It would also show evidence of that approach and deployment. The lack of evidence is a common weakness in many responses. I can remember reading, on a draft of two categories I wrote for Thermo King's application in 1990, the notes of a hired gun Baldrige examiner. His most frequent comment was: "Is there evidence of this?" It may have sounded good, but where was the proof? Specific numbers, examples, and matrices are good ways of providing evidence.

"Results," the third dimension, refers to the measures of your company's success with its approaches and deployment. Are your positive indicators going up? Are the adverse indicators going down? How fast? Is it sustained? How do your trends compare to those of your competitors and of world leaders?

When an examiner scores your application, he or she evaluates your results based on the following:

- what quality and performance levels are demonstrated, how important are they, what are the rate and breadth of improvement, and is the improvement sustained

- how do the results compare to industry and world leaders

- do the improvements result from the company's quality practices and actions

Examiners use the three evaluation dimensions of approach, deployment, and results to score an application. The "Scoring Guidelines" matrix in Figure 3.2 shows how an examiner scores a response.

Very few items ask for all three dimensions. Most ask for approach and deployment. Six items—6.1, 6.2, 6.3, 6.4, 7.4, and 7.5—ask for results, but these six items add up to 330 points.

The weight given to "results" helps examiners and judges to differentiate applicants. As companies begin their quality journeys, many are implementing well-conceived approaches on a broad basis. In fact, it can be hard to distinguish these companies from companies whose approaches have proven effective over time—until you compare results. It's like the

SCORE	APPROACH	DEPLOYMENT	RESULTS
0%	•anecdotal, no system evident	•anecdotal	•anecdotal
10—40%	•beginnings of systematic prevention basis	•some to many major areas of business	•some positive trends in the areas deployed
50%	•sound, systematic prevention basis that includes evaluation/ improvement cycles •some evidence of integration	•most major areas of business •some support areas	•positive trends in most major areas •some evidence that results are caused by approach
60—90%	•sound, systematic prevention basis with evidence of refinement through evaluation/ improvement cycles •good integration	•major areas of business •from some to many support areas	•good to excellent in major areas •positive trends—from some to many support areas •evidence that results are caused by approach
100%	•sound, systematic prevention basis refined through evaluation/ improvement cycles •excellent integration	•major areas and support areas •all operations	•excellent (world-class) results in major areas •good to excellent in support areas •sustained results •results clearly caused by approach

Figure 3.2 A matrix of the Baldrige scoring guidelines.

saying, "All cats are gray in the dark." Giving weight to the results is like stepping on a tail: the ensuing "bark" tells you all you need to know.

Approach/deployment/results, or A/D/R to Baldrige junkies, have given many applicants fits. Until 1991, applicants were confused about which items required which dimensions. That was clarified in the 1991 Application Guidelines (which is now two booklets, "Criteria" and "Application Forms and Instructions"). Still, the dual requirement of responding to an item at the same time you are trying to explain a systematic, well-deployed approach can be frustrating. We will look at ways to accomplish this in Chapter 14.

The first Application Guidelines in 1988 said little about how applications would be evaluated. Since then the explanations, like the criteria, have improved. The 1988 criteria had 62 items and 278 areas to address.

Table 3.2 The Evolution of the Baldrige Criteria

1988 Criteria: Item 1.1 Senior Corporate Leadership	**1992 Criteria: Item 1.1** Senior Executive Leadership
Describe the major roles of the CEO, COO, CQO, and other key executives in quality improvement processes. Include specific examples of sustained and visible executive involvement in the development of an effective corporate quality culture. a. Demonstration of continuous, meaningful leadership and involvement in addressing quality issues b. Direct interaction by these executives in many levels of the organization c. Involvement in external quality-related activities (i.e., speeches, professional societies, etc.) d. Evidence that executive leadership has resulted in improved product or service quality	Describe the senior executives' leadership, personal involvement, and visibility in developing and maintaining a customer focus and an environment for quality excellence. a. Senior executives' leadership, personal involvement, and visibility in quality-related activities of the company. Include: (1) reinforcing a customer focus; (2) creating quality values and setting expectations; (3) planning and reviewing progress toward quality and performance objectives; (4) recognizing employee contributions; and (5) communicating quality values outside the company. b. Brief summary of the company's quality values and how the values serve as a basis for consistent communications within and outside the company. c. Personal actions of senior executives to regularly demonstrate, communicate, and reinforce the company's customer orientation and quality values through all levels of management and supervision d. How senior executives evaluate and improve the effectiveness of their personal leadership and involvement

The 1992 criteria have 28 items and 89 areas to address. "It started out more like a checklist and is moving more and more to becoming an integrated system for learning how to serve customers better," says Reimann. The evolution from checklist to integrated system is apparent when you compare the criteria from 1988 to 1992 (see Table 3.2).

The criteria have also evolved from being manufacturing oriented to being more applicable to all types of organizations. When the criteria were being designed in 1987, the manufacturing sector provided nearly all of the input. Deming, Juran, and other quality experts had made their marks working primarily with manufacturers. The American Society for Quality Control promoted manufacturing quality. Nearly all the input into the criteria came from people who knew manufacturing, and the criteria reflected their bias.

The criteria have become more generic with input from service companies and small businesses, which are taking a more systematic approach to quality. "Manufacturing applications were impressive from the start," says Kent Sterett, a Baldrige judge from 1988 through 1991. "Most service companies are late to the quality journey, but they seem to be able to move more rapidly than manufacturing."

"The growing strength of the service applicants is one of the more important stories in the award program," says Reimann. "It's a combination of companies getting better and becoming more systems oriented and the fact that the criteria have become more relevant as we've learned."

The problem with small businesses has been the lack of transferable knowledge. Remember, one of the objectives of the award program is to make available "detailed information on how winning organizations were able to change their cultures and achieve eminence."

"We're finding that small businesses are much more intuitive in planning and information systems," says Reimann. "They're based on information and fact but there's no paper trail, and if the knowledge isn't transferable, it is probably not a good basis for an award."

Many small business owners decline to apply for the Baldrige Award because they cannot document the processes requested by the criteria. That problem is being addressed by the Board of Examiners, which has used site visits of small businesses to evaluate how well the criteria apply. Their findings are being used in 1992 to train examiners to focus on what is appropriate to expect small businesses to do.

The criteria continue to be improved because they are constantly being evaluated. Reimann and his staff review the feedback reports Baldrige examiners write for applicants. They go out on site visits with the examination teams. They ask for ideas from applicants, examiners, and quality experts. Every year, soon after the winners have been announced, they pull in members of the Board of Examiners for one day to talk about the criteria. They welcome and listen to any comments, suggestions, hints, or criticisms that may lead to improvements.

"The award and the quality movement are about organizations learning," says Reimann, "and we're an organization that ought to be doing a lot of learning ourselves. When I talk to companies with good quality systems, I ask them, 'What part of your story can't you tell with our criteria?' or, 'What story am I asking you to tell that you feel is irrelevant or is getting in the way of your quality?'"

With input from so many sources, it is not surprising that Reimann estimates he spent 400 hours revising the 1991 guidelines. It is hard to imagine any other quality methodology that is exposed to such widespread scrutiny and debate on a regular basis.

The result is a tool that organizations can use to diagnose the condition of their quality systems, identify their strengths and weaknesses, and plan their improvements. It is not a prescription for improving quality, although many companies wish it were. For companies not far along the quality path, the criteria can be very intimidating. The scope of the system extends beyond what most organizations have considered "quality issues." Reading the criteria for the first time, senior executives and other managers often feel lost in a quality maze, bumping into one wall after another: quality objectives, benchmarking, quality planning, employee involvement, reducing cycle time, measuring quality improvement and customer satisfaction—the list is formidable.

One common response is to call those who administer the Baldrige program and ask for the prescription that cures the headache. Where do we go for help with benchmarking? What is the best way to integrate quality planning with business planning?

People ask, but Reimann and his staff will not answer. "My feeling is that giving a prescription would not only be mischievous, it would be fundamentally wrong," says Reimann, "because there isn't one path that fits all. I think there's a certain laziness and lack of patience when you expect that something as culturally based as quality can be reduced to a formula of 'Here's what you do.'"

That brings us back to the idea of do-it-yourself quality. It would be nice if someone would walk through the door, prescription in hand, and set the company sailing toward Baldrige Award-winning quality. It would be nice, but it would probably cost a fortune. The Baldrige Award winners have incorporated quality beliefs and processes from a variety of sources into their corporate cultures. They have taken what they needed from the quality smorgasbord, kept some and declined others, always with their own tastes, their own sense of themselves, in mind.

The criteria are not perfect, but they are the best description of a total quality system on the market (and they're free!). To understand the scope of that system you need to understand the elements within each of its major categories, beginning where most experts say a quality system must begin, with leadership.

PART TWO

———————————— ✦ ✦ ✦ ————————————

The Baldrige Categories

CHAPTER 4

Leadership

You may have heard this story. Around Baldrige campfires it is met with knowing nods. It is a story of senior executive leadership, best told by the senior executive who led, Roger Milliken.

As chairman and chief executive officer of Milliken & Company, Roger Milliken initiated his company's quality resurgence during the 1980s, an effort recognized by a Baldrige Award in 1989. When he accepted the award, Milliken described a turning point for the organization:

> ... Almost a decade ago, I remember a manager looked at me and said, "There are only five managers in this room who know how to listen" (and there were over 400 people there). That was a disturbing eye-opener, and I believed him. At the end of the conference and after some practice, I jumped up on one of those little banquet tables and, raising my right arm, asked them to raise theirs and repeat after me:
>
> *I will listen.*
>
> *I will not shoot the messenger.*
>
> *I recognize that management is the problem.*
>
> It was a breakthrough moment.
>
> That day we started to commit—unfortunately, not quite all of us—and to embark upon an entirely new approach to quality. One of leadership through listening and coaching, and one of increased recognition for the efforts that make up a true and effective quality process of continuous improvement.
>
> Without realizing the magic of what we were about to do, we were indeed beginning to enable and empower each and every one of our associates to do what they know and can do best.

After he climbed off the banquet table, Roger Milliken set about being the solution instead of part of the problem. He started by deciding that the first four hours of every policy committee meeting—a group of senior executives that met for two days every four weeks—would be devoted to quality.

At the first meeting after this decision, each of the four division presidents was asked to talk about his quality initiatives. One by one, they discussed a few steps being taken in their divisions and what they expected to be done. Each had an hour to talk. Each was done in minutes, after which there was silence. One person in attendance, who didn't even have to speak, remembers how excruciating the silences were. The senior executives quickly got the message that this quality business was not going away. At the next meeting—and at every meeting in the 10+ years since then—they have had something to talk about.

QUALITY LEADERSHIP

Milliken's experience mirrors the experiences of other Baldrige Award winners and quality leaders. The transformation to world-class quality is not possible without committed, visionary, hands-on leadership.

Just ask the quality guru of your choice. Dr. W. Edwards Deming's 14 Points for Management outline what total quality leadership means. Point #2 states, "Adopt a new philosophy. We are in a new economic age. Western management must awaken to the challenge, must learn their responsibilities, and take on leadership for change."

Dr. J. M. Juran has devoted an entire book to leadership, called "Juran on Quality Leadership." Philip Crosby's first of fourteen steps of quality improvement is "management commitment."

Armand Feigenbaum wrote that leaders can only implement quality if they instill the following:

Quality attitude: the deep recognition that what you are doing is right. It is the strongest emotional motivator, and the basic driver in true quality leadership;

Quality knowledge: an understanding of today's customer-driven markets and how to serve them;

Quality skills: the development of the work and teamwork habits that build in quality throughout the organization. It is what makes quality programs stick.

Quality experts agree on the role of leadership because they agree on the source of the quality problem: the company's quality system. Because only management can fix the system, it is a management problem. Or as Roger Milliken said, "management *is* the problem."

This is not a message most managers want to hear, which is why they hunt for other possible causes. Workers have always been an easy target: if they only worked harder or smarter; if they only cared about what they were doing; if they only did exactly what we told them, our quality problems would vanish.

Outside forces are convenient: the competition is bigger; has more money; is well entrenched; the Japanese have an unfair advantage; we are in a recession.

When these excuses fail, some try putting quality in its place: stockholders only care about profitability; we are focusing on innovation; Baldrige Award winners do not have that great a bottom line.

To paraphrase John Kenneth Galbraith, "Faced with the choice between changing and proving there is no need to do so, most get busy on the proof." Or in this case, on excuses, blaming, and finger pointing.

Many senior executives stand defiantly against total quality management in the face of strong winds of change. Autocratic leadership may have been accepted by employees in the past, but that was before they were asked to think about what they were doing, to help speed it up or improve quality, to get involved. Awakened to the joy of contributing with their minds as well as their hands, employees will no longer settle for putting in time. They chafe against the bonds of mind-numbing tasks. They know what needs to be fixed, and they grow weary waiting for their managers to empower them to fix it.

No group has been more frustrated with senior management than quality professionals, who have long struggled to find effective strategies for involving management in quality. John Cooney, manager of Xerox's National Quality Communications and Promotions Office, has been sharing the Xerox story with companies since Xerox won the Baldrige Award in 1989. He has heard the plea.

"The most frequent concern expressed by companies we talk to is leadership," says Cooney. "If the leader's fingerprints aren't on the quality strategy, the propensity for failure is great."

Quality systems fail because of management's apathy and ignorance. For a long time, management could afford to be apathetic about quality because profitability could be bought by sheer volume and besides, it had a quality department in charge of that quality stuff. As a result, management ignored quality with obvious consequences: ignoring leads to ignorance.

The first category of the Baldrige criteria does not reward apathy or ignorance. On the contrary, it recognizes leadership as the driver of a company's quality system. If your company's leaders are merely passengers, no one will drive you anywhere, and total quality management will not even be on your map. But if your leaders believe, as others do, that quality products and services are your ticket into the competition, they have their work cut out for them. They must lead the change.

"A lot of executives make the mental commitment," says Donald Grimm, president and chief executive officer of Hybritech, a San Diego–based biotechnology firm. "They think quality is good and say so. Others add a spiritual commitment—you can tell they really believe in quality. But the key is *physical* commitment. Will you, the CEO, put your body into the process? Will you participate in training? Take part in teams? And get out of your office every day to give people face-to-face support and guidance?"

"Total quality is just too big a change to bring about using anything less than all three dimensions of leadership," Grimm says, "mental, spiritual, and physical."

"As today's corporation evolves, it will need 'renaissance managers'— people whose vision encompasses all the activities of the global enterprise." George Fisher, Motorola's president and CEO, described the "manufacturing renaissance" in a speech at the Stanford Manufacturing Conference in April 1988. "If you are to be a successful [renaissance manager], you will demonstrate creativity and technological flair and a deep understanding of the world's markets and political and economic forces. You will weld together a team that solves very specific customer needs. You will be a knowledge engineer, able to grasp a problem and know what technologies are most appropriate for a specific application. You will demonstrate an ability to envision your strategic intent and energize your organization. You will create an environment that enables your team to succeed. You will attract the best and brightest people to this environment. You will exert a positive influence beyond your company—in your community and in your profession. Above all, you will let your imagination transcend conventional boundaries."

That is an intimidating list of qualifications. Where does one find the da Vinci School of Renaissance Management? A good place to start—a good place to assess your role in your company's quality improvement process—is to measure that leadership against the Baldrige criteria.

The dimensions of quality leadership are measured in category 1.0. As described in the Baldrige Criteria booklet, the category "examines senior executives' *personal* leadership and involvement in creating and sustaining a customer focus and clear and visible quality values. Also examined is how the quality values are integrated into the company's management system and reflected in the manner in which the company addresses its public responsibilities."

Item 1.1, "Senior Executive Leadership," is worth one-half of the category's 90 points and focuses specifically on the company's highest-ranking official and his or her direct reports. The item asks about senior executives' leadership, personal involvement, and visibility in quality-related activities; about the company's quality values; about the senior executives' personal actions to demonstrate, communicate, and reinforce the company's customer orientation and quality values; and about how senior executives evaluate and improve their leadership.

"Most companies fall short in active, visible commitment of senior managers," says Robert McGrath, a quality consultant and past Baldrige examiner who teaches a Baldrige self-assessment workshop for ASQC. "They're not living the commitment to quality, even though they may be preaching it. That comes through in the application."

Reading the description of item 1.1, most senior executives believe they could score quite well. They suspect they may be a little weak when it comes to spreading the quality gospel, but when you talk about promoting it within the company, they see themselves as "dogs on the bone of quality."

GETTING SENIOR MANAGEMENT INVOLVED

The fact is, that many companies, even those just beginning the quality journey, receive decent scores for the first item and the first category. Senior management is initiating change, and that effort can be reflected in their responses to the category.

Most companies, however, fall short in two critical areas: (1) the president, chairman, or CEO is a high-profile quality zealot, but his or her direct reports are little more than quality parrots; and (2) senior executives talk a good game, but very few "put their bodies in the process."

Nothing can sabotage a quality movement faster than managers who are not engaged in it. Milliken has said it faced three barriers to change: upper management, middle management, and front-line management.

When Roger Milliken asks his division presidents to report on quality initiatives in their divisions, he involves them in Milliken's quality movement. When Xerox's top 25 senior operating executives worldwide meet regularly for 15 months to develop the company's quality policy, strategies, and plans, they are involved. When all of Cadillac's executives agree to be the first to take any division wide training key to Cadillac's success, they are involved. When the top 340 executives of Federal Express set aside nine full days each year to participate in total quality training, they are involved.

"Executive participation in quality training is not symbolic," says Larry McMahon, FedEx's vice-president of human resources. "We're preparing our officers, directors, and managers for active, participatory quality leadership."

D. Otis Wolkins is GTE's vice-president of quality services and marketing administration. GTE hired him in 1984 to put the company on a quality improvement path.

"Until 1984, GTE had a short-term view with no thought of using quality as a strategic weapon," says Wolkins. "We had a quality vision and policy and no understanding of how to get there. We didn't know quality. My job was to close the ignorance gap."

Wolkins consulted with quality leaders in the United States and Japan, taking ideas that fit GTE's culture and needs. He borrowed what was good from companies at the forefront of the quality movement, such as process improvement from IBM and vendor quality processes from 3M.

Using what he learned, Wolkins began shaping a quality improvement process that fit GTE's culture and goals. The initial phase of that process was a three-day course called, "Quality: The Competitive Edge."

The first group to take the course was the chairman and his staff.

"The senior executives spent half of each day in lecture and the other half working on their business unit strategies." Wolkins says. "Day one focused on what quality is. Day two was on tools and techniques, looking at what others were doing. On day three we discussed the executive's role in the quality improvement process."

In 1987, GTE began using quality as a competitive weapon. "The training permanently changed the executives who took it, and it changed our corporation," Wolkins says. "Every action since then has been an outgrowth of that course."

David Garvin, author of *Managing Quality,* taught the course to GTE's senior executives. In his book he writes:

In a growing number of companies...a new vision has begun to emerge. It embodies a dramatic shift in perspective. For the first time, top managers, at the level of presidents and chief executive officers, have expressed an interest in quality. They have linked it with profitability, defined it from the customer's point of view, and required its inclusion in the strategic planning process. In the most radical departure of all, many have insisted that quality be viewed as an aggressive competitive weapon.

To arm that weapon, senior managers must act on their belief. Some call it "walking the talk," and it's absence is a critical weakness in companies struggling to improve quality. Donald Grimm described it as a "physical commitment." You cannot study the Baldrige Award-winning companies without coming to this conclusion: *A company cannot convince its customers, suppliers, or employees that it is committed to continuous quality improvement unless its senior executives participate in the quality improvement process.*

It is not enough just to create a "quality mission." It is not enough to say you are committed, then delegate the job to other people or departments. And it is surely not enough to proclaim that employees deserve the credit for improvements in quality and customer satisfaction, and that management exists to help the front-line people do their jobs—and then pay executives 100 times more than these employees, and lay off the so-called "valuable" employees when the economy weakens. At that point the quality program becomes what the employees knew it was all along: a way of manipulating them into working harder for the bottom line, not working together for the customer.

Baldrige Award-winning senior executives "walk the talk." They spend the time learning what quality means and how it can be achieved, then train those who report to them, beginning a cycle that reaches everyone in the company. They establish goals, objectives, and measures. They participate in cross-functional teams formed to improve quality in a particular process or area. They meet frequently with customers, suppliers, and employees. They break down the barriers that set them apart from their coworkers, inviting everyone to work together toward a common goal.

Physical commitments by senior executives are so rare that, when they occur, they shock an organization. Tom Malone succeeded Roger Milliken as chief executive officer of Milliken & Company. He decided that his private offices separated him from his coworkers, so one night he had his desk moved out into the middle of the floor. No partitions. Nowhere to hide. No delusions of superiority. How long do you think Malone's managers kept their private offices when the boss stopped using his?

Today, Milliken has no private offices and an abundance of conference rooms. It also has a sense of enthusiasm, teamwork, and pride most senior executives only dream about.

KEY INDICATORS OF QUALITY

A study of Baldrige applications reveals some common attributes shared by our country's quality leaders. These *key excellence indicators* exist in companies that have achieved world-class quality. They provide a terrific synopsis of what it takes to win a Baldrige Award.

The key excellence indicators for the first item in category 1.0, which examines "senior executives' leadership, personal involvement, and visibility in developing and maintaining an environment for quality excellence," are the following:

- Leaders have a missionary zeal about quality. They are highly visible and are very committed to and knowledgeable about quality.

- Leaders set "leapfrog" goals to make dramatic gains in quality, such as Motorola's Six Sigma quality goal by 1992.

- Winning companies are nondenominational, getting ideas from anyone who is doing it better than they are.

- All senior managers are accessible to customers, suppliers, and employees.

- Leaders in winning companies use clear, easily remembered values that can be communicated effectively.

The Westinghouse Commercial Nuclear Fuel Division, which won one of the first Baldrige Awards in 1988, had the following mission:

The Commercial Nuclear Fuel Division exists to serve our customers' needs. We are committed to excellence in our products and service.

To achieve excellence, we must be competent and motivated people who seek opportunities and implement innovative ideas.

In everything we do, we conduct ourselves with openness, integrity, and respect for the individual and society.

You can be sure.

Based on this mission, the division's goal was "to be internationally recognized in the marketplace as the highest-quality fuel supplier."

Motorola prints its corporate objective and key beliefs, goals, and initiatives on a laminated card the size of a credit card, which it hands out to all employees and anyone else who would like one. On one side the card says:

OUR FUNDAMENTAL OBJECTIVE

(Everyone's Overriding Responsibility)

Total Customer Satisfaction

The back of the card outlines how this objective will be achieved:

Key Beliefs—*how we will always act*
- Constant Respect for People
- Uncompromising Integrity

Key Goals—*what we must accomplish*
- Increased Global Market Share
- Best in Class
  —People
  —Marketing
  —Technology
  —Product
  —Manufacturing
  —Service
- Superior Financial Results

Key Initiatives—*how we will do it*
- Six Sigma Quality
- Total Cycle Time Reduction
- Product and Manufacturing Leadership
- Profit Improvement
- Participative Management Within, and Cooperation Between Organizations

In their missions, goals, and objectives, quality leaders share a fondness for brevity, clarity, and strong statements. This is the Xerox Quality Policy:

> Xerox is a quality company. Quality is the basic business principle for Xerox. Quality means providing our internal and external customers with innovative products and services that fully satisfy their requirements. Quality improvement is the job of every Xerox employee.

Each company's approach to communicating its quality values is different, yet each effectively captures the culture and vision of the company.

Item 1.1 of the Baldrige criteria asks for the applicant's quality values and how senior executives project those values throughout the company. Item 1.2 asks how the company evaluates and improves awareness and integration of its quality values.

Cadillac, which won the award in 1990, described several strategies for pushing its values throughout the organization. First, Cadillac's mission statement:

> The mission of the Cadillac Motor Car Company is to engineer, produce and market the world's finest automobiles, known for uncompromised levels of distinctiveness, comfort, convenience and refined performance. Through its people, who are its strength, Cadillac will continuously improve the quality of its products and services to meet or exceed our customer expectations and succeed as a profitable business.

Cadillac uses three primary strategies to integrate its quality values into day-to-day business management:

- A change in culture to recognize teamwork and employee involvement as competitive advantages

- A focus on the customer, both internal and external

- A disciplined approach to planning that puts everyone in the company to work in the continuous improvement process

Zytec's senior executives use the feedback from three different employee surveys, monthly reviews of each department's progress on plans tied to the corporate goals and strategies, and informal discussions with employees in a variety of situations to analyze how well the company's quality values are being adopted.

THE MANAGER'S ROLE

Item 1.2 in category 1.0 focuses on a company's managers and supervisors. "Management for Quality" examines how a company's "customer focus and quality values are integrated into day-to-day leadership, management, and supervision of all company units."

For managers to be quality leaders, they must assume a different role: the "renaissance manager" described by Motorola's Fisher. Managers change from being bosses to being coaches, from talking to listening, from criticizing to supporting, from dictating to facilitating. They translate senior management's goals and strategies into practical, achievable steps. They invite the people they manage to participate in that translation and in the quality improvement process. They learn that being a manager is different than it used to be; it requires a new attitude and new skills.

At the same time, organizations are getting flatter by eliminating levels of management—especially during the times of recession. Companies intent on empowering their employees are eliminating layers of management to push decision making to the front lines. The message to middle managers is that being a manager is not enough: *you must be a quality leader.*

"Our last major hurdle is middle management," says Paul Noakes, vice-president and director of external quality programs for Motorola. "It's hard for them to turn over power. In some cases their jobs are in jeopardy. They don't necessarily have all the training they need, although we've been addressing that problem for the last six years. What we've found is that good managers work the process."

"The major change in the quality movement is the change in the manager's role," says Frank McCabe, vice-president of corporate quality and process technology for Digital Equipment Corporation. McCabe drew a typical control chart. "Before, the manager's role was to help control the variables in a process." McCabe then drew another control chart, to the right of the first chart and significantly lower. "Now, the manager's role is to improve the process dramatically, through such things as JIT. In this way, the manager makes it possible to move to the next level."

Baldrige Award-winning companies tend to have flat organizations; more of their employees are adding value to the products and services the company provides. Managers add value by helping to improve processes and by involving and encouraging the employees they manage.

It is a skill most managers need to learn. In *Kaizen,* Masaaki Imai writes that "American managers put forward their own ideas nine times for every one time they build on, improve, or support other people's ideas in meetings . . . less than half the level of supportive behavior seen in groups from Singapore, Taiwan, Hong Kong, and Japan."

For managers to be effective, they must be trained in listening, statistical thinking, problem solving, and team skills. They must be involved and encouraged by their managers, just as they are being asked to involve and encourage those they manage. And they must be evaluated on and rewarded for their new management behaviors.

One of the key excellence indicators for the leadership category is that "the leaders of successful companies have introduced systems whereby managers are becoming more like coaches than like bosses." Preaching teamwork or customer focus is not enough. Senior management must change the infrastructure to allow managers to succeed, encouraging and reinforcing managers' efforts to become top-notch coaches.

Although "becoming a coach" almost sounds like fun, it is, for most, a scary prospect. Being a manager is like being a parent: anyone believes he or she can do it because we have all had parents and managers and we can do what they do. Now we are telling people that that is not what managers do. That is not how you lead the quality improvement process. Item 1.2 asks how the company's customer focus and quality values are part of its day-to-day leadership.

PUBLIC RESPONSIBILITY

The last item in category 1.0 focuses on corporate citizenship. Item 1.3, "Public Responsibility," asks how a company "includes its responsibilities to the public for health, safety, environmental protection, and ethical business practices in its quality policies and improvement activities, and how it provides leadership in external groups."

If a company apportions pages in its application according to how many points an item is worth, an applicant would have roughly $1\frac{1}{2}$ pages to respond to item 1.3, which is worth 20 points. Even the worst environmental, ethical, and safety offenders can fill a page-and-a-half with a positive description of how they carry out their public responsibilities.

However, they should not deceive themselves into thinking that they can gloss over irresponsible public behavior. During the selection of companies to receive site visits, NIST evaluates the ethical conduct of the finalists.

"We have a responsibility on behalf of the government to prevent embarrassment to the award or to those presenting it," says Curt Reimann. "If a company performs poorly in item 1.3 and item 1.3 is important to that company and its industry, it will be judged harshly."

The Baldrige judges consider an award winner a role model for the nation. A company may score in a range that would make it a candidate for the award, but if it is a poor public citizen, it is a poor role model, and it will not win.

Corporate citizenship and responsibility are elements within a company's quality system, and that makes them leadership issues. Leadership drives the quality system. The senior executives at leading quality companies know that quality problems and quality improvement are quality *system* issues, and that they alone have the power to change the system.

That does not mean that leaders must have all the answers. On the contrary, quality leaders use the system to improve it. They listen and learn from customers, suppliers, and employees (Baldrige categories 7.0, 5.0, and 4.0), and analyze data and information from processes, benchmarking, and customers (categories 2.0, 5.0, 6.0, and 7.0).

Leaders use this information to lead the company's quality planning process (category 3.0). They involve all employees in continuous improvement (category 4.0), use leapfrog goals and cycle time reduction to improve their processes (category 5.0), and keep everyone's eyes on the prize: customer satisfaction (category 7.0).

Leaders are like pilots on a plane: they are guiding the flight of which they are a part, using their charts, instruments, and coworkers to reach their destination successfully. First-time quality leaders, like first-time pilots, often feel overwhelmed at even beginning such a journey.

Pilots take flight lessons. Leaders take quality lessons. The leaders of Federal Express take nine days of quality training a year. Zytec's leaders have taken courses in statistical process control, problem solving, just-in-time manufacturing, Six Sigma, statistical thinking, and customer service, and have taught courses on customer service, quality, communication, and leadership.

Another way to learn is to listen—to customers, employees, suppliers, and quality companies. As you will see in the next few chapters, Baldrige Award winners are good at listening.

All of this information gathering will illuminate what your company needs to do to improve quality. The next question is, How?

"After three years of learning about the Baldrige criteria and how we and world-class companies apply them, our units are beginning to understand *what* is meant by 'world-class,'" says Ronald Abrahams, corporate vice-president of quality and regulatory affairs for Baxter Healthcare. "They want to know *how,* but we don't give them the prescription. Instead, we stress continuous improvement using the PDCA cycle and benchmarking."

PDCA stands for plan-do-check-act—then plan again, in a continuous cycle. World-class companies use the PDCA cycle throughout their organizations for continuous improvement. In the do-it-yourself quality toolbox, the PDCA cycle is often the first tool to be grabbed, a combination tape measure, hammer, screwdriver, and wrench.

The Baldrige Criteria booklet calls PDCA "key learning cycles," noting that they "are explicit and implicit in every part of the criteria. The primary dynamic characteristic of the criteria is their inclusion of cycles of continuous improvement." Managers, supervisors, front-line workers, departments, and teams can use the PDCA cycle to plan, design processes, select indicators, deploy requirements, solve problems, and improve processes.

Senior executives embrace the PDCA cycle as a systematic approach to implementing and leading the quality improvement process. It works like this:

- Plan. Gather facts and data to define the problem or the "gap" between where you are and where you want to be. Benchmark processes with best in class. Involve those who can add value to the plan in the process. Formulate a plan.

- Do. Implement the plan. Make sure the plan includes a way to measure its success.

- Check. Check internal and external indicators to see if the plan is achieving the desired goals.

- Act. If the plan is successful, document and communicate the new process. If it is unsuccessful, refine the plan or develop a new plan—which takes you back to the "plan" part of the cycle.

Finally, *be patient.* The improvement cycle takes time. Changing attitudes and instilling new values take time. Quality takes time.

"You do this because quality is the right thing to do," says GTE's Wolkins. "Your gut tells you it's the right thing to do. There isn't a person in the company who doesn't believe quality has impacted the bottom line positively."

For many senior managers, believing is a lot easier when it is based on solid information. The second Baldrige category, "Information and Analysis," examines the scope of your quality system's information and how that information is used to support continuous improvement.

CHAPTER 5

Information and Analysis

To manage quality you must measure it. Category 2.0 of the Baldrige criteria examines "the scope, validity, analysis, management, and use of data and information to drive quality excellence and improve competitive performance." It also wants to know if your data, information, and analysis system supports the improvement of your customer focus, products, services, and internal operations. Some call it "management by fact," as opposed to management by intuition, management by wishful thinking, or management by blind luck.

Cadillac proudly states that its "quality improvement process rests on a strong foundation of systems for collecting, disseminating, and analyzing data and information."

In its response to Baldrige item 2.1, Xerox wrote, "Of Xerox' 375 major information systems supporting our business, 175 relate specifically to the management, planning, and evaluation of quality."

A matrix in Zytec's application identified 85 different types of quality data segmented by purpose (see Figure 5.1): customer-related; internal operations and processes; employee-related, safety, health, and regulatory; quality performance; and supplier-related. It also listed other data used for proactive process improvements beyond what was shown in the matrix.

A quality system is built on a foundation of fact—which may be one reason the quality systems of many U.S. companies are wobbly. According to Curt Reimann, director of the Baldrige program, applications for the award since its inception have shown that the area of information and analysis is "a serious national problem."

The problem is that many organizations don't measure quality or analyze the data when they do measure it. They don't measure progress toward their quality goals. They cannot identify the cause of quality problems. They have no database on which to plan or evaluate improvements. When they do measure quality, they don't analyze the data for use

71

Customer-Related	Internal Operations and Processes	Quality Performance
Delivery Time—% On Time		Internal Audit Failures—Total/
Corrective Action Request—	Audit Failures—Total/	Department
Total	Department	Quality of Service Providers—
Reliability Test Failures—Total	Quality of Service Providers—	PPM
Visits—Total	PPM	Defective Services/Products—
Warranty Repair—% Return	Cost Reductions—$	PPM
Product Lead Times—Days	Defective Products/Services—	Delivery Times—% On Time
Customer Satisfaction Level	PPM	Test Failures—%
Market Trends—Various	Production Shipments—% On	Customer Satisfaction—Level
Accounting Processes—Various	Time	Training/Instructor Effectiveness
Internal Yield—% and Parts Per	Inventory Turns—#/Year	—Various
Million (PPM)	Material Staff vs Receipts—$	Product Design Margin—Various
Critical Product Parameters—	Design Cycle Time—Weeks	Inventory Accuracy—%
Process	Part Count/Product—Total	Team Accomplishments—Various
Capability Index (Cpk)	Material Cost/Product—$	Benchmark Parameters—Various
Product Nonconformities—PPM	Production Lead Time—Days	
Reliability/Design Margins	Excess Inventory—$	**Employee-Related**
Mean Time Between Failures	Labor % of Sales—%	
(MTBF)—Hours	Computer Integrated Mfg.—%	Lost Time Accidents—Total
Cost Reductions—$	Product Internal Yield—PPM	Customer Visits—Total
	Testing—Failure Rate	Manufacturing Skills Training—
Supplier-Related		Hours
	Safety, Health and	Employee Development—Hours
Defective Product/Service—	**Regulatory**	Implemented Improvement
PPM		System—Participation
Delivery Time—% On Time	Insurance Standards	Quality Training—Hours
Cost Reductions—$	Compliance	Corporate Culture Satisfaction
Dock-to-Stock Parts—%	Regulatory Agency Data	Level Survey
Supplier Base—Total	Hazardous Material Usage/	Baldrige Criteria Implementation
Material Reject Records—Total	Control	Level Survey
Critical Parameters by	Safety Training Effectiveness	Wage/Salary Survey Program
Commodity—Cpk	Audit Nonconformities	Schedules—Accuracy
SPC Training & Implementation		Classroom Training Index
—Level		

Figure 5.1 A matrix showing Zytec's list of quality data.

in planning, reviewing performance, improving processes, or comparing performance with that of competitors.

Measurement has been more of a problem for service companies than for manufacturers, and an even greater hurdle for small businesses. Manufacturing processes tend to consist of tangible, identifiable, chartable steps. Service processes are harder to pin down, as manufacturers themselves have discovered: even those manufacturing companies that excel at measuring their manufacturing processes tend to be weak in measuring support processes in legal, accounting, marketing, sales, and so on.

MEASURING QUALITY

Companies confused about how to measure nonmanufacturing processes need not be discouraged. It can be done, as a few companies have shown.

For example, Banc One measures the intangible interactions between bank personnel and customers by "shopping" each other. Bank people "shop" other bank people, then complete simple forms that ask questions such as, "When you approached the bank representative, did he or she offer a prompt, friendly greeting?" "During the transaction, did the representative use your name?" "What did the representative do to create a memorable experience?" Banc One's goal is nine out of ten positive answers, a 90 percent "shop."

Small businesses typically use far fewer measurements than large corporations because everyone at a small business is closer to the process. "I don't collect data for on-time delivery at this time," says Maureen Steinwall, president of Steinwall, Inc., a small Minneapolis thermoplastics manufacturer. "I don't collect that data because I'm so close to the daily process. I know if I'm on time. Besides, we don't have extra staff available to collect and analyze that data. A lot of my data collection began two years ago because that's when it became important for me to watch."

"Once it becomes clear that certain data adds value, it will be collected," she says. "For example, we have always prided ourselves on being good housekeepers. The question is: How do you know you're doing a good job? Prove it to me. Quantify it. By developing a measure, we've been able to quantify a subjective system."

Many companies struggle with how to develop measures. Honeywell created a guide to total quality management for its managers, called "The Honeywell Quality Improvement Owner's Manual," which explains the six elements of the Honeywell Total Quality Systems Model: top management leadership; culture change; division needs assessment; quality training; improvement process and techniques; and *specific goals and measures*.

The manual identifies the following "Principles of Measurement":

1. Measurement must be specific. You need to know exactly what you want to measure.

2. Measure the outputs of highest value to the customer. This entails converting customer information into measures, which means you must first know exactly what your customers expect.

3. Measures can be applied to all performance dimensions, external as well as internal. It is not enough to achieve an internal goal if you fail to meet customers' expectations or your competitors' performance.

4. Understand the game before you decide how you will keep score. Tracking the wrong measure will not improve your quality.

5. Measure process as well as results. If you just measure results, you will always be fixing mistakes instead of preventing them.

6. You can't hit tomorrow by shooting at yesterday. You can't even hit tomorrow by shooting at today. The science of anticipating future customer and process requirements is called "leading the duck."

7. There is no single perfect measure. First identify the indicators for your objective, then measure all those indicators.

Federal Express uses specific measurements on a grand scale. The company tracks events that negatively affect a customer as they happen using their service quality indicator (SQI). Twelve types of events are weighted by degree of importance to the customer: a lost package is ten points, a package delivered late on the wrong day is five points, an invoice adjustment is one point, and so on.

FedEx's goal is an SQI score of zero. SQI results are broadcast weekly over the company's private television network. Identifying actual failures creates an intense focus on the relatively few service breakdowns.

Twelve cross-functional teams—one for each type of event that leads to customer dissatisfaction—analyze the data from failures or complaints and implement improvements. Two of these corporatewide teams have over 1,000 employees in various subteams working on improvements. In addition, managing directors are developing local SQI measurement systems that support the corporate SQI and their critical success factors.

Federal Express practices management by fact, not management by wishful thinking. SQI fits with the company's other customer measures to help it improve the quality of its services.

BENCHMARKING

In the information age, high-quality information is a competitive advantage. Baldrige item 2.1 examines the base of quality data and information you use to plan, manage your business, and evaluate quality. Item 2.2

broadens the scope of that information to competitive comparisons and benchmarking.

Companies have been scrutinizing competitors ever since there were competitors. When they weren't comparing price, product features, price, sales approaches, or price, they looked at product quality—especially if they did not compare well in the other areas.

Total quality management demands a broader view of competitive comparisons. They are still being made on product and service quality, but they have been extended to include customer satisfaction and other customer data, internal operations, business processes, and support services.

Much of this information is gathered by *benchmarking*.

Benchmarking is the process of understanding your performance, comparing it against the performance of best-in-class companies, learning how they perform better, and using that information to improve. The last two steps in this definition make benchmarking a major contributor to quality improvement.

Benchmarking is arguably the one area in the Baldrige criteria that has stumped the greatest number of applicants. Until very recently, many companies did not know what benchmarking was or believed that it meant comparing results.

I remember Thermo King, a 1990 Baldrige site visit company in the manufacturing category, performing a hasty telephone survey of a half dozen companies to get a number—in this case, the time it took to fill a parts order—for a benchmarking comparison in their application. The number came in handy in the "Quality Results" section of the examination, but it told Thermo King nothing about how to improve the process.

"The most difficult thing about benchmarking has been that most people interpret competitive benchmarking as how do our results compare to theirs," says Mary Lo Sardo, MetLife's assistant vice-president, corporate quality. "It's the *process* we need to be looking at."

Benchmarking has been called "the power tool of quality." It is the difference between teaching yourself how to hit a golf ball and taking lessons from Jack Nicklaus. One leads to inefficient mechanics and frustration, the other to a Six Sigma swing and hope for improvement.

Benchmarking is a power tool because it promotes quantum improvements in processes and because it motivates people. Working the same process day after day, tinkering with improvements suggested by the same team members, it is natural for new ideas to dry up. Xerox describes it as "building a box around ourselves." When you benchmark others, you cut windows in the box.

The effect inspires the habitants of the box, like letting in fresh air and sunlight to a person in solitary confinement. A world of potential exists out there, filled with people who share the same problems but have created different solutions. Some of those solutions will work for you. Others will stir your thoughts and lead to fresh approaches. Still others will point out the strengths in your processes, the things you can proudly tell others about.

Not everyone feels comfortable using power tools, especially the first time. Benchmarking is like any new situation we confront: we worry about whether our questions will be dumb, whether the way we do things will sound inferior, and whether the people we contact will be too busy for us.

All of these are possible, but what most people find is that peers in other companies are just like they are: proud to be asked, willing to share, and eager to learn themselves. They also find that seeing a better way spurs continuous improvement, injects a sense of urgency into an otherwise complacent atmosphere, and involves employees.

"We found that we could cut the cost of the semiconductor circuit board-connector packages used in disk drives and controllers by 65 percent if we adopted best-in-class practices," stated Digital's Bob Paul. "A 65 percent reduction in cost sounds like a lot, but on the strength of our benchmarking studies we know it's an attainable goal. Everyone in the organization is committed to that goal and knows that they will be measured against it. But it is a goal they set themselves."

"We learned that it's not enough to benchmark individual steps in the manufacturing process," Paul added. "You have to look at the potential savings that are possible when you optimize the entire process."

In addition to the 65 percent reduction in cost, Paul estimated a potential increase in their world-class quality by a factor of two. The ability to make this statement suggests the level of measurement taking place at Digital.

Baldrige item 2.2 asks for the process you use to choose companies to benchmark, the scope of your benchmarking, how you use benchmarking data to improve, and how you improve your benchmarking process. The item is worth 25 possible points, but that amount is misleading. *The information gained from benchmarking affects your entire quality system:*

- Category 3.0 asks how you use benchmarking data to develop strategic quality plans. If you know what factors are important to your customers, benchmarking these factors will help you set stretch goals.

- Category 4.0 examines how your human resource plans are derived from your strategic plans. It also asks how your trends in employee well-being and morale compare to key benchmarks.

- Category 5.0 asks how benchmark data are used to improve your processes.

- Category 6.0 expects benchmark comparisons of your product and service quality results, operational performance, business processes results, support services results, and supplier quality results.

- Category 7.0 asks you to compare your customer satisfaction results with those of competitors and world leaders.

You cannot win the Baldrige Award without benchmarking. If you do not compare your processes and results with others, in and out of your industry, you cannot prove how good you are. As one wag put it: "How do you know you're not the cream of the crap?"

The best Baldrige Award applicants tend to be benchmarking demons. As Curt Reimann notes, they "try to find anybody who is doing anything better than they are. They then try to find a way of introducing this into their own system." They don't worry about "following the leader" because they are not followers; they adapt what they learn to their processes, refining and improving until they have created an even better model. Besides, if someone else is doing it better than you are, it is better to learn from the leader than to fall even farther behind.

The benchmarking frenzy began with Xerox. When Xerox counted its benchmarking studies for its 1989 Baldrige application, it stopped at 279. Of course, it helped that Xerox had been doing benchmarking for almost 10 years.

Xerox began benchmarking because it was losing market share in the copier business. It tore apart Japanese copiers to find out why they were better and discovered that the *processes* used to make the copiers were better. In fact, Xerox's cost to make their copiers equaled the selling price of the Japanese copiers.

Such discoveries led to process improvements and to a broader use of benchmarking. Today, the Xerox 10-step benchmarking model is used by all departments and has been widely adopted by companies in all types of industries.

The Xerox 10-Step Model

1. Identify what is to be benchmarked. It can be tangible, such as a product, or intangible, such as customer satisfaction.

2. Identify comparative companies. Some companies, such as Wallace, ask their customers who they should benchmark. Some delegate the search to the team working on improving the process. To use a sales analogy, it is like developing a list of prospective buyers, qualifying those on the list, then contacting them to see if the process should continue. It is the hardest part of the selling process and the hardest part of benchmarking.

3. Determine data collection method and collect data. This usually involves face-to-face discussions with people from the company you are studying.

4. Determine current performance levels. You must collect data on your existing processes for comparison.

5. Project future performance levels. Once you know a performance gap exists, you need to set new performance goals and estimate how long it will take to close the gap.

6. Communicate benchmark findings and gain acceptance. Recommendations go to management. When they are endorsed, they are communicated to employees.

7. Establish functional goals.

8. Develop action plans.

9. Implement the plans and monitor progress.

10. Recalibrate measurements. Close the loop by returning to step 1.

Other companies have modified the Xerox model or developed their own. Digital follows four steps: know your operation; identify the best; incorporate the best; and gain superiority.

Alcoa uses six steps: decide what to benchmark; plan the benchmarking project; understand your own performance; study others; learn from the data; and use the findings.

AT&T's Material Management Services Division has a 12-step process. The first six steps remove any obstacles that could undermine the benchmarking process, including assuring buy-in from the group that wants the benchmarking done, identifying a deadline, determining the scope of the project, and preparing the benchmarking team. The last six steps outline the process.

Whether your company uses four, six, ten, or twelve steps, the benchmarking process follows a similar path: commit to doing it, identify what and who to benchmark, know yourself, study others, and use what you learn to improve quality.

Opening the process to best-in-class helps companies to get around the problem of benchmarking competitors who are either reluctant to share or unwilling to provide anything of substance. The most quoted example in Baldrige circles involves Xerox benchmarking L.L. Bean. As the story goes, Xerox's logistics and distribution unit wanted to find examples of superior warehousing systems. As it looked, the name L.L. Bean kept surfacing. Even though it was in a different industry, a closer look at its warehousing and distribution system revealed strong similarities.

Xerox benchmarked L.L. Bean and incorporated what it learned. As a result, Xerox estimates that 3 to 5 percent of its 10 percent productivity gain could be attributed to benchmarking Bean.

Here is another example. In the late 1980s, Motorola's finance department benchmarked First National Bank of Chicago's check-clearing operations. It applied what it learned about electronic data transfer and other techniques to its processes for closing the books each month. In 1989, Motorola required 8,000 fewer labor hours to audit its books than it needed in 1986, despite a sales increase of more than 50 percent.

The scope of benchmark data showing up in Baldrige applications suggests a steady increase in benchmarking outside a company's industry. "We've always benchmarked well against competitors and ourselves," says Jean Otte, vice-president of quality management for National Car Rental System, "but we never thought to go to companies like American Express or Federal Express. Now we are. It helps that we have a lot to offer them as well, such as our highly sophisticated reservation center, an excellent training program, and an automated process for measuring customer satisfaction."

Information sharing is not necessary for benchmarking—but it helps. Companies with world-class quality processes are seeing a rapid increase in requests for benchmarking information.

"Our reputation as a Baldrige finalist has increased benchmarking requests tenfold," says Beverly McClure, assistant vice-president of corporate quality at USAA, an insurance and financial services association.

Motorola, Federal Express, American Express, Paul Revere Insurance Group, Xerox, IBM, and others report similar demands. An unexpected benefit of benchmarking is the development of partnerships in other areas of business. Companies that would have had little contact without benchmarking are discovering common goals and obstacles.

Some are forming partnerships and consortiums to tackle common causes. GTE, AT&T Bell Labs, and NYNEX have a consortium currently focused on sharing human resources information. Digital, Motorola, and Xerox have agreed to work together to address the collective needs of their suppliers. Their consortium is supported by Boeing and Sematech, an association of 14 semiconductor manufacturers.

Small businesses seem to have the most trouble with benchmarking. Their processes are not on the same scale as those of the larger, more visible corporations. They do not have the resources to devote to a long-term benchmarking process. And often, their businesses change too rapidly for benchmarking data to be useful.

"We can't benchmark L.L. Bean," says Maureen Steinwall, "but we can bounce ideas off our neighbors. That's not as systematic as Baldrige demands, but it works for small businesses."

David Mitchell, president of David Mitchell & Associates, a small computer consulting company located in St. Paul, admits that benchmarking for his company has been very hard. He is looking to fix that. "We're exploring options for benchmarking," Mitchell says, "including forming a benchmarking group in the Twin Cities. We do some benchmarking with larger companies, so we might be able to get them to participate as well."

Some small businesses are using the examiner feedback reports on their Baldrige applications to benchmark their progress in critical areas. The feedback report and how companies are using it are described in Chapter 15.

WHO TO BENCHMARK

The biggest stumbling block for prospective benchmarkers is identifying who to benchmark. Two groups are trying to do something about that on a national level. The American Productivity and Quality Center in Houston is creating a benchmarking clearinghouse that companies can call to find out who is best-in-class for various processes.

The American Quality Foundation and Ernst & Young have undertaken a cross-industry, cross-cultural study to identify and compare the best international quality management practices. Early results of the study were presented at the 1991 Quality Forum VII. The International Quality Study[sm] is described as "a comprehensive database that can be used by companies everywhere to benchmark their own quality performance against 'best practices' around the world."

The final item in Baldrige category 2.0 asks what you do with all the data you collect. Item 2.3, "Analysis and Uses of Company-Level Data," examines "how quality- and performance-related data and information are analyzed and used to support the company's overall operational and planning objectives."

The first two areas to address connect directly to Baldrige categories 6.0 and 7.0. They want to know how you aggregate and analyze your operational performance data and your customer- related data and how you use what you learn in each of these areas to develop priorities and key trends. The third area to address asks how you use key cost, financial, and market data, and the last area to address discusses how you evaluate and improve your analysis.

Baldrige Award-winning companies analyze their data to support key quality and customer service objectives, company-level strategies, decision making, and evaluation. For example, Cadillac performs its analyses using trend charts, control and run charts, projections, simulations, design of experiments, status reports, surveys, forecasting methods, reliability analyses and projections, and regressions analyses.

The analysis of data is one area in which many companies seek outside help. Skills in implementing and using analysis tools must be learned, and unless a company has someone on staff who can teach them, the company must turn to quality experts for training. You cannot "do it yourself" until you have learned the basics.

Expert assistance may also be needed with the types of data to collect and analyses to perform. The 1992 Baldrige Criteria booklet states that "a major consideration relating to use of data and analysis to improve competitive performance involves the creation and use of performance indicators."

You should choose indicators that reflect the factors that determine customer satisfaction and operational performance. Zytec selects quality-related data based on the criteria established by its principal corporate objectives (its 1991 objectives were to become a Six Sigma company by 1995, to reduce cycle time, to improve service to customers, and to win the Baldrige Award). The matrix earlier in this chapter shows the data Zytec chose based on these objectives. Zytec uses quality function deployment, strife testing, the seven "old" and seven "new" statistical problem solving tools, and other analysis tools to evaluate performance, track progress, and initiate improvements.

World-class companies use key indicators to drive customer satisfaction and quality improvement throughout their organizations. Federal Express's service quality indicator is a perfect example. The focus on these indicators forces every division, department, group, and individual to align all activities toward common goals.

The next category zeroes in on the process companies use to define their goals: the strategic planning process.

CHAPTER 6

Strategic Quality Planning

Strategic business planning is an essential part of running a business. Few would say the same about strategic quality planning. In fact, most would question what quality planning is and assume, because they don't know, that it cannot be all that important.

Quality leaders disagree. They see business planning and quality planning as essential elements in their strategic planning process. As one Baldrige Award winner says, "At Cadillac, the business plan *is* the quality plan."

Category 3.0 of the Baldrige criteria looks at how you integrate all key quality requirements into your strategic business planning. It examines your planning process, your short- and long- term plans, and how performance requirements are deployed throughout your company.

STRATEGIC BUSINESS PLANNING

Strategic business planning is the process of answering a few very basic questions:

- What business are we in?

- What are our customers' expectations?

- What are our strengths and weaknesses?

- How do they compare to those of our competitors?

- What must we do to succeed? To excel? To be a world-class leader?

Companies typically respond to these questions by focusing on their products and services or their bottom lines, but to be a quality leader a company must break out of this narrow perspective. Companies with integrated quality and business plans broaden their thinking to include the total needs and expectations of their customers.

A systematic planning process touches every part of a company's quality system. The outline of a typical planning process shows its dependence on the entire system (related Baldrige items are in parentheses):

Strategic quality planning begins with broad quality goals and the principal strategies for achieving them (3.2). Senior management determines goals and strategies (1.1, 3.1) using data about current and future customer requirements and expectations (7.1, 7.6), the company's current quality levels (6.1, 6.2, 6.3) compared to the competition (2.2), process capabilities (5.2, 5.3), and supplier capabilities (5.4).

Next, short- and long-term plans are deployed (3.1) to all units (4.1, 5.1) and suppliers (5.4), resources are committed (3.2, 5.1, 5.2, 5.3, 7.1), and performance relative to plans is reviewed (1.2, 2.1, 2.3, 4.1, 4.2, 4.3, 4.4, 5.1, 5.2, 5.3, 5.4, 5.5, 7.1, 7.2, 7.3, 7.6).

It's not that you cannot separate the best quality planning process from a company's business planning—you cannot separate it from the business. In world-class companies, planning is not a distinct activity designed to nail down financial targets; it is the way quality goals are translated into day-to-day activities. That is what Baldrige category 3.0 measures.

"The scores for this category are generally low, primarily because most companies use old-fashioned short-range planning to produce profits rather than short- and long-range planning to improve quality," says Robert McGrath, a Baldrige examiner for three years and the lead instructor for the ASQC's Baldrige self-assessment course.

Cadillac uses its business planning process to align activities, guide internal processes, and achieve specific short- and long-term quality improvement goals (see Figure 6.1). The four-month process begins with an executive staff review of Cadillac's mission and strategic objectives. This is the alignment phase.

Information gathering takes the form of a situation analysis, involving input from all areas of the company. Based on this information, the executive staff drafts the next year's business objectives, a process that takes four to six weeks. The draft is widely reviewed, then finalized and shared with top union and management leaders. A summary of the business plan is distributed to all employees. For 1991, the business objectives were organized under five headings: Quality, Competitiveness, Disciplined Planning and Execution, Leadership, and People.

Functional staffs and plant quality councils develop goals and action plans to support the business objectives, involving almost every employee

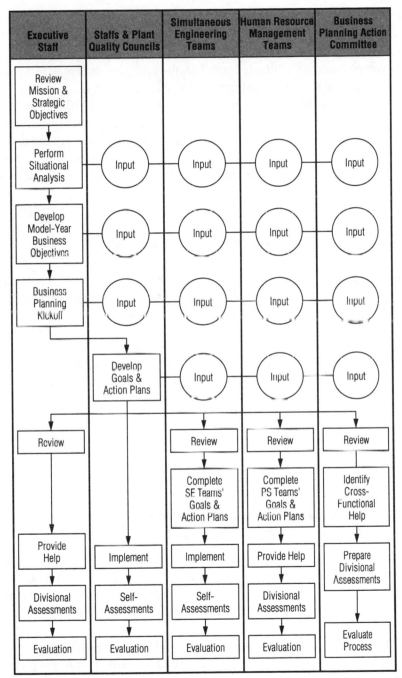

Figure 6.1 Cadillac's business planning process model. (Courtesy of Cadillac)

in this six- to eight-week process. The executive staff reviews all goals and action plans to make sure they are aligned with the objectives and that they encompass all important areas. The entire business plan is communicated to all employees at Cadillac's annual State of the Business meeting in early December, and Cadillac implements the plan in January.

Throughout the planning process, the executive staff, plants, and functional staffs do product and process benchmarking to establish standards for major programs. They also involve suppliers and dealers in the process. The cross-functional Business Planning Action Committee coordinates the planning process and recommends areas for improvement, which are then incorporated into the next year's process.

MANAGEMENT BY PLANNING

Zytec improved its planning process dramatically in 1989 after a senior management benchmarking trip to Japan, where they learned about *hoshin kanri*—what Zytec calls "management by planning."

"Before we implemented management by planning we didn't have any connection between our long-range plan, our budget, and our annual objectives," says Zytec CEO Ron Schmidt. "They're all tied together now."

Zytec's planning process takes the quality and service needs of customers and drives them through the organization and to its suppliers. The process involves three steps:

1. Data is gathered.

2. Goals are set by long-range strategic planning (LRSP) cross- functional teams.

3. Detailed action plans to implement these goals are developed by departmental management by planning (MBP) teams.

The Deming approach to setting goals and developing plans for quality leadership requires that planning be based on data. Each functional area in Zytec collects data by soliciting customer feedback, conducting market research, and benchmarking customers, suppliers, competitors, and industry leaders (see Figure 6.2).

Long-range strategic planning begins when senior management identifies strategic issues. Each issue is assigned to a small strategic planning group, which researches the issue and prepares a report identifying what has been examined and how progress will be measured.

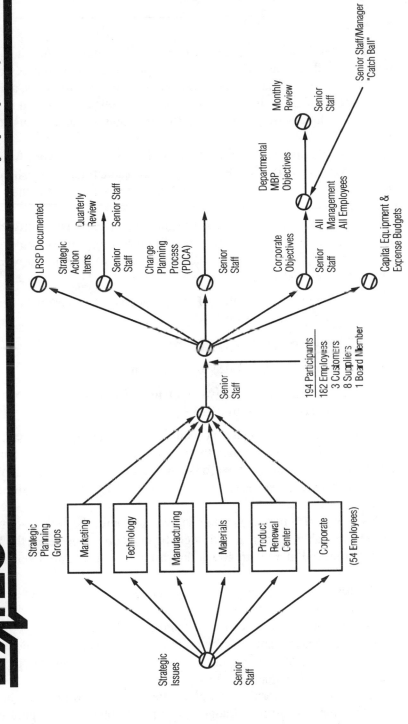

Figure 6.2 Zytec's long-range strategic planning process. (Courtesy of Zytec)

Their reports are critiqued at two off-site, one-day planning meetings attended by all managers, all exempt employees, representatives of the nonexempt and multifunctional employee work force, customers, and suppliers (a total of more than 194 participants in 1991). At the end of these meetings, a document incorporating the presentations and discussions is written.

The people attending the meeting brief the rest of the work force, involving everyone in the LRSP process. At the same time, Zytec shares the LRSP with major customers and suppliers, who are asked for their reactions to the plan.

When agreement is reached on the company's five-year quality vision, the focus shifts to short-term planning. To guide this process, senior management uses the LRSP to set broad objectives for the teams to work on. For 1991, Zytec's objectives were:

1. Improve the quality of our products and processes to become a Six Sigma company by 1995.

2. Reduce our total cycle time.

3. Improve our service to our customer.

4. Improve Zytec so we win the Malcolm Baldrige National Quality Award by 1995.

Using the LRSP and Zytec's corporate objectives as a road map, each major functional area identifies the key performance measures that will help it monitor its progress toward becoming the "best of the best." When work units convert these measures to action plans, Zytec's major strategies become measurable goals.

Each goal is supported by a detailed work plan for the next year that includes measurable, specific monthly goals. In its first three years, the MBP process produced more than 400 action-oriented plans at all levels of the company.

To prevent conflicts between departments, Zytec's senior executives manage an ongoing exchange of information and negotiation with each MBP team, a process referred to as "catch ball." They also meet with representatives of each team to agree on their objectives and to review their detailed plans and measurements. In this way, the maximum energy is focused on Zytec's key quality issues.

Finally, the short-term action plans are converted to financial benchmarks. Detailed department budgets, manpower plans, and capital plans are established that support the objectives.

Throughout the year, senior management reviews monthly goals and progress toward those goals. Each department describes its progress in achieving its objectives, then reviews the action plan for one of its four objectives. Successes are commended, problems are discussed, and new actions or possible solutions are proposed.

"The LRSP is a year-round process," says Schmidt. "In January we have the departments present one of their success stories for the past year and one of their MBPs for the coming year. At the same time, senior management is identifying strategic issues for next year's long-range strategic plan."

Zytec constantly reviews and improves its planning process. Participants suggest improvements when a major step in the process is completed. Zytec's chief financial officer keeps the feedback in a journal and publishes it for participants. The feedback has helped refine the process, expanding employee participation, involving customers and suppliers in the process, improving facilities that are used for the planning meetings, and training participants in methods of organizing their ideas.

Because of the broad involvement in and cross-functional development of the LRSP and MBP, Zytec's direction for the future, both short- and long-range, has broad consensus and support. Zytec's planning process demonstrates the key excellence indicators for Baldrige category 3.0:

- The business plan and quality plan are completely integrated.

- The planning process anticipates present and future customer expectations, focusing on targets derived from customer requirements.

- The plan is deployed to all units.

- The plan incorporates the abilities of suppliers.

Intel follows a similar management by planning process that incorporates quality and business planning into one plan (see Figure 6.3). Like Zytec, the process begins with the identification of corporate objectives. Intel's business groups then create strategic objectives that support the corporate objectives. Teams within the business groups translate each of the strategic objectives into strategies and tactics, which are then addressed with projects and activities—all aimed at achieving the corporate objectives.

To help clarify the connections, business groups use a consistent numbering system. A strategic objective is "1." A strategy to achieve that

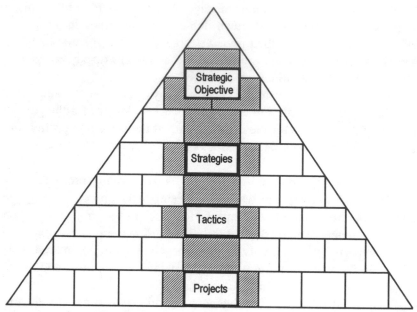

Figure 6.3 The Intel management by planning system. (Courtesy of Intel)

objective would be "1.1." A tactic to achieve that strategy would be "1.1.1." And so on.

"It's easy to understand your role in all this," says Scott Pfotenhauer, total quality manager for Intel's Semiconductor Product Group. "Our goal is to have 85 to 90 percent of our activities supporting our corporate objectives. With management by planning, it's clear whether or not your activities support the corporate objectives."

Paul Revere Insurance Group's planning process reflects a different approach, with similar results. In 1984, Paul Revere started a quality idea system that included recognition for significant achievement. As the process matured, employees requested a planning and evaluation system that would better accommodate both short- and long-term activities. The company responded by introducing a goal-setting and self-assessment structure that expands on the original quality idea model.

At the beginning of the year, division and department managers draft operating plans based on the company's business plan. They then circulate the drafts among their people for reaction and input.

The final operating plan has both short- and long-term goals. Individuals set objectives based on the operating plan. Quality teams, both existing teams and new teams formed to address new issues, set challenging and meaningful goals that align with their departmental operating plans.

Currently, the company requires its teams to set at least 50 percent of the goals with hard dollar or quantifiable measures. This goal-setting structure enables teams to plan either short- or long-term activities as needed, and also allows them to pursue "quick-hit" quality ideas.

Quality analysts and senior managers help teams to set goals that match their job functions and abilities. They also help to identify measurements. "Setting goals is relatively easy," says Penny LaFortune, quality analyst. "Setting measurements is the toughest part. That's when the departments and teams contact us. What's most important is that we set company measurements first, then department measurements that are in alignment."

Measurements are identified as bronze, silver, and gold standards of achievement, modeled after the Olympics. A team must demonstrate that it has not only met but exceeded all customer expectations to earn a level of recognition and reward.

"At Paul Revere the quality planning process is not a separate entity," says LaFortune. "We have 100 percent involvement. Everybody in the company feels he or she can make a difference."

Banc One Corporation's quality planning process is tied directly to the Baldrige criteria. Each affiliate of Banc One develops its own annual quality plan. The internal assessment is done by each department in a medium- to large-sized bank, and by the entire organization in smaller banks.

"We distribute the planning document in the middle of the year and provide training and consulting for anyone who wants them," says Charles Aubrey, vice-president and chief quality officer. "We recommend that each bank complete its quality plan before its business plan, then revisit the quality plan after the business plan is reviewed. That way most things in the quality plan get integrated into the business plan."

The quality plan usually begins with a calculation of the cost of poor service, as shown in Table 6.1. The lost revenue and excess numbers are referred to at the end of the quality plan with two boxes: one for the estimated revenue *not* lost because this quality plan is implemented; the other for estimated cost *not* incurred because the plan is implemented.

The quality plan asks banks and departments to commit to quality goals correlated with the Baldrige criteria. For example, under "Leadership" the team completing the plan must commit to the following: a number of quality councils; a number of managers and officers attending quality training; the time the CEO, COO, CQO, and department heads will devote to quality; the number of people attending quarterly CQO conferences; the

Table 6.1 Banc One Quality Plan

Lost Revenue Estimate		Your Estimate	Ave. Bank
A.	Annual Revenue (Interest and Noninterest Income)	$_____	
B.	Number of Customers or Accounts:	#_____	
C.	Percentage of Dissatisfied Customers or Accounts (Range 5–45)	x_____	25%
D.	Number of Dissatisfied Customers or Accounts (C × B)	=#_____	
E.	Percentage of Dissatisfied Customers or Accounts Likely to Switch (Range 60–90%):	x_____	75%
F.	Number of Dissatisfied Customers or Accounts Who Will Switch (D × E)	=#_____	
G.	Revenue Per Customer or Account (A/B):	=$_____	
H.	**Potential Revenue Lost through Poor Service Quality (F × G):**	=$_____	
Excess Expense Estimate			
A.	Annual Operating Expense (Noninterest Operating Expense)	$_____	
B.	Percent of Expense to Do Things Over Again and Placate Dissatisfied Customers (Range 15–40%):	x_____	25%
C.	**Potential Excess Expense Due to Poor Service Quality (A × B):**	=$_____	

total direct expense of quality activities; and so forth. The team must also list action plans or steps to accomplish the goals, with an expected date of completion. The action plans are reviewed quarterly for progress.

Banc One's 1991 quality plan covers all the Baldrige criteria. Each statement correlates directly with a Baldrige item, which is noted in the planning document.

In addition to training, Banc One teaches quality planning by example. "First, we gave everyone an example of the most aggressive quality plans we have in the Banc One system," says Aubrey. "It's always helpful to find out what other banks in the system are doing. I then created a realistic model of what a world-class bank would look like. For those banks that are already the best, seeing what 'world-class' means can be very helpful."

World-class companies plan how they will improve their quality systems. When little or no planning takes place, companies are susceptible to "program of the month" temptations, to false starts, dead ends, wrong turns, and unnecessarily long journeys. Without a plan to guide and integrate every effort, a company cannot move as one toward meeting its customer and company performance requirements.

"I find that the people who prepare the best quality plans do the best jobs in quality," Aubrey concludes. "It's not the plan itself, it's their commitment to quality."

The next chapter considers how a company's commitment to quality is embraced and shared by its most valuable resource: its people.

CHAPTER 7

Human Resource
Development and Management

In his book, *Kaizen*, Masaaki Imai wrote, "When speaking of 'quality,' one tends to think first in terms of product quality." "Nothing could be further from the truth. In Total Quality Control, the first and foremost concern is with the quality of the people."

Frank Caplan is a senior Baldrige examiner and owner of a quality consulting firm in Issaquah, Washington. He sees a lot of companies having problems with the human resource part of their quality systems. "I can name 10 companies that are good at serving customers and horrible at treating employees," Caplan says. "The first thing that happens in any downturn is that people get laid off because we're more worried about the quarterly report than how we treat people."

For many companies, a downturn isn't needed to treat employees like commodities. Business magazines are littered with executives' quotes that convey insensitivity toward their people. For example, consider the following quotes by John Trani, who took over GE Medical Systems in 1986. According to an article in *Fortune,* "Trani gave himself 60 days to analyze the business and formulate a vision that would change the company's unacceptable paradigm. First, says Trani, 'half the middle managers went home. They were doing non-value-added work that just didn't have to be done.'"

The article also quotes Trani as saying, "People come to me and ask, 'Why was I good enough yesterday but not today?' It's simple. In 1954, Roger Bannister won world acclaim for breaking the four-minute mile. Today high-schoolers can do that. The standard is always changing, but there's always a top ten and a bottom ten."

The question begs another answer: "You are not good enough today because we did not lead, involve, empower, train, and reward you. Our fault, not yours. But you're going to pay anyway."

Caplan offers a contrast that captures the essence of the fourth Baldrige category. "When I was a kid we lived in Bethlehem, Pennsylvania," he says. "My grandfather and uncles worked in the steel plants there. During the Depression, Bethlehem Steel got its employees together in large groups and said, 'It looks to us like this depression is going to be a long-term proposition. We're afraid the economy as a whole is in trouble. We want you to help us think very carefully about how to deal with each other and the company in these circumstances.'"

"I remember my grandfather talking about this at the dinner table that night. He said, 'We decided that those of us who had the most seniority will only work two or three days a week if times get really bad, so the rest of the people can be kept on the payroll.'"

Times got bad. Steel companies let people go to the degree, Caplan remembers, that "one out of three people on Pittsburgh's streets was a laid-off steel worker." But nobody got laid off by Bethlehem Steel.

EFFECTIVE HUMAN RESOURCE STRATEGIES

High-quality companies treat their human resource as a resource, not a commodity. They struggle against the corporate mentality that separates upper management from other employees, the quick-fix option of getting rid of people to save money, and the tendency to focus on the job and forget about the person. None of them wins all these struggles all the time. But their people remain committed to respecting each other and working together toward a common goal.

Globe demonstrated its commitment to its employees by initiating a companywide profit-sharing program, eliminating time clocks at its main facility, responding to quality-related questions within 24 hours, reviewing the company's financial performance with every employee, and eliminating layoffs.

Federal Express is committed to a policy of limiting layoffs as much as possible. Several years ago FedEx discontinued its electronic mail service, a decision affecting 1,300 people. Not one lost his or her job.

The people who work at companies like Globe and Federal Express see each other as internal customers. Some companies use that term. Others just practice the concept. MBNA America, for example, carries the internal customer concept further by shunning the term "employee." It says *people* work at MBNA and that managers manage efforts, not people. Milliken calls its employees "associates," as do Wallace Company and a growing number of companies across the country. That may seem like semantics to some, but it points out how far companies are willing to go to break the hierarchy implied by the terms "manager" and "employee," a hierarchy that restricts rather than releases the potential of the human resource.

Tom Oliver, a senior vice-president for Federal Express, says, "I know that if we can keep bringing out the best in the people of Federal Express, we'll succeed in improving the quality of our service, reducing costs, and building our competitive advantage. And that's exactly what the quality improvement process does. It brings out the best in us."

Baldrige category 4.0, "Human Resource Development and Management," asks how you bring out the best in your people. Specifically, it "examines the key elements of how the company develops and realizes the full potential of the work force to pursue the company's quality and performance objectives." Also examined are the company's efforts to build and maintain an environment for quality excellence conducive to full participation and personal and organizational growth.

For many companies—even quality leaders—the responses to this category are a mixed bag. They may be doing something in areas that bring out the best in their people, such as teams, suggestion systems, training, recognition, and measurement of employee satisfaction, but their efforts tend to be disorganized, inconsistent, and hard to measure. They lack a systematic approach and full deployment to all employees.

ALIGNMENT

A systematic approach to using your human resource begins by aligning human resource plans with your company's quality goals, strategies, and plans. Baldrige item 4.1 wants to know about this alignment. What will you need to do in such areas as training, development, employee involvement, empowerment, and recognition to achieve the short- and long-term goals identified in item 3.2? What are your human resource quality improvement goals? How do you use employee-related data to improve your employees' effectiveness?

At Cadillac, the people part of the business planning process is fully integrated and tied to the goals identified in the plan and in item 3.2.

Zytec can show how the company's guiding philosophy, Deming's 14 Points for Management, is translated first into long-range plans, then long-range strategic objectives, and finally into short-term human resource objectives. The process follows a traceable path that identifies quality improvement goals for human resources at the same time that it aligns those goals and the rest of its human resource plans with Deming's Points and the company's long-range strategic plan.

IBM Rochester's human resource strategy is guided by three factors:

1. An IBM basic belief: respect for the individual.

2. The Rochester site vision for people: enabled, empowered, excited, and rewarded.

3. The goal to shift from a product-driven quality focus to a market-driven quality focus.

Based on these factors, IBM Rochester's human resource strategy has three initiatives: formal education and communication (IBM Rochester spends five times the national average for education); customer contact (all employees are given opportunities for regular contact with customers); and participation initiatives (these include empowerment programs, job flexibility, recognition, and compensation).

EMPLOYEE INVOLVEMENT

"Employee Involvement" is item 4.2 in the human resources category. It examines "the means available for all employees to contribute effectively to meeting the company's quality and performance objectives."

Employee involvement has been a big enough issue for a long enough time that it has its own acronym: EI. Employees have always been involved in doing the work that makes a company's processes function; now they are being given ownership of the processes. That's EI.

Milliken has 17 plants that are being run completely by self-directed teams. That's EI.

In 1991, Milliken's associates submitted 663,000 ideas for improvement, or an average of 52 ideas per person. That's EI.

Any Zytec employee can spend up to $1,000 to resolve a customer complaint without prior authority. That's EI.

In 1989, 75 percent of all Xerox Business Products and Systems employees were actively involved in quality improvement or problem-solving projects. That's EI.

IBM Rochester measures "technical vitality," its term for employee participation in such things as articles written for professional journals, patent applications, and inventions. From 1986 to 1989 the number of activities nearly tripled, to 1,100. That's EI.

At Cadillac, the number of hourly and salaried employees working on teams increased 600 percent from 1985 to 1989. That's EI.

Employee participation at Wallace increased the same amount. In 1991, Wallace had 116 teams in place, and most of the company's 280 employees serve on several teams. That's EI.

As these examples suggest, the two most common means of employee involvement are teams and suggestion systems. Teams take many forms: by task, process, department, division, or company; cross-functional and cross-departmental; formal and informal; short- and long-term. They typically form to solve a problem or improve a process, and they usually disband when they complete their mission.

A work unit is a team. For example, at Cadillac's very traditional Grand Blanc sheet metal plant, the stamping line asked if it could compete in the national Quick Die Change competition. (For those who have never been inside a manufacturing plant, a die is the part of a machine that stamps, cuts, or molds material—in this case sheet metal—into a particular shape.) Management gave them the go-ahead, but said it could not provide any funding, although it did provide training. When the team started, it took them 10 to 12 hours to change a die. By their first competition, they had cut the time to 4:59—not hours and minutes, but minutes and seconds. The next year they had it down to 3 minutes, 46 seconds. They cut the cycle time from over 600 minutes to less than 4 minutes because they assumed ownership of the process. That is the power of teams.

Executives in the United States fell in love with teams when they first saw quality circles in Japan. The current love affair sees the team in a different light: trained, empowered, focused on specific problems or opportunities, and contributing to dramatic quality improvements.

The Paul Revere Insurance Group thrives on quality teams. It assigns new employees to quality teams on their first day of employment. Team leaders are trained through Paul Revere's Team Leader Institute, given broad responsibilities, encouraged to share information at the Team Leader Conference Day, and recognized for their leadership at a Team Leader Reception. Team members are also trained, involved, and recognized.

The success of the team approach has inspired American business to levels of teamwork that approach those of the Japanese. But in another area of employee involvement, individual contributions, U.S. business still lags far behind; *U.S. companies average one-half suggestion for improvement per employee per year*. Milliken got 52 per associate in 1991. Citizen Watch in Japan averages 201. The management of Nissan, which receives 19 suggestions per employee per year, seriously considers any suggestion that saves at least 0.6 seconds. That's about as long as it takes to say the word "empowered."

Many American companies have tried various suggestion systems, with little success. The problem is that nobody makes suggestions. Even paying for suggestions has not helped.

In *Kaizen*, Masaaki Imai outlines three stages a suggestion system should go through:

1. Management helps workers provide suggestions that improve the workers' jobs and the work area.

2. Management stresses employee education so that workers can provide better suggestions.

3. Management focuses on the economic impact of the suggestions.

Notice that all three stages describe management actions. "Getting productive ideas from employees is not so much a matter of having creative employees as it is one of having supportive management," Imai writes. "If a manager cannot get the workers to introduce productive ideas, most likely he is the problem, not the workers."

Milliken, which got more than 660,000 ideas in 1991, does not have a suggestion system. It has opportunities for improvement, or OFIs. "We solicit ideas," says Bill Hogg, dealer development director. "Our process encourages, evaluates, and implements ideas. But there are no financial rewards for these ideas, and most ideas aren't cost savers."

Why would people submit 52 ideas a year if they were not going to get paid for them? Because they care about their jobs and their company and because their ideas are taken seriously.

Milliken has a policy it calls 24/72. When someone submits an OFI (an idea), his or her supervisor must respond within 24 hours. The response may just be acknowledgment that the idea was received. Within 72 hours, the supervisor must have a plan to act on the idea, and share that plan with the employee. In 1990, Milliken *implemented* about 400,000 ideas. If each one saved just $5, the OFIs would have saved Milliken a cool two million in one year.

According to Imai, "Japanese managers are willing to go along with a change if it contributes to any of the following: making the job easier; removing drudgery from the job; removing nuisance from the job; making the job safer; making the job more productive; improving product quality; saving time and cost. This is in sharp contrast to the Western manager's almost exclusive concern with the cost of the change and its economic payback."

As Milliken has shown, not all Western managers are concerned with the financial aspect of suggestion systems. And look where it gets them.

Teams and suggestion systems empower people. Baldrige item 4.2 values empowerment, which is why Baldrige Award winners excel at employee involvement. Zytec involves nearly all of its employees in short- and long-range strategic planning. It empowers them to spend up to $1,000, without authorization, to serve customers. It empowers hourly workers to make changes in a process with the agreement of only one other person. It authorizes sales people to travel whenever they feel it is necessary for customer service.

Zytec's production workers designed a multifunctional employee (MFE) system. They identified tasks which, when mastered, would make an employee more flexible and increase his or her pay. An employee group monitors and improves the system. All non-MFE employees work with their managers to develop personal action plans focused on improved performance. This program was also developed by an employee team.

Through these and other activities, Zytec empowers its employees to improve quality, in line with Deming's 14th Point, which states that management must "put everybody in the company to work to accomplish the transformation."

If you are not interested in a transformation, you are probably not interested in employee involvement. Once you start along the path of empowerment, it is very hard to turn back. It's like prying the lid off a well-sealed can of worms. When the worms turn, leaders had better be ready to lead, because grabbing back all the power by slapping the lid on makes for a very unhappy and unproductive work force.

Consider a typical situation: You receive bad parts from a supplier, and your product, which requires those parts, is due to the customer in a few days. Here is the likely solution: You call the customer to explain the problem and the reason for the delay. You promise that the product will be shipped as soon as possible.

Here is another solution: Your front-line, blue-collar workers decide, on their own, to fabricate the parts they need. They arrange their own shifts, over a weekend, to get the job done. As a result, they meet the customers' expectations for high-quality products delivered on time.

The first solution costs customers and the second solution costs money. Which costs more? Many companies, however, do not even have the second option because it requires employee involvement. In this case, the second solution happens to be the actual response of a GTE facility, where empowered employees took personal responsibility for GTE's commitment to customer service.

As companies flatten their organizations, eliminating layers of management, they must give employees more responsibility. If the managers are not in place to monitor the employees, then employees must be trusted to do the jobs on their own. Employee involvement makes this possible.

For small businesses, employee involvement is not as big an issue. "Empowerment is why small businesses are successful," says Maureen Steinwall, president of a 50-person thermoplastics company. "We're all close to our challenges and our customers." But although empowering employees to act is less of a problem for small businesses, Steinwall finds that technical training is more difficult. "We need to incorporate more training, but that's tough to do because our training budget as a percent of payroll is much higher than that of most large corporations."

Many companies, including small businesses, begin their quality improvement journey with training. Wallace started with quality awareness training. John and Sonny Wallace, the company's chief executive officer and president, led sessions for all employees that explained Wallace's new direction and covered such subjects as team-building skills, problem solving, and statistical process control. During the next three years, Wallace invested more than $700,000 in training its 280 employees, an average of $2,500 per employee.

One reason that Globe Metallurgical was the first small business to win a Baldrige Award was the 1,260 total hours of training in quality techniques its 210 employees received. That was 1,260 hours in the classroom instead of on the shop floor—a significant amount for a small company.

EMPLOYEE TRAINING

Baldrige item 4.3 focuses on employee education and training—not training related to the employee's job, which is a given, but training that employees need to achieve their quality objectives. The item asks how you know what types of quality and related training to provide, how you utilize the knowledge and skills your employees acquire, what quality and related training your employees have received, and how you evaluate and improve the effectiveness of that training.

When it comes to training employees, one of the best U.S. role models is Motorola. Motorola began its focus on training in 1980, when it established the Motorola Training and Education Center. In 1989 Motorola changed the Center's name to Motorola University, reflecting a change in focus from the needs of the organization to a broader education relevant to the company, the job, and the individual.

Motorola's commitment to employee education grew out of the realization that it needed better-educated employees to compete. "We learned that line workers had to actually understand their work and their equipment," William Wiggenhorn, president of Motorola University, wrote in *Harvard Business Review,* "that senior management had to exemplify and reinforce new methods and skills if they were going to stick, that change had to be continuous and participative, and that education—not just instruction—was the only way to make all this occur."

The course they took demonstrates the fits and starts so common to training programs and to all long-term quality improvement activities. As Wiggenhorn noted, "We had thought progress would be made in leaps, but it took place one step at a time."

Motorola started with an intensive, one-time course for its executives. When the desired cultural changes did not materialize, the Motorola Training and Education Center was formed. It developed a five-part curriculum that included courses in statistical process control, problem solving, presenting conceptual material, effective meetings, and goal setting. A typical Motorola plant invested 20 hours of employee time in this program. It, too, failed, primarily because employees were not motivated to learn and senior managers were not learning what was being taught to those they managed. Motorola changed its training program with two initiatives: hiring and training its manufacturing talent more carefully, and training upper management and line workers in the same concepts.

Motorola was now five years into its focus on training. From 1985 to 1987, Motorola's top 200 executives each spent 10 days learning about manufacturing, five days on global competition, and two days on managing cycle time. These major components were then cascaded down through the company.

However, a component Motorola had not anticipated was missing: elementary reading and math. The company discovered the problem as it prepared its Arlington Heights, Illinois, plant to become a new cellular manufacturing facility, converting it from working with radio technology to cellular technology. Only 40 percent of the facility's employees passed a simple math test.

The problem, it turned out, was that the 60 percent who failed could not read the questions. Motorola quickly established a standard for new hires based on seventh grade math and reading skills, then set about learning how many of its existing employees could meet that standard. "Documenting installations one by one," Wiggenhorn says, "we concluded that about half of our 25,000 manufacturing and support people in the United States failed to meet the seventh grade yardstick in English and math."

To address the problem, Motorola turned to community colleges. But it did not turn the problem over. Instead, Motorola sees schools and colleges as suppliers and works with them to improve the quality of their "products," Motorola's employees. Motorola and its educational partners exchange faculty, jointly develop curriculum, and share lab equipment.

In addition to its $60 million annual education budget, Motorola invests in schools that are willing to be Motorola suppliers. It provides summer internships, encourages the schools to use its labs for all their students, sponsors a planning institute for superintendents from 52 school districts in 18 states, and finds Motorola employees who are willing to work with the schools.

All of this expands the traditional view of corporate training to roles that may be more appropriate for a university. Motorola University, that is. "The word university is undeniably ambitious," says Wiggenhorn, "but Motorola management has always tried to use words in ways that force people to rethink their assumptions."

American executives have long assumed that training costs money. Excellent companies like Motorola would say that it saves money.

IBM Rochester spends an amount equal to 5 percent of its payroll on training. It focuses that money on two areas: quality information and processes and specific, job-related training. It calls employee education the catalyst that makes quality happen, the reason revenue per employee increased 35 percent from 1986 to 1989 while the time it took to develop a new mid-range computer was cut in half.

Every Xerox employee receives 28 hours of quality training. Cadillac and Motorola average 40 hours of quality-related education per employee per year. Milliken averages 76 hours per employee per year. Like IBM Rochester, they understand that do-it-yourself quality is not possible without trained do-it-yourselfers. You can point them toward the goal, arm them with the tools, and nudge them with high inspiration, but if they don't know what they are doing, quality will suffer.

QUALITY RECOGNITION

Baldrige item 4.4 in the human resources category evaluates how your employee performance, recognition, promotion, compensation, reward, and feedback processes support your quality and performance objectives.

Recognition is another strength of quality companies. Paul Revere Insurance Group uses a host of approaches to recognize quality efforts: quality gift certificates for employees who achieve their quality measures; quality coins and ice cream tokens, given spontaneously by managers for service beyond the expected, which are redeemable for a free lunch or ice cream at the company's cafeteria; year-end awards to individuals and teams for service excellence; the company's annual Quality Celebration, which marks the end of each quality year; Qualifest, an opportunity for quality teams to share information with other employees; presidential citations, given to individuals who communicate effectively with their customers and provide service excellence; and Team Leader Conference Day, a special day for team leaders to network and share ideas.

At Banc One Corporation, the number of quality awards presented has risen from 272 in 1986 to 15,394 in 1990. The awards include the Chairman's Quality of Customer Service, Annual Quality Plan Performance, Best of the Best, Great Impressions, We Care Award, and the Witty Award (for "Whatever It Takes, Thank You"). The best quality improvement projects are further recognized by being included in a Best of the Best book. The 1990 edition described 276 team projects, roughly half of which identified cost reductions and/or revenue enhancements that totaled nearly $12 million.

Many companies are creating quality awards based on the Baldrige criteria. Cargill, Baxter Healthcare, Intel, 3M, and others evaluate the quality improvement efforts of plants, departments, work units, and divisions using an exact or modified version of the Baldrige criteria. Their awards are described in detail in Chapter 10.

For quality companies, aligning recognition with quality objectives has been relatively easy. Aligning performance measurements with quality objectives has been more difficult, and the few that do accomplish it tend to focus it on management, marketing, and sales people. An exception is Cadillac which, in line with Deming's philosophy, eliminated its traditional employee rating systems and instituted a performance development planning process.

At Federal Express, the bonuses for management and professionals are tied to performance on the three corporate objectives: people, service, and profit. An annual employee survey determines performance on the people objective. If workers don't rate executives at least as high as the previous year, no executives receive year-end bonuses. Measurement for the service objective is the service quality indicator. Profit is self-explanatory.

Federal Express initiated this performance measurement system in 1988. The company did not meet its goals in 1989, so no bonuses were given to upper management. When you consider that bonuses can account for up to half a senior vice-president's expected income, you can see how such a system would focus management's attention on the continuous improvement of its quality system.

GTE aligns performance with quality objectives through incentive compensation, computed as follows: 35 percent for meeting quality objectives; 35 percent for meeting financial objectives; and 30 percent for "other."

"Our quality objectives are based on our customers' perceptions of quality," says D. Otis Wolkins, vice-president of quality services. "We have an outside consulting firm do a statistical sample monthly in each of our market segments. Our customers tell us what's important, and we turn their input into objectives. If you miss the objectives, you can miss up to 35 percent of your bonus."

QUALITY WORK ENVIRONMENT

Baldrige item 4.5 in the human resources category asks how you maintain "a work environment conducive to the well-being and growth of all employees." It addresses employee health, safety, satisfaction, and ergonomics. It examines mobility, flexibility, and retraining to support employee development, and it asks about special services, facilities, and opportunities your company makes available to employees. It looks at how you determine employee satisfaction, and requests trends in your key indicators of employee well-being and morale.

"What we have seen repeatedly in the companies that do well in the competition for this award," says Curt Reimann, Baldrige program director, "is that they have lower turnover, accident, and absenteeism rates."

For companies turning to their work force to improve quality, retention of employees, like retention of customers, has become critical to their success. The successful quality companies promote the health and safety of their employees. They work to keep morale high, and they use a variety of tools to measure employee satisfaction.

At Cadillac, illness and injury rates have improved by more than 33 percent, while workers compensation cases have been cut in half. Milliken measures its disabling incidence rate per 200,000 hours worked. From 1985 to 1988, it cut that rate in half to a level 3 times lower than the textile industry average and 12 times less than the average for all industries.

As you would expect, the measures of employee satisfaction for excellent companies often show that 90 percent or more of the people are happy with their jobs. Absenteeism, grievances, strikes, and other signs of discontent are low. Employee turnover at Cadillac is 0.3 percent per year. Xerox improved its turnover rate by 36 percent in three years.

The results reflect the quality companies' concern for the well-being and morale of their employees. They strive to consider each person as an individual, a resource to benefit from rather than a commodity to be used. They implement processes to prevent accidents. They anticipate and correct issues that may increase turnover. And they seek total employee satisfaction because they know it is vital to total customer satisfaction and to total quality.

Excellent companies use change to their advantage. People change, and companies that ignore that fact end up with an unhappy—and unproductive—work force. Quality companies help their employees to develop as workers and as people. They design employee assistance programs that respond to the identified, not imagined, needs of their employees, and they create programs that help their companies and their employees serve the community.

The degree to which your employees are involved, empowered, trained, and satisfied will be apparent in the success of your business. The processes that produce your products and services, examined in the next Baldrige category, depend on people to function effectively and efficiently.

Not commodities. People.

CHAPTER 8

Management of Process Quality and Quality and Operational Results

At last, that part of the quality system the old-timers live for: process design and control. Enough of that soft human resources and strategic planning stuff. We have the data we need and we're tired of waiting at senior management's doorstep for financial crumbs. Leave us to our processes. Let us measure, analyze, and tinker. We *are* the do-it-yourselfers, the quality pros, the leaders of the Quali T Rap.

> Cycle time and SPC,
> Poka yoke, JIT,
> Scatters, fishbones, runs, and flows
> Numbers. Concepts. On your toes!
> Pareto and the "vital few,"
> CIM and CAD/CAM, too,
> QFD and DOE,
> Cpk's and Taguchi,
> Automation, EDI,
> And yes! Six Sigma! My, oh, my.
> Implement the Quali T Rap!
> Implement and close the gap.
> Quali T Pros can teach the tools
> To all those other corporate fools.
> Yes! Quali T Rap is on a roll!
> We're in control! We're in control!

Until recently, only quality professionals could appreciate the terms and acronyms so carefully arranged on the quality platter. The American Society for Quality Control, our country's largest collection of quality professionals at about 100,000 strong, has spent much of its nearly 50 years feeding quality philosophies and tools to its members without so much as giving outsiders a taste. Not that outsiders really wanted a taste.

Global competition changed that. Executives who didn't know they had a quality manager suddenly wanted to be one themselves. Some even added a title: CQO (chief quality officer). Quality has moved from the back room to the board room, and quality managers have gone from their control charts to their company's organizational charts.

The first place that people look internally for quality is in the quality of the processes used to produce a product or service. A statistical process control chart is visible proof of quality improvements. A trend chart indicates progress. A flow chart shows process improvements.

While many service companies struggle with Baldrige category 5.0, manufacturing companies wallow in it. It is not uncommon to see a first draft of this category that is as long as the whole application is supposed to be.

The trouble for quality professionals is that category 5.0 is worth 140 of the examination's possible 1,000 points, and the items that relate to the processes that produce their products or services account for only 75 points, less than 10 percent of the total for what might be 100 percent of their quality improvement efforts.

Yet even in its strongest area, U.S. companies often compare poorly to their Japanese counterparts. In his book *Managing Quality,* David Garvin compares U.S. and Japanese factories in the room air conditioner industry.

> Overall, the Japanese plants had distinctly superior production and work force management. Their manufacturing processes were more stable and predictable, and tight control was the norm. Strict process limits had been established using statistical techniques; handling damage, worker inexperience, and other sources of variability had been regulated to the extent possible; rigorous audits and tests ensured that deviations were quickly discovered and reported; and long production runs built up learning and accumulated experience. The resulting manufacturing operations had few defects that could be traced to process-related problems.

Garvin's description highlights key elements in Baldrige category 5.0: using statistical techniques to control processes; performing audits and tests to assess quality; and the elimination of defects. The category begins at the starting point for products and services: the customer.

DESIGN QUALITY

Baldrige item 5.1 examines how you design and introduce new and improved products and services and how you design your processes to meet key product and service requirements. It is fed by item 7.1, which asks what the most important factors in maintaining and building relationships with your customers are; by category 3.0, which identifies your improvement priorities; and by category 4.0, which assesses the capacity of your employees to design high-quality products, services, and processes.

How you determine your customers' needs and expectations is covered in item 7.1. How you convert those needs and expectations to products, services, and processes is the focus of item 5.1.

Do-it-yourself tools exist for this purpose. Digital uses voice of the customer tools. Cadillac employs a process called simultaneous engineering. IBM applies tools such as conjoint analysis. Early steps in Motorola's Six Sigma process identify customer needs and define the process for doing the work. The Xerox delivery process incorporates customer requirements at each step.

One of Digital's tools is called contextual inquiry. It puts Digital employees in their customers' shoes through a powerful interactive process:

1. Talk with users in their work context. Explore the nature of their initial responses to the relevant products and services.

2. Watch them work. Let them do the talking. When you form a new understanding of what they are doing or experiencing, briefly share that with users. Together theorize about the user's experience.

3. Summarize functions or features found usable or missing. Clarify any emergent issues. Accept surprise! Be ready to take on a new challenge to our technology and creativity.

"Contextual inquiry helps us go beyond what we get when we ask customers what they need," says Frank McCabe, vice-president of corporate quality and process technology for Digital. "We watch them work. We talk to them. And then we use the data we gather for quality factor development."

QFD (more commonly known as quality function deployment) uses matrix charts to define and prioritize customer wants and needs and to fo-

111

cus efforts on meeting the customer's true desires. "It's like auto makers watching people in a supermarket parking lot," McCabe says. "They want to see how a car's trunk is used in real life, if it opens the right way, if it holds enough, how it could be improved." They are "listening" to the voice of the customer.

Cadillac's simultaneous engineering approach uses cross-functional teams to bring a car to market. The teams follow a four-phase process, beginning with concepts for vehicles that integrate customer needs and expectations, business plan objectives, and future product and process technology plans.

The degree of integration illustrates the linkages between Baldrige categories and items referred to earlier. Excellent companies focus their entire quality systems on serving customers. Item 5.1 is a Baldrige pulse point that examiners use to learn if a company is actually living its commitment to customers.

At IBM Rochester, customers are involved throughout the product cycle. Customers review future product plans through customer and business partner councils. Every day, customers visit an executive briefing center at Rochester that is supported by development and manufacturing teams. An independent worldwide user group of 6,000 customers meets regularly to present its requirements, and IBM Rochester's Software Partner Lab gives customers a chance to see if their requirements are being met. Customers are contacted 90 days after receiving IBM Rochester's AS/400 system to find out how they like it. As one customer said, "Do you realize that 90 percent of what I suggested last fall is now in the product? I feel like I'm part of the development team."

PRODUCTION AND DELIVERY

Once the products, services, and processes have been developed, the next step is to produce. Baldrige item 5.2 examines how you manage your product and service production and delivery processes to meet quality requirements and to continuously improve.

Much of the "Quali T Rap" being bandied about describes activities in these areas. Statistical process control (SPC) and design of experiments (DOE) are tools for controlling and improving processes. *Poka yoke,* a Japanese term meaning "mistake-proofing," describes methods of preventing defects. Cycle time refers to the time it takes to complete a process or a step in that process. Just-in-time (JIT) and *kanban* (a signboard system used to feed parts to JIT production) help reduce inventories and overproduction, the most serious waste problems in manufacturing.

Prevention is characteristic of an excellent quality system. The root causes of process upsets and defects are routinely tracked down and corrected. Cadillac, for example, uses its Quality Network Five-Step Problem-solving Process to right the upsets and eliminate the causes.

Cycle time reduction is also a common focus for quality leaders. Wasteful steps in a process are targeted and eliminated, and necessary steps are streamlined and improved. The goal is to speed up the delivery of quality products and services to customers. In the process, inventories are reduced, waste is removed, and quality is improved.

In early 1991, Bill Lesner, one of three people who led Cadillac's Baldrige Award-winning application process, and a dozen other Cadillac employees met to consider what Cadillac will look like in the year 2010. At one point during the discussion, as the participants were getting frustrated by the limitations of their own thinking, the facilitator took them to one side of the room and asked them to form a circle. He pulled a tennis ball from his pocket, handed it to one of the people, and told the group to throw the ball around the circle so that each person touched the ball once. They did, but it took some time. They did it a few more times until they started to get the hang of it. The facilitator pointed out that their last try had taken 20 seconds from the time the first person threw the ball until the last person touched it. He asked how fast they thought they could do it with their best effort.

"We said we could do it in 13 seconds," Lesner says, "and then we went ahead and did it in 11 seconds. We applauded our effort and the facilitator said, 'That's great. Toyota does it in two seconds.'"

"We couldn't believe it. It wasn't possible. Then we thought about the process and realized we didn't have to stand so far apart; we could tighten the circle. And we could rearrange the order so that, basically, we handed the ball to the next person. We rolled the ball around our circle and, sure enough, we did it in two seconds."

I heard Bill tell this story during a speech to another company's managers in St. Catharines, Ontario. Later that day Bill and I were talking about benchmarking when he mentioned hearing that Japanese automakers were aiming to fill a customer's car order in two days. Cadillac was working hard to reduce its own cycle time, which was then at about six weeks.

One month later, an article in *Fortune* pointed out that "in Japan, Toyota buyers can select any combination of features and colors they desire on Monday morning, and pick up the car on Friday afternoon."

Excellent companies are zealots about reducing cycle time because it enables them to compete. As a car buyer, how would you feel if you ordered a new car to your specifications on Monday and were told you could pick it up on Friday? Or on Wednesday? Compare that to how you would feel if you were told it would be six weeks. American buyers accept six weeks now, but those expectations will change.

In the global marketplace, the Japanese cycle time superiority gives them a competitive advantage, and not just in their ability to deliver a product in four days that it takes an American company 42 days to deliver. Cycle time reductions demand that you improve every process. Like Lesner's group, it forces you to look beyond the obvious solutions, to make revolutionary instead of evolutionary changes. As the Baldrige Criteria booklet notes, "Response time improvements often 'drive' simultaneous improvements in quality and productivity."

Motorola is a champion of cycle time reduction. Robert Galvin, the chairman of Motorola, wrote in a special report to *Financial Executive* magazine:

> At Motorola, we've realized that we can change our cycle times by huge amounts. Not just 5 or 10 percent. In fact, we hardly take a serious interest in less than a 50 percent improvement.

As an example, Galvin refers to Motorola pagers that offer a variety of features in several million combinations. It used to take 44 days to produce a pager to a customer's order. The finished product, made to customer specifications, can now be at the shipping dock in one hour and forty minutes.

Excellent companies routinely realize cycle time reductions of 80 and 90 percent. They also realize that the speed of the cycle depends on factors that feed the cycle.

"We've dramatically reduced our cycle times, up to 80 percent in manufacturing," says Digital's Frank McCabe. "However, if you don't get vendor cycle times reduced at the same speed, you're going to get caught."

Six Sigma Quality

To bring their suppliers up to speed, Digital, Motorola, Xerox, and Boeing have formed a consortium to train them. They are also working to reduce cycle times in the nonmanufacturing areas of their companies.

For Motorola, cycle time reduction throughout the company is driven by its commitment to Six Sigma quality. Six Sigma is a standard; it means

3.4 defects per million of anything produced. If you send out a million invoices and only three have mistakes, you are doing Six Sigma quality. If you fill a million customer orders and only three are wrong, you are doing Six Sigma quality. Statistically, Six Sigma is virtual perfection.

Most companies work at a four sigma rate. That's 6210 defects per million. A Six Sigma manufacturer's defect levels are 200 times better than a four sigma manufacturer. A four sigma manufacturer spends more than 10 percent of its sales dollar on repair, whereas a Six Sigma manufacturer spends less than 1 percent. According to Motorola, "a four sigma supplier cannot directly compete with a Six Sigma supplier and survive."

Motorola's process for achieving Six Sigma quality in nonmanufacturing areas exemplifies the type of systematic approach to ensuring the quality of product, services, and processes sought in the Baldrige criteria. It can be applied to any business, large or small, manufacturing or service. Motorola calls it "Six Steps to Six Sigma."

1. Identify the product you create or the service you provide.

   What do you do? The answer is your product or service, which you supply to external or internal customers.

2. Identify the customer for your product or service, and determine what he or she considers important.

   For whom do you do your work? Your customers will tell you what they require to be satisfied. Failure to meet the customer's critical requirements is a defect.

3. Identify your needs to provide product or service so that it satisfies the customer.

   What do you need to do your work? By answering the first three questions, you sketch a system that enables you to convert requirements (inputs) into products or services (outputs) that satisfy your customers.

4. Define the process for doing the work.

   How do you do your work or process? A process is an ordered sequence of human or machine operations designed to produce a desired result. Those who perform or manage the tasks in a process define those tasks, not a quality expert or consultant.

115

5. Mistake-proof the process and eliminate wasted effort.

   How can you do your work better? The answer has two thrusts: (1) mistake-proofing, which means identifying potential defects, then implementing solutions that make those defects less likely to occur; (2) the elimination of waste, which includes nonvalue-added activities and essential activities performed at less than peak efficiency. As a result of these activities, the revised process is mapped, with specific measurements for defects and cycle time, and inputs from suppliers are reviewed with changes communicated to the suppliers.

6. Ensure continuous improvement by measuring, analyzing, and controlling the improved process.

   How perfectly are you doing your customer-focused work? The common metric is "defects per unit of work," which can then be translated to a sigma level. Actual performance versus goals is plotted and publicized.

MANAGING SUPPORT SERVICES

By carrying out the steps to Six Sigma, a company could easily answer all the items in category 5.0 of the Baldrige criteria, including item 5.3, which examines the quality of business processes and support services such as finance and accounting, sales, marketing, information services, purchasing, and research and development. It is a systematic approach to ensuring the quality of all goods and services.

It is also an approach to world-class quality and worldwide success. As Galvin says, "when Motorola decided to reach for total, perfect quality, all of these improvements became wealth-creating phenomena. And this wealth turns into seed and savings for investment globally."

Motorola's goal is Six Sigma quality in 1992. Some functions and departments have already achieved that goal. The company's drive for Six Sigma quality in manufacturing alone returned $750 million in cost of quality savings in 1990, and $1.5 billion from 1986 to 1990. In the nonmanufacturing areas, where implementation of the steps to Six Sigma is proceeding more slowly, Motorola estimates that it can save an additional $1 billion a year.

Improving nonmanufacturing processes (or nonprimary service processes for service companies) is one of the weakest areas in the quality systems of nearly every company. Most focus, justifiably, on the processes that produce their products and services. When they turn their attention to business processes and support services, they see the results of those departments—profit and loss statements, legal opinions, computer print-outs, sales figures, and R&D breakthroughs—and not the processes required to deliver those results.

Item 5.3 asks how you manage these processes to meet current requirements and continuously improve quality, and it expects that you will demonstrate a systematic approach and wide deployment in your responses. Few companies can meet these expectations.

SUPPLIERS' ROLE IN QUALITY

Baldrige item 5.4 asks about another contributor to the quality of your products, services, and processes: your suppliers. It examines "how the quality of materials, components, and services furnished by other businesses is ensured and continuously improved." In this item and in item 6.4, the term "supplier" includes distributors, dealers, and franchisees as well as those that provide you with materials and components.

The most common response to this item is the inspection of goods and services when they are received. Quality leaders strive to eliminate this nonvalue-added step—and to proactively prevent defects rather than reacting to defective parts—by certifying the quality of their supplied goods and services. This requires investing in the quality improvement processes of key suppliers, which in turn requires paring down the number of key suppliers to make such investments possible.

Quality leaders treat their suppliers as partners, as an extension of their organizations. They involve suppliers in planning, product development, and process improvement. They train suppliers in quality tools and techniques. They offer incentives and recognition for quality performance, and they reward key suppliers with a bigger slice of the pie—in some cases all of the pie. Furthermore, they demand that suppliers commit to improving quality and achieving results at a pace that will allow the quality leaders to meet their quality and customer satisfaction goals.

This change in relationships has stressed suppliers. Motorola's largest sector used to have 4,000 suppliers. It now has 1,000 and will settle around 350 when the ones that have been grandfathered are phased out, which means that 3,650 ex-Motorola suppliers will have to make up for the missing business somewhere else. But where? Other quality leaders are making equally dramatic slashes in their supplier lists. *Only those suppliers who can compete on quality, price, and close working relationships with their customers can hope to survive.*

In such situations it would be easy for a large company to abuse its suppliers. If I am your most important customer and I tell you that I want you to guarantee higher quality products delivered faster at competitive prices—and if you don't I have ten other suppliers eager for my business—your life just got more difficult.

If I then tell you how I want you to go about ensuring the quality of your products and services, as Motorola did, you may rebel—as some of Motorola's suppliers did. In 1989, Motorola told its suppliers that they would have to apply for the Baldrige Award within five years or Motorola would no longer be their customer. "We worked hard at our application," says Paul Noakes, "that's why we dictated that our suppliers had to apply. We want them to get better."

Motorola holds seminars and workshops to help its suppliers get better. Monthly seminars discuss the Baldrige criteria, the strengths and weaknesses of applicants, a comparison of Baldrige with ISO 9000 and the Deming Prize, and Motorola's requirements of suppliers, and include presentations by suppliers who have applied for the award. Motorola University offers several courses for suppliers, including four it calls essential: Understanding Six Sigma; Manufacturing Cycle Management; Design for Manufacturability; and Practical Implementation Strategies for Design of Experiments. Motorola is also part of a consortium that is establishing a network of supplier training centers.

Despite this support, some Motorola suppliers chafed at what they perceived as a heavy-handed way to tell them how to run their businesses. One supplier, quoted in the *Washington Post,* said, "I don't need that award to make this company successful. I already have a high-precision, quality part. It's more documentation and inspection frequency. It means hiring more people. It means storing and retrieving more information. They say this will save you money. Maybe in the long term, but up front, people have to buy the hardware and software. And it wouldn't change our quality level, to be honest with you."

Robert Galvin, Motorola's chairman, has heard the complaints. "I remember attending a supplier presentation by the president of a small company," Galvin says. "After his presentation, he told me he had been very upset when he got my letter telling him he had to apply for the Baldrige Award. In fact, he tore the letter up."

The president described to Galvin how he had told his head of sales to kiss off Motorola. The next day, the head of sales came back and said he would forget Motorola if the president wanted, but did the president know that Motorola represented 20 percent of their industry? The president did not know that. He sent for a copy of the Baldrige criteria, and when they arrived he dug into them.

"He got them under his fingernails," Galvin says. "Now, a year later, he raves about the benefits of applying. He said, 'We needed a kick in the tail. These are the best standards I've seen. I'm a Ph.D. and we're a good company, but I discovered I had a lot more to learn. I couldn't have made this presentation today—I wouldn't have had the reliability measures— without the Baldrige criteria.'"

Another Motorola supplier concurs. "The Baldrige Award became a rallying point for us," says Grant Hollett Jr., president of Cherry Electrical Products. "It brought together many of the elements that we were doing to improve quality, cost, and customer satisfaction, and made us more aware of what we were doing internally to reach those goals."

Motorola, IBM, Xerox, and other quality leaders expect their suppliers to work with them to improve quality. They are not asking them to do more than they themselves are doing. Pressured by competition, these quality leaders implement total quality management, guided by the Baldrige criteria, throughout their organizations. The pressure is passed along to suppliers but they are not abandoned to fend for themselves. Quality leaders work with them as partners toward shared goals, through quality improvement processes that are requested in Baldrige item 5.4. They provide direction, requirements, audits, certification, training, incentives, recognition, and rewards.

In return, they get results. Xerox's 1989 Baldrige award-winning application noted that production-line defective parts had been reduced 91 percent since 1982. Cadillac's 1990 award-winning application reported that the number of suppliers delivering just in time had increased by 425 percent since 1986. Zytec's 1991 award-winning application showed that supplier quality, measured in parts per million, had improved 47 percent from July 1989 to December 1990.

QUALITY ASSESSMENT

The final item in category 5.0, item 5.5, asks how you assess the quality and performance of all of your systems, processes, practices, products, and services. This includes such assessment tools as audits, surveys, testing, and a self-assessment using the Baldrige criteria.

Thermo King, a subsidiary of Westinghouse, scored high in its 1990 Baldrige application for its total quality fitness review (TQFR), a regularly scheduled quality system audit administered by the corporate quality department. TQFRs are performed at least once a year until an organization (plant or department) achieves certification (a score of 80 or better out of a possible 100). The process examines whether the organization's quality program plan responds to Thermo King's corporate quality program plan, whether its procedures respond to its quality program plan, whether actual performance conforms exactly to written procedures, and whether results are effective.

TQFR findings and recommendations are the primary input to the divisions' and plants' annual quality improvement plan. The team that conducts the next TQFR checks the prior report and the organization's response to verify that the proposed actions were taken, closing the loop.

TQFRs and other types of audits help a company perform internal assessments. If they measure the right indicators, these assessments should predict quality and customer satisfaction. The results of the assessments and of other key measures are requested in category 6.0, Quality and Operational Results.

QUALITY AND OPERATIONAL RESULTS

Category 6.0 asks for the results of the approaches described in categories 1.0 through 5.0. It is *not* concerned with customer satisfaction or other customer data, which are requested in items 7.4 and 7.5.

Category 6.0 is unusual because it focuses solely on results. Unlike the other six categories, 6.0 is filled with charts and graphs. Each of its four items asks for trends in key indicators and how those trends compare to the results of competitors, industry leaders, and other benchmarks.

The 1992 Baldrige Criteria booklet devotes a page to explaining the "pivotal role" of category 6.0: it "provides a focus and purpose for all quality system actions"; "represents the bridge between the quality system and the customer"; and provides "key information (measures of progress) for evaluation and improvement of quality system processes and practices."

The following description of items 6.1 through 6.4 is excerpted or paraphrased from the 1992 Baldrige Criteria booklet:

6.1 Product and Service Quality Results

This Item calls for reporting quality levels and improvements for the product and service attributes that truly matter to your customers and the marketplace (the results of the approaches described primarily in Item 5.2). The attributes are identified by the customer-related Items ("listening posts") that make up Category 7.0. If the attributes have been properly selected, improvements in them should show a strong positive correlation with customer and marketplace improvement indicators (requested in Items 7.4 and 7.5). *The correlation between quality and customer indicators is a critical management tool.* It is a device for focusing on key attributes and anticipating changes in the marketplace or the attributes themselves.

6.2 Company Operational Results

This Item calls for reporting performance and improvements in your quality and productivity. It focuses on attributes that best reflect overall company performance, including "generic" attributes (such as cycle time, internal quality, and the use of labor, materials, energy, capital, and assets) and "business-specific" attributes (such as rates of invention, environmental quality, export levels, new markets, and financial indicators clearly connected to your quality and performance improvement activities).

6.3 Business Process and Support Service Results

This Item calls for reporting performance and improvements in the quality, productivity, and effectiveness of your business processes and support services (the results of the approaches described primarily in Item 5.3). In this Item you can demonstrate "alignment": how your support units link and contribute to overall quality improvements (reported in Item 6.1) and overall improvement in your operational performance (reported in Item 6.2).

6.4 Supplier Quality Results

This Item calls for reporting quality levels and improvements in the key indicators of supplier quality (the results of the approaches described primarily in Item 5.4). The term "supplier" refers to external providers of products and services, "upstream" and/or "downstream" from the company—which means distributors, dealers, and franchises

121

are also considered suppliers. The focus should be on the most critical quality attributes from your point of view.

All four of 6.0's items ask how your trends compare with those of competitors, industry averages, industry leaders, and/or other key benchmarks. *Without some form of benchmarking, you will not be able to make these comparisons* and without the comparisons you will be hard pressed to score very well in this category. That could prove costly, because category 6.0 represents a possible 180 total points, the second most valuable category in the Baldrige examination.

"Companies have two problems with this category," says Robert McGrath, a quality consultant and former Baldrige examiner. "They don't measure enough parameters to show improvement and they don't have benchmarks."

Even those companies that measure enough parameters often do not have enough data points to show the direction of the trends. Three years of data are considered necessary to suggest a trend. Five years or more are better. Less than three years may be acceptable, but it is certainly not ideal.

Examiners and judges use results to differentiate quality leaders from quality wannabees. As applicants get better at describing their approaches, examiners struggle to make distinctions between processes that sound equally effective. Results make the distinctions for them. If trends are flat or going in the wrong direction, impressive-sounding approaches quickly lose their luster, but if the payoff for impressive-sounding approaches is impressive results, the application will score well. As one examiner said, "You can't glamorize poor results."

Baldrige category 6.0 measures the quality of the system you use to meet your customers' expectations. In that respect, it is a predictor of customer satisfaction. If you know what your customers want and need, if you have translated those expectations into product, service, and process features, and if you then measure the quality of your work, you can anticipate having satisfied customers.

The final Baldrige category represents the goal of your entire quality system: customer focus and satisfaction.

CHAPTER 9

Customer Focus and Satisfaction

J aws clenched, we ease onto thin ice. The warning sign is cryptic. It says, "Customer Satisfaction."

Some companies interpret customer satisfaction this way: "We have customers, therefore they must be satisfied."

Or: "We continue to show a profit, which means we have satisfied customers."

Or: "We don't get many complaints, so our customers must be satisfied."

Or: "We survey thousands of customers each year with little negative response. We have satisfied customers."

Actually, what they have is the delusion of customer satisfaction. Thin ice, for sure.

Take, for example, a story reported in *The Wall Street Journal*. Dean Witter Reynolds, a subsidiary of Sears, Roebuck and Co., sent out 1.1 million customer service questionnaires. Only 278 were returned. A company spokesman said it was an indication of customer satisfaction. (You can hear the ice cracking.) Of the 278 who responded (that's .03% of the total sent), only 102 said they were pleased with Dean Witter's service. (Welcome to open water.)

"On a positive note," Robert Gardiner, chairman of Dean Witter Financial Services, wrote to his staff, "the fact that 35 percent of those [who responded] were complimentary about DWR's services bears significance that we are meeting many clients' needs adequately." (The fact that only one out of every 10,000 customers had anything positive to say suggests that even the thin ice was an illusion.)

Federal Express provides a contrast. It tracks 12 types of events that its customers have told it are important and communicates performance on these events through its service quality indicator (SQI).

Federal Express knows exactly what its customers expect. It has designed a quality system based on those expectations. It measures progress toward meeting customer expectations and continually improves the processes that make that possible. Unlike companies that assume they have satisfied customers, Federal Express has planted its "Customer Satisfaction" sign firmly in solid ground.

Baldrige category 7.0 examines your relationships with your customers, your knowledge of their requirements and of the key quality factors that determine your competitiveness, and your methods of determining customer satisfaction. It also asks you to show just how satisfied your customers are. It is the largest category in the Baldrige criteria, with 6 of the the criteria's 28 items and 21 of its 89 areas to address. Its 300 possible points account for 30 percent of all possible examination points.

Most companies new to the criteria figure they will skate smoothly across the fragile ice of category 7.0. C-r-a-c-k…"Companies are not nearly as good in this category as they should be," says Robert McGrath, quality consultant and former Baldrige examiner. "They've always known that customers are important, but there's a real lack of measurement. They're good when it comes to knowing market share, but weak in complaint management. And they don't take the time to discover if they are objective in their evaluations."

In other words, most companies are not systematic about meeting customers' requirements and expectations. According to Baldrige category 7.0, these are the questions an effective customer satisfaction "system" must answer:

Item 7.1: How do you manage your relationships with your customers, in cluding determining customer requirements, defining and communicating service standards, handling complaints, and choosing and supporting customer-contact employees?

Item 7.2: What commitments do you make to your customers to promote confidence in your products, services, and relationships?

Item 7.3: How do you determine customer satisfaction?

Item 7.4: How satisfied are your customers?

Item 7.5: How do your customer satisfaction results compare with those of your competitors?

Item 7.6: How do you determine the future requirements and expectations of your customers?

Category 7.0 is considered the "goal" of the entire quality system described by the Baldrige criteria. As Motorola's laminated cards say,

"Our Fundamental Objective (Everyone's Overriding Responsibility): Total Customer Satisfaction." Baldrige Award winners know their customers well, and they translate that knowledge into products and services that meet and exceed customer expectations.

A new word has become popular because it captures the notion of exceeding customer expectations: delight. We don't just want to satisfy our customers, we want to delight them.

Digital divides customer needs into three categories: satisfiers, dissatisfiers, and delighters. Delighters are the hardest to identify because you have to listen to customers to know what will delight them. But as Digital notes, "delighters create markets. People spread the word when a product meets needs they didn't recognize themselves until someone provided them with a better product or service than they ever expected."

MANAGING CUSTOMER RELATIONSHIPS

Baldrige Item 7.1 examines how you determine what will satisfy and delight your customers. It is the most important item in the Baldrige criteria, the first item many examiners look at, because without a sound, systematic process for listening to your customers, your company cannot know what will please them. As a result, your leaders make uninformed and misguided guesses based on incomplete data. You gather data that have nothing to do with customer satisfaction, and you produce quality plans using inaccurate assumptions. You invest people and resources in activities that you assume are important, but that contribute little to serving customers. You develop products and services that serve imagined needs, but miss your customers' real needs.

Without the firm foundation of a high-quality process for determining customer requirements and expectations, your entire quality system can tumble.

"High-scoring companies are very, very proactive in terms of customer expectations," says Curt Reimann, director of the Baldrige program. "The winning companies have a clear picture of their customers' requirements."

IBM captures the importance of this step with its slogan, "Market-Driven Quality." You cannot be driven by your markets unless you know what those markets demand. IBM Rochester uses a matrix to identify the elements it knows are important to customer satisfaction (see Figure 9.1). It strives to provide *total customer solutions* by responding to all of these elements.

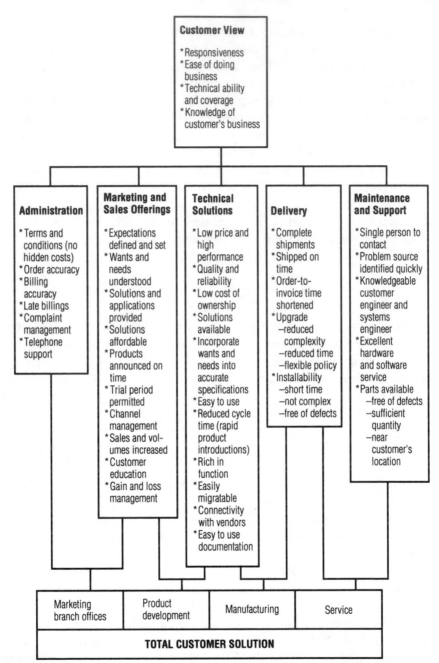

Figure 9.1 A matrix of IBM Rochester's total customer solution. (Courtesy of IBM Rochester)

Once the elements are identified, you need to attach customer needs and wants to them. One survey isn't going to cut it, nor is a belief that you intuitively know your customer's needs because you talk to them regularly. It requires a systematic process of gathering data from a variety of sources.

Cadillac has a market assurance process that uses segmentation schemes and other market research techniques to integrate the voice of the customer into its product development programs. Simultaneous engineering teams use this data in product design. Cadillac collects customer feedback on new vehicle concepts during product and feature clinics, and its customer councils unite current vehicle owners and vehicle team members to talk about product satisfaction and areas for improvement.

In its Baldrige application, Xerox identified several sources of information about customer requirements, including data that details the needs of different market segments, the company's customer satisfaction measurement system (CSMS), information collected at various points in the product delivery process, benchmarking, product user groups, and data collected by the sales, service, and administration personnel who have daily contact with Xerox customers. One of these elements, CSMS, has been in place since 1981. Each month Xerox mails 55,000 surveys to customers, asking them to rate Xerox equipment, sales, service, and customer administration performance.

Another source of Xerox's information is its copiers themselves. Between 20,000 and 30,000 Xerox copiers worldwide have microprocessors connected to phone lines that automatically report diagnostic status and problems directly to Xerox service offices. The microprocessors also tell Xerox in real time how their copiers are being used, reporting such things as whether volumes are increasing or decreasing and the frequency of use of features such as enlarging or two-sided copying. The data collected by the copiers becomes an integral part of Xerox's customer satisfaction process.

Zytec relies on 18 different processes to gather data and information from and about customers. Many of these processes provide several types of data. For example, in 1990 Zytec participated in eight different demographic surveys that helped identify product and service quality features valued by customers. The company shares the results of these and other data-gathering processes with its customers to get their reactions to the findings.

Based on the surveys and customer input, Zytec identified product quality, product reliability, and on-time delivery as the "vital few" features its customers value most. Depending on the complexity of your products and services and the nature of your customer groups, you may have a significantly different list.

CUSTOMER CONTACT

Knowing what is important to your customers is only one aspect of your relationship with those customers. As with all relationships, a customer relationship thrives or withers because of the *people* involved in it.

A survey quoted in *U.S. News and World Report* of why customers change suppliers found that 68 percent switched because of indifference by one of the supplier's employees. Quality leaders understand that the key to customer service is relationships, people serving people.

Westinghouse Commercial Nuclear Fuel Division creates customer service plans for each client, then reviews those plans with the client quarterly.

Zytec empowers every employee to spend up to $1,000 without approval to service a customer. This authority is clearly stated in the "Service America" training that all employees receive. A case study in Zytec's training materials describes how a Zytec repair technician exercised this authority to serve her customers. She was repairing about 20 printer power supplies a month under warranty for a problem the technician could not duplicate with her equipment. She bought a $600 printer to test her repair before shipping the power supplies to the customer, and the repair process was modified. The customer was happy, as were four other customers who benefited from the improved process. No Zytec managers participated in the decision.

Wallace identified 72 processes that contribute to quality service to its customers. It then assigned each process to a team to assess and improve it.

According to its Baldrige Award-winning application, Xerox customers rate the professionalism of the company's service personnel at 99 percent—the same rating they give sales telephone follow-up. Telephone waiting time improved 28 percent in three years, to 16 percent better than the industry standard. Refunds for sales reversals dropped 29 percent, and billing transaction quality improved 35 percent.

At Globe, customer complaints decreased by 91 percent from 1985 to 1987. In 1985, Globe received 44 complaints and 49,000 pounds of returned product. In 1987, it had 4 complaints and no returned product.

Like many quality leaders, Cadillac does not rely on complaints as its sole source of customer feedback. The company surveys *every* Cadillac customer. If a customer does not respond or responds negatively, he or she gets a personal follow-up call.

IBM Rochester calls every AS/400 system customer 90 days after the customer gets a new system. The customer's likes, dislikes, and comments are entered in a database for analysis and improvements. IBM contacts dissatisfied customers and customers with concerns to better understand the source of the problem and initiate action to correct it. Thirty days later, the same customers are called back to make sure they are satisfied.

COMMITMENTS TO CUSTOMERS

Baldrige item 7.2 looks at your commitments to your customers regarding your products and services, which might include guarantees and product warranties. Embedded in the item is a direct connection with your product and service quality, and thus area 7.2(b) asks how improvements in the quality of your products and services over the past three years have been translated into strong commitments.

Cadillac provides an example. As its quality improved, Cadillac expanded its warranty coverage from one year or 12,000 miles in 1988 to four years or 50,000 miles in 1990. From 1986 to 1990, Cadillac's warranty costs for the first 12 months or 12,000 miles decreased nearly 30 percent. Cadillac also established a consumer relations center and has set the benchmark with its roadside service program.

Total customer service contributes to total customer satisfaction. Customer service as defined by the Baldrige criteria means establishing service standards based on customer expectations, empowering employees to provide quality service, seeing complaints as opportunities to improve service, and making commitments that reflect the quality of your products and services.

"The top runners in the award competition have had definite service standards linked to key customer requirements such as timeliness, courtesy, and responsiveness," says Reimann. "Excellence in the area of customer satisfaction requires the empowerment of the front-line worker. Also important is the technological and infrastructure support for the front-line employees so they don't have to give the endless runaround to customers."

MEASURING SATISFACTION

The payoff for excellent customer service, together with high-quality products and services, is a high level of customer satisfaction. Baldrige items 7.3, 7.4, and 7.5 examine how you measure customer satisfaction and what those measurements show.

After IBM Rochester applied for the Baldrige Award in 1989, it formed a customer satisfaction team to collect all customer satisfaction information at one central place where it could be analyzed, correlated, and distributed. It is a closed loop process for managing complaints and measuring customer satisfaction that IBM Rochester's customers now want to buy for their own use (see Figure 9.2).

For Baldrige Award winners, the proof of just how successful their quality systems have become is in their customer satisfaction results:

- From 1983 to 1989, Milliken received 41 major customer quality awards, including a record five General Motors Mark of Excellence manufacturing awards. It was voted the outstanding residential carpet manufacturer in the United States in 1988.

- Each year from 1987 to 1990, Cadillac ranked as the number one domestic make on the independent J.D. Power and Associates Customer Satisfaction Index, improving 42 percent during that time. Cadillac has the highest repurchase loyalty of any automobile manufacturer, foreign or domestic. In 1990, Cadillac displaced Honda in third place for the total industry.

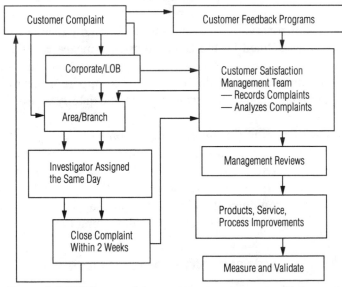

Figure 9.2 IBM's complaint management process. (Courtesy of IBM Rochester)

- In an independent survey of power supply manufacturers, Zytec ranked number one against its competitors and exceeded the industry average in 21 of 22 attributes considered important by its customers.

- Wallace's market share increased from 10.4 percent in 1987 to 18 percent in 1990.

- In 1987, the year before Westinghouse Commercial Nuclear Fuel Division won the Baldrige Award, 90 percent of the orders placed were by existing customers.

- From 1982 to 1987, customer retention at Xerox remained consistently above industry standards, a trend that correlated with Xerox's overall improvement in customer satisfaction.

Quality leaders understand that customer satisfaction is essential to retaining customers, which can give profits a critical boost. "Retention of customers is important because it costs more to get a customer than to keep one," says Charles Aubrey, chief quality officer for Banc One.

In 1982, MBNA America, a credit card company based in Delaware, committed itself to keeping every one of its customers. By 1990, its defection rate was 5 percent, one-half of the average rate for its industry. Without making any acquisitions, MBNA's industry ranking rose from thirty-eighth to fourth. Its profits in 1989 were 16 times what they were seven years earlier.

According to an article in *Harvard Business Review,* "it is common for a business to lose 15 to 20 percent of its customers each year. Simply cutting defections in half will more than double the average company's growth rate."

How do you cut defections in half? A good place to begin is by assessing how well you are meeting your existing customers' requirements and expectations. One of the best tools for that do-it-yourself project is the Baldrige criteria. The next chapter describes how companies are using the criteria to focus on their customers' requirements.

ANTICIPATING EXPECTATIONS

Another way to cut defections is to anticipate future customer requirements and expectations, a process you must describe for Baldrige item 7.6. This is the last item in the Baldrige examination, a request for the process you use to determine the shape your quality system will take in the months and years ahead.

As with all Baldrige items, you must have a systematic approach to this item to score well. The item asks you to describe how data from current customers is projected, how potential customers figure into the process, and how technological, competitive, societal, economic, and demographic factors and trends are considered.

What you learn in this process will drive your quality improvement process. As the Baldrige Criteria booklet states, "improvement is driven not only by the objective to provide better quality, but also by the need to be responsive and efficient. It demands constant sensitivity to emerging customer and market requirements, and measurement of the factors that drive customer satisfaction."

Or as Will Rogers said, "Even if you're on the right track, you'll get run over if you just sit there."

PART THREE

---✦ ✦ ✦---

A Baldrige Self-Assessment

CHAPTER 10

Do–It–Yourself Quality Assessment

The value of the Baldrige criteria as a self-assessment tool is often missed—even by Baldrige advocates.

Charles Aubrey is a senior Baldrige examiner, president-elect of the American Society for Quality Control (ASQC), and chief quality officer for Banc One in Columbus, Ohio. He has seen the value of the Baldrige criteria as a true measure of a company's quality system, both through the applications he has evaluated and the site visits in which he has participated.

As a quality professional, Aubrey had his doubts about the Baldrige self-assessment workshops springing up across the country. He put his doubts to the test when he accepted an offer from a friend, who is a Baldrige examiner, to help teach a two-day Baldrige self-assessment workshop. The participants were white-collar executives from one department of a major oil company.

"They had no formal quality training," Aubrey says. "During the workshop, they learned about the criteria, did their own assessment of their department, and were amazed at what the assessment revealed. They were enlightened. They walked away with a 32-item action plan, which was a long way from just reading the criteria."

Aubrey was enlightened, too. "I think a Baldrige self-assessment is a very effective tool," he now says. So effective, in fact, that he is developing an internal two-day self-assessment workshop for Banc One.

"The Baldrige criteria help an organization that's intensifying its quality drive know where it is in all areas," says Frank McCabe, Digital's vice-president of corporate quality and process technology. "It's a very empowering self-assessment."

Digital applied for the Baldrige Award in 1988. Although it has not reapplied, the company continues to use the Baldrige criteria to assess its quality system. "The Baldrige criteria help you develop your total quality management approach," McCabe says. "They stimulate internal competition. And you learn through applying. We've asked a number of groups within Digital to prepare applications, then scored them. We use the feedback to improve quality."

Across the country, in all industries, and in government agencies, school systems, and nonprofit groups, organizations are discovering the value of using the Baldrige criteria to assess and improve quality. This is the Baldrige program's greatest strength and surest benefit. If you do nothing else with the Baldrige criteria but use them to assess your quality system, you will understand your quality system better, recognize your opportunities for improvement faster, and improve quality quicker than competitors who choose to grope their way to quality along an uncharted path or along someone else's path.

To realize these benefits, you must do the assessments properly. In this chapter, we will look at how other companies have used the criteria as their do-it-yourself tool for improving quality. Although self-assessment sounds like a job for diligent bean counters, a nit-picky kind of project that "big picture" people avoid, it actually illuminates the big picture like no other assessment tool.

USING THE CRITERIA TO IMPROVE

Ask any executive how he or she feels about quality and you will get an enthusiastic endorsement. Probe into the quality system at that executive's company and you will hear declarations like "quality is a way of life here," "quality is our top priority," or "quality is the key to our success." Seek substance for such claims and you will find it in stories of heroic efforts, spectacular quality improvements, and glorious successes.

In most cases, what you have are traces of a quality system, bits and pieces that reassure management that quality exists but provide no evidence that it is systematic or effective, or that it can be sustained.

This anecdotal approach to describing a quality system fails to answer several key questions:

- How good are we really?

- What exactly are we doing in quality?

- How effective have our efforts been?

- What do these efforts have to do with each other and with our success?

- How can we get the most for our efforts?

- How can we make sure our efforts are helping us to achieve our goals?

- What are we missing?

You cannot answer these questions accurately without a thorough assessment of your entire quality system, and the results of that assessment will reveal your opportunities for quality improvement.

The Baldrige criteria quantify quality for managers. Before the criteria came along, it was the rare manager who thought of quality in terms of planning, process management, employee involvement, and customer satisfaction. How many considered the real value of quality data and information? How many knew how well they were leading the quality improvement process in their companies? How many had a clear sense of where their quality systems were and where they needed to go?

With the criteria, quality is no longer a "squishy" subject. The criteria provide a framework for your total quality management system, identifying the key elements in a quality system and how those elements fit with your overall business efforts.

The criteria give you a credible tool, developed and improved by national quality experts, that you can use to assess your quality system. The self-assessment generates objective feedback which you can translate into short- and long-term action plans. You can then use the Baldrige criteria to measure your progress over time.

If you put the criteria to work for your company, you *will* make progress. You will quickly learn which areas urgently need improvement, so you can allocate your resources more wisely. You can begin a continuous improvement process that wins over skeptical employees, strengthens relationships with customers and suppliers, and improves profitability. You can discover the joys of sharing effective approaches within your company and with other quality leaders. And you can become a quality role model, a dynamic organization, a lean team hungry to be better—and eager to take on the next challenge.

3M provides an excellent quality model. The company incorporates the Baldrige criteria into Q90s, its global strategy for achieving excellence in every 3M business and support unit. 3M Quality Services developed the Q90s global management system to meet several critical goals:

- a plan to keep improving all operations continuously

- a system for measuring these improvements accurately

- a strategic plan based on benchmarks that compare the company's performance with the world's best

- a close partnership with suppliers and customers that feeds improvements back into the operation

- a deep understanding of the customers so that their wants can be translated into products

- a long-lasting relationship with customers, going beyond the delivery of the product to include sales, service, and ease of maintenance

- a focus on preventing mistakes rather than merely correcting them

- a commitment to improving quality that runs from the top of the organization to the bottom

3M adopted the Baldrige criteria because it serves these goals. As 3M chairman and CEO A.F. Jacobson said, "The Baldrige criteria are the best road map to quality I've ever seen."

In 1988, Quality Services presented its Q90s plan to 3M's executive conference, consisting of the CEO, his direct reports, the division vice-presidents, and the international manufacturing directors. 3M's quality experts explained to the conference that the focus of Q90s is on understanding the customer's present and future expectations, then empowering all employees to participate in meeting these expectations. It would be implemented through self-evaluation, using the Baldrige criteria as the standard of excellence.

"At the meeting we had the executive conference score category 1.0," says Ron Kubinski, quality manager at 3M. "We worked very hard at positioning this as evolutionary, and as needing champions and changes for it to continue."

The executives became Q90s champions. Jacobson developed his own personal Q90s plan with objectives for each item in Baldrige category 1.0 (1990 criteria):

1.1 Senior Executive Leadership

- Position Q90s as the umbrella program to meet customer expectations. All other programs will have as an objective meeting customer expectations for quality, value, and sustainable corporate performance.

- See that the senior executive management is trained and motivated to promulgate the Q90s process worldwide.

- Position Q90s as a principal feature in all executive conference, management committee, and functional council meetings.

- Position Q90s as the dominant corporate goal in our annual report.

1.2 Quality Values

- Prepare appropriate statements of vision, mission, and policy to demonstrate 3M's quality values in our diverse operations.

- Measure the penetration of quality values in our organization as part of employee surveys.

1.3 Management of Quality

- At a minimum, visit the following number of locations to discuss quality goals, self-analysis, and quality action plans: 12 business or staff units; 18 U.S. and subsidiary plants; and 12 subsidiary head-quarters locations.

- Help develop an overall measurement of Q90s progress for corporate management.

1.4 Public Responsibility

- Promote quality and awareness of the Baldrige process as a 3M spokesperson to outside audiences.

- Encourage employee involvement in state, local, professional, and industry quality-improvement activities.

- See that the principals are operative in the areas of environmental protection, employee and community health and safety, and other areas of community responsibility.

- See that the corporate ethics are maintained at the highest level.

The list demonstrates Jacobson's understanding of the Baldrige criteria and his personal commitment to improving quality at 3M. His willingness to "put his body in the process" is surely envied by quality professionals under the thumb of less enlightened CEOs.

Jacobson shared his personal plan with all senior managers and encouraged them to create their own plans for achieving the Q90s objectives. At the same time, 3M Quality Services provided full Baldrige examiner training to 140 Q90s coordinators worldwide and sessions explaining Q90s to every business unit management team. Within six months everybody knew what Q90s was about, and within a year every business unit had done a self-assessment.

"The business units did a self-assessment using the Baldrige criteria," says Kubinski. "We use the criteria as they are because they're so good, we don't want to mess with them."

The self-assessment process was driven by an internal champion and a corporate Quality Services person. Teams, formed at the division level, were made up of senior management and their staff and, separately or together, functional groups of employees. The teams received one-half to one day of training on the criteria, then were told to do the assessment for their situations. Each person on the team scored and responded to each Baldrige area to address with strengths and weaknesses.

"It was fascinating to watch the self-analysis because that's where the buy-in to Q90s came," says Kubinski. "Employees had a chance to participate and to determine what they can do and what management can do."

The next step was a one- to three-day consensus meeting that would prioritize the key areas to address, and form teams to "close the gap."

"3M has changed because of the assessment part of Q90s," Kubinski concludes. "It brings into play all we've been doing, but now we're more balanced. And our progress is measurable."

"Q90s will ultimately provide a disciplined process to examine everything 3M does in terms of how it serves the customer," Jacobson said in *Traffic Management* magazine. "It takes quality out of the realm of anecdotes and into the realm of measurement."

3M's approach to using the Baldrige criteria is important for many reasons, not the least of which is the way it involves senior management in the process. The best way to appreciate the value of the criteria is to wrestle with what they mean and how they apply to your company. This is a time-consuming process that most executives would rather delegate. But without some understanding of the power of the criteria to transform an organization, a Baldrige self-assessment lacks the energy of leadership and risks becoming just another "quality program of the month."

3M Quality Services gained the support of top management by creating an entire management strategy around the Baldrige criteria, then involving the executive conference in applying the criteria to their role as leaders. Once the need for such a system was clearly established, the solution was apparent. And when the CEO developed a personal plan based on Q90s, the system was embedded in 3M's culture.

Like 3M, other companies have internalized the Baldrige criteria by developing ownership among senior management. Paul Revere Insurance Group, for example, applied for the Baldrige Award in 1988 and received a site visit, but did not win. After taking time to study the examiner feedback and implement improvements, the company decided to use the criteria to integrate quality into their business practices.

"I gave the other senior staff members the assignment of explaining a Baldrige category," says G. Robert Lea, Paul Revere's vice-president of human resources and quality. "They had to become expert in a category and on a section of our quality plan. This was a turning point for them, the first time they realized that quality isn't just a human resources or quality department thing."

CASE STUDIES

One of the best ways to teach the Baldrige criteria is to use a case study (available through NIST and ASQC; see Appendix B). Baldrige examiners are trained with case studies, which are fictional applications the examiners use to interpret the criteria and to evaluate and score the responses. A case study provides real life answers to the less tangible Baldrige items and areas to address, and it forces examiners to wrestle with the criteria and assess the responses.

A case study can do the same for senior management—especially when the case study is an application from senior management's own company. Some companies, such as Motorola, create full-blown applications at the group level. Others, such as Corning, have their business units prepare reports of their self-assessments.

From March to July, 1990, Corning trained 1,500 managers in a new self-assessment process. The two-day sessions taught them how to interpret the Baldrige criteria, develop key indicators, perform a gap analysis, identify the vital few objectives, and plan how to achieve those objectives and measure progress toward their goals. The self-assessments of all Corning business units, including staff functions, were then presented to the senior executive committee in a one-day quality review in late October.

"The assessment teams also physically reviewed their final reports with their senior executive on the operating or executive committee level," says Tom Bloomer, director of quality management, "and the reports were communicated throughout the organization. Since then we have been deploying the vital few and initiating improvements."

One of those improvements has been the development of key result indicators, quality measures of customer satisfaction as defined by the Baldrige criteria. Progress on these indicators is reported to senior leadership quarterly.

"For the first time we're measuring ourselves on legitimate quality measures," says Bloomer. "Senior management is taking strong stands on stretching our goals so that we move faster and farther. We're seeing some real leadership coming out of the executive committee."

This executive leadership focuses on areas that are stressed in the Baldrige criteria. "Business units saw for the first time that they had a way to measure quality. It was a real eye-opener," Bloomer says. "The assessments caused us to take a systematic approach to benchmarking, to look at new techniques for process improvement, to stress the service factors associated with customer satisfaction, to integrate business and quality planning, and to look more closely at deployment from top to bottom. Really, it caused us to significantly focus on and measure quality for the first time."

Following a 15- to 18-month schedule, every Corning unit is reassessing its progress relative to the Baldrige criteria. "It reinforces that we have a lot of work to do," says Bloomer. "People are saying, 'Boy, we're making a lot of progress, but boy, we still have a long way to go.'"

This type of self-assessment process works because it helps senior management to recognize the scope of its quality system and confront its strengths and weaknesses. Issues such as quality planning, benchmarking, and full deployment rarely surface before a company is exposed to the Baldrige criteria. Once exposed, leaders are "cursed with new knowledge"; they can no longer feign ignorance about quality and focus only on financial performance, because now they know the condition of their company's quality system—and the need for leadership to improve it. Executives lose credibility quickly when they say they are committed to quality and customer satisfaction, then ignore the gaps exposed by their own assessment.

Of course, the "Baldrige curse" also has its positive side. Rather than wondering where the problems are, you have a list of areas for improvement. You know what quality means, the level of quality that exists in your company, and what you can do to improve it. Now you have a reason to empower your employees and energize your company, and you have a new do-it-yourself tool that you can use to become a quality leader.

QUALITY MANAGEMENT

To wield that tool, *senior management must be involved in the self-assessment process*. Ideally, that would mean participating on the teams that interpret the criteria, gather information, and write reports. At the very least, it means acquiring a working knowledge of the criteria and analyzing the self-assessment reports for accuracy and direction.

McDonnell Douglas uses the Baldrige criteria to improve quality at all six of its companies and its corporate office, which is considered another company. The presidents of these companies and their staffs have all had five or six hours of training on the Baldrige criteria, and senior staffs champion the Baldrige assessments being done within their companies, which are coordinated by respected members of upper management. The McDonnell Douglas Missile Systems Company applied for the Baldrige Award in 1988, and its experience spurred a corporatewide effort to integrate the company's various quality initiatives under one "total quality management" roof.

In 1989, McDonnell Douglas encouraged its companies to use the Baldrige criteria to assess their quality improvement efforts. Two companies wrote applications, one in bullet form and the other as a narrative report. Another company conducted a survey based on the criteria, and other companies studied the criteria but did not do formal assessments.

In early 1991, McDonnell Douglas decided that all of its companies would use the Baldrige criteria as an assessment of their total quality management and as a template for improvement. Scores on the 1991 applications will be used as baselines to measure improvement in subsequent annual assessments. Senior management has a personal stake in using these assessments to improve quality because a portion of each executive's incentive compensation is based on how well his or her company improves from year to year.

"We want to focus all of our energy and effort on *improvement*," says Steve Detter, director of total quality management and a Baldrige examiner. "Each company has gone through training sessions on the criteria, how to assess, and how to develop a report and improvement plans. A corporate assessment team, together with others in the company and five external Baldrige examiners, will evaluate the applications. There will also be site visits at all seven companies."

"We're not after the score or the report," Detter says. "We're after improvement."

Many companies begin, as McDonnell Douglas did, by trying to weave the Baldrige criteria into their existing quality improvement processes. Marriott Hotels, for example, overlaid the Baldrige criteria on their five-year quality improvement plan to find gaps in the plan.

"We're using the Baldrige framework to check our own thinking," says Greg Behm, vice-president of total quality management for Marriott's Hotels and Resorts Division and a Baldrige examiner. "At present, senior executive staff and operations vice-presidents as a team are using the Baldrige criteria to evaluate where we are in the TQM process in such areas as employee involvement, training, and customer focus. We aren't doing a detailed self-assessment, but are using the criteria more as a blueprint."

Other companies use the Baldrige criteria—and the Baldrige application process—to drive their quality plan. Grand Trunk Railroad began building its quality process in late 1990. "We've held basic two-day Baldrige training for the owners of our quality plan—our vice-presidents, assistant vice-presidents, and directors," says Edward Strauss, director of quality. "In all we've trained 370 management people and 115 union chairmen."

"We went through each item in each category, asking questions like what do we do, where do we stand, how would we score Grand Trunk, and what does a Baldrige examiner look for? Our vice-presidents have told us they know we have a long way to go and the Baldrige criteria are a good road map for us. Now they're committed to the journey."

Motorola is using the Baldrige application process to assess quality in 1991. "We have 24 applications—full 75-page ones—from the group level (usually two or three divisions) and from internal groups like MIS, legal, finance, and the Motorola Institute," says Paul Noakes, vice-president and director of external quality programs. "We trained 94 examiners internally to evaluate the applications, but we aren't conducting site visits. Our goal is to find problems, then develop work plans to fix them."

National Car Rental pushes the process to its field managers. "We hold employee involvement workshops all over the country," says Jean Otte, corporate vice-president of quality management. "Field management must read the Baldrige criteria and come to the workshops ready to discuss opportunities for improvement. We go through the criteria category by category and develop actions plans right in the workshops."

National Car had already conducted similar workshops in their home office, and they are cascading the criteria from their field management to the field offices. "Part of the city managers' responsibility is to conduct these workshops with the level under them and with their quality councils," says Otte, "which makes the process cross-functional."

GTE began its quality improvement journey by training senior management (for a description of how they did this, see Chapter 4). All GTE units are now using the Baldrige criteria to assess where they are on that journey. Because every business unit has a different quality strategy, the criteria also give GTE a way to compare units.

One GTE business unit does a monthly operations audit on the Baldrige criteria. To speed up this process, it has translated the criteria into statements using its own business unit language. When it finds a gap, it normally forms a team to address it.

BALDRIGE SURVEYS AND QUESTIONNAIRES

Similarly, several companies have translated the criteria into concise statements or questions to make them more "user-friendly." Consider the effort required to respond to one of the criteria's 89 areas to address:

> 1.2(c):types, frequency, and content of reviews of company and work unit quality plans and performance. Describe types of actions taken to assist units which are not performing according to plans.

Thinking through just this one area to address takes time. A team or individual must be clear about what is being requested, then try to figure out where to look for answers. People must be interviewed. Data must be collected. All of the information gathered must then be organized and distilled into a concise written response, which is reviewed and revised until it accurately represents what the company does.

Not every company feels it has the time or resources to do this. Those that have gone through the process of applying for the Baldrige Award talk about it taking from 10,000 to 50,000 hours. *They also say that the time was well spent because they ended up with a complete picture of the strengths of their quality systems and the areas they needed to improve.* We will discuss the benefits of completing an application in the next chapter.

Companies that translate the criteria into statements or questions usually do it to measure progress by surveying managers and/or employees.

If writing an application provides the full panorama of your company's quality system, completing questionnaires based on the criteria produces snapshots of the current state of that system.

Contrast the effort required to respond to area 1.2(c) with that needed to answer "yes" or "no" to each option under the following statements:

1. Departmental quality plans and progress toward goals are reviewed in these types of ways:
   - through formal written reports
   - through formal presentations at meetings
   - through informal meetings or discussions
   - through some other method

2. Departmental quality plans and progress toward goals is monitored by:
   - the department head
   - departmental planning board, or equivalent
   - all managers
   - all supervisors

3. Review of departmental quality plans and progress toward goals takes place:
   - annually
   - quarterly
   - monthly
   - weekly
   - daily

4. For those areas in our department that are experiencing difficulty in meeting quality goals, our department offers:
   - consultant support
   - additional training
   - additional resources
   - other

Any manager or supervisor could respond to these statements. If the managers or supervisors in a department, division, group, or company were given the same assessment to complete, you would have a quick appraisal of your quality system. However, you would *not* have a thorough examination of that system.

Baldrige assessment surveys take the pulse of your quality system; the Baldrige application process studies every element in the system. By its nature, a survey narrows the possible responses to an item to those that the survey writers believe are most important. For example, statement #1 asks if awareness of quality values is being measured by surveys. This is not the only way to measure awareness of quality values, but it is the most important way according to the survey writers (and presumably the company).

By its nature, a Baldrige assessment survey is prescriptive. It cannot ask questions about every possible response to an area to address, so it focuses on the company's priorities. By contrast, the Baldrige criteria are essentially nonprescriptive. They invite an infinite variety of responses, which is one reason the application process is so difficult.

The statements presented on the previous page were taken from a self-assessment instrument developed by MetLife. Actually, MetLife created two instruments: a long form and a short form. The long form, from which the four statements were taken, consists of 1,200 items; the short form has 200. Approach and deployment statements require a yes or no response. Statements that focus on results ask whether trends are up, down, or flat, or if there is no data.

"The assessment takes the wording of the Baldrige criteria and translates it into terms our people can use," says Mary Lo Sardo, assistant vice-president for corporate quality. "The assessment becomes diagnostic. Departments can identify where their strengths are and where they have opportunities for improvement, which becomes the basis for action plans. They don't have to call us in unless they need us for consultation."

Assessments are completed at the departmental level, which may include anywhere from 10 to 5,000 people. In some cases, a department head uses the short form in a Quality Improvement Council meeting. When a weak area is discovered, the department can use the long form to zero in on the areas that need improvement.

"Some have been frustrated by the self-assessment because they didn't have the data to respond," says Lo Sardo, "but that was part of our aim, to show where we weren't doing enough. People are beginning to realize that there's more to total quality management than having teams. It's an integrated system. That's been sobering for some, which is the value of it."

Like MetLife, Solectron translated the criteria into statements, except that those responding to Solectron's assessment must rank the extent of approach and/or deployment for each statement. Each of Solectron's 17 organizations completes a self-assessment annually.

"Organizations use the assessments to identify strengths and weaknesses and to develop action plans," says Tom Kennedy, vice-president of quality and technical operations. "Corporate quality also pulls together the responses to all the assessments to identify areas we need to improve as a company."

Ford developed a survey based on the Baldrige criteria, with adjustments to reflect the automobile environment. Each of more than a hundred items receives a rating of 1 to 4 for approach, deployment, and results, so that the group responding could get up to 12 points on an item.

"We distributed the survey to 38 upper-level managers," says Dan Whelan of Ford's corporate quality office. "The survey took each person or group about three hours to complete, a process that triggered discussions and quality initiatives."

At the IBM laboratory in Santa Teresa, California, managers score their operations quarterly, using questions derived from the Baldrige criteria plus questions dealing with innovation, speed, and leadership.

STATE AND COMPANY QUALITY AWARDS

Some companies abbreviate the writing part of the process by applying for state quality awards. In Minnesota, for example, applicants must respond to the Baldrige criteria in 35 pages or less. (See Chapter 17 for more information on this and other state awards.)

Many companies are developing internal awards based on the Baldrige criteria. In 1991, each of IBM's seven lines of business assessed and scored itself using the criteria. The assessment may or may not include a formal application, at the business line's discretion. Internal examiners verify the accuracy of the scores, possibly by site visits. Those that score in the 500 to 625 range receive Bronze Awards; those in the 626 to 750 range get Silver Awards; those with 751 to 875 points earn Gold Awards, and those with 876 or more points get the Chairman's Award.

Intel handed out its first Intel Quality Awards in April 1991. One executive-staff-level group and up to three organizations within these groups are eligible for the annual award.

"The Intel Quality Award marries a Baldrige assessment to how well a group or organization is performing to the six Intel values," says Royce Johnson, director of total quality for the Architecture and Applications Group. Applicants first complete a self-assessment based on the Baldrige criteria and scoring system. If they score 500 or more points they proceed to the next step, a detailed assessment of their strengths and weaknesses compared to each of the Intel values: results orientation, risk taking, discipline, customer orientation, quality, and a great place to work.

The group or organization prepares a six-page summary of these strengths and weaknesses, which it presents to an executive review committee that includes the chairman of the board and two Intel employees who are also Baldrige examiners. The committee selects the winners.

"We did some mapping between the Baldrige criteria and our values," says Johnson. "Looking at the two together gave us a good idea of how well we're performing to our values and getting the results we want."

Honeywell initiated an internal quality recognition process, Honeywell Quality Value, in 1991. It uses the Baldrige Award process exactly with one exception: there is no limit on the number of winners.

"When the process was announced it turned everyone's attention to Baldrige," says Arnold Weimerskirch, director of corporate quality. "There was an immediate need for training."

Training began with general managers and their staffs scoring the 1991 case study used to train Baldrige examiners (available from ASQC; see Appendix B). The general manager and his or her staff then met as a group to review their scoring, assess their division, and develop action plans based on their assessment.

"They start cracking on their improvements, too," says Weimerskirch. "And it's not always in their weakest areas, because in some cases, it may benefit them more to improve on their strongest areas. For example, it may be more beneficial to help Cecil Fielder [Detroit Tigers baseball slugger] hit five more home runs than to work with him on stealing bases."

The second response to the announcement was that Honeywell divisions began using the Baldrige criteria as an assessment. "There is a feeling among many divisions, similar to that of many companies considering the Baldrige Award, that you shouldn't apply for recognition until you're ready," Weimerskirch says.

Although Control Data patterned its quality award program after the Baldrige program, it made significant changes to involve more people and to align the program with corporate goals. Individuals, teams, departments, and business units submit 20-page applications to an internal board of examiners. The 22-member board, which includes 14 quality professionals and 8 executives, evaluates the applications, reaches consensus on scoring, and conducts site visits.

The criteria for the Control Data Quality Award include 11 categories, four more than the Baldrige criteria. "We decided on 11 areas so that we could role model what we as a company need to promote," says Gary Floss, a vice-president of quality for Control Data, senior Baldrige examiner, and leader of the internal award effort. "That is, an intense focus on customer requirements and a stronger discipline using the Plan-Do-Check-Act cycle."

Baxter Healthcare's Baxter Quality Award was designed to institutionalize a continuous improvement process into the company's strategic thinking and planning cycle. The purpose of the Award, stated in the Award's guidelines, "is to reinforce Baxter's common culture of meeting customer needs and requirements; provide Baxter operations with a world-class standard for comparison; recognize and promote quality excellence; increase quality, awareness, understanding, involvement, and improvement."

The process begins when an applicant compares its performance to the Baldrige criteria. Baxter business units ranging in size from a division to a manufacturing plant to a service center may apply, as may corporate staff groups.

First, the applicant performs a quality self-assessment. This requires that the unit understand the criteria, gather and analyze data, and determine pluses and minuses. "It puts them in a position to assess their own organizations," says Joseph Tsiakals, director of corporate quality operations, "and that's a significant part of the BQA process."

Based on the assessment, applicants submit quality reports. Finalists are chosen and site visits conducted, after which Baxter's Senior Management Committee selects the award recipients based on recommendations by the BQA Steering Council.

This is only the first stage of Baxter's continuous improvement process, the "check" phase of the Plan-Do-Check-Act (PDCA) cycle. Baxter *Acts* on the assessments by having unit or division management review the feedback reports and self-assessment information, evaluate strengths and areas for improvement, and prioritize the opportunities for improvement against business needs and resources.

The *Planning* step focuses on incorporating these prioritized improvements into short-term corrective actions and short- and long-range plans, allocating resources, and assigning responsibility. So all that is left is to *Do* it: implement the plan, manage the improvements, and recognize successes.

The PDCA cycle starts over again when a unit *Checks* itself against the Baldrige criteria.

Baxter is also using the award as a means of sharing best-demonstrated practices. "We put together a matrix of what they are and where to find them," says Debra Owens, director of corporate quality strategy and planning. "We identified the best practices in each category and provided the names of contacts. Our analysis of the reports also gives us a broad picture of Baxter's progress toward world-class performance and leadership."

"The Baxter Quality Award builds on our Quality Leadership Process," Owens concludes. "With the Baldrige criteria, management knows what total quality management looks like. They can identify the gaps and implement improvements."

As any do-it-yourselfer who has tried to pound in a nail with the handle of a screwdriver instead of a hammer knows, a job goes more smoothly when you have the right tool for the job. Do-it-yourself quality is no different.

Assessing your quality system demands a complete understanding of the dimensions of that system and their relative importance. As more and more companies are discovering, the Baldrige criteria are the best tool for performing that assessment. *Whether you write an application that responds to the criteria, answer statements or questions derived from the criteria, or submit an entry for an internal award based on the criteria, the key strategy is to use the criteria to improve quality.*

As Baldrige Award winners, applicants, and nonapplicants have discovered, using the criteria produces immediate and long-term benefits. In the next chapter, companies that have used—and continue to use—the criteria describe what the assessment process has meant to them.

CHAPTER 11

Using the Assessment to Improve

When Corning trained its managers in how to interpret and use the Baldrige criteria, it held one of its two-day training sessions in Farragut, England. The afternoon of the second day focused on planning how to achieve the quality improvement objectives the group of 60 had set.

At the end of the planning process, the managing director stood in front of the group and said, "The staff and I owe you the next steps."

"We know what needs to be done," an employee responded. "Just don't get in the way."

"That was the epitome of what we were trying to accomplish," says Tom Bloomer, director of quality management. "It happened over and over again. People came into these self-assessment meetings grumbling and walked out saying, 'Wow, this is great!'"

The managing director probably walked out saying, "Wow, what have I gotten myself into?" Many managers are used to controlling the agenda, deciding what is important and who should do it. To effectively use the Baldrige criteria to improve your quality system, you must release some of that control and empower people. You must give them the opportunity to analyze what needs to be improved, the training to study the problem and suggest solutions, and the authority to initiate change. And you must get out of the way.

Managers across the country are empowering employees because quality improvement pays, and because it is not possible to improve quality dramatically and continuously without employee involvement. Motorola cannot achieve Six Sigma quality through the dictates of management; it must train and involve its employees. Federal Express cannot achieve a perfect score on its Service Quality Indicator unless every employee provides perfect service.

A thorough assessment of your quality system using the Baldrige criteria *will* improve quality at your company. The *degree* to which it is improved depends on the degree to which management is committed to quality.

153

The catch-22 is that most managers need proof of just how much quality pays before fully committing time and resources to it, but they can't get the proof without a constantly improving quality system—which requires time and resources.

Enlightened leaders cut through this dilemma by a "leap of faith." That's what Ron Schmidt, CEO at Zytec, called its decision to pursue quality relentlessly. Dr. J. M. Juran calls it "the faith of the true believers," a faith managers get by "witnessing the miracles." Lord knows, there are certainly enough miracles to choose from in the quality arena these days.

This chapter is a testament to the value of using the Baldrige criteria to improve quality. It is the gospel according to those who have witnessed the miracles, an epistle to the skeptics, the doubters, and the unconvinced.

The message it carries is the power of going through the Baldrige application process *whether or not you submit your application.* The same benefits can be gained from writing an application for a state award. Slightly less benefit is realized by using surveys based on the Baldrige criteria, unless the surveys are an interim measure and do not replace writing an application.

The benefits drop off significantly when companies attempt to use only parts of the criteria, answer verbally or in brief outline form, or have employees respond to the criteria without senior management involvement or action. Companies that have tried these approaches have little to show for their efforts.

For those who produce an application, the process involves and motivates people throughout the organization; provides a proven quality system; focuses that system on the customer; assesses quality; demands data; provides feedback; encourages sharing with quality leaders; stimulates change; and builds financial success. Each of these benefits has been realized by companies that have gone through the application process.

THE APPLICATION PROCESS
INVOLVES AND MOTIVATES PEOPLE

Corning saw immediate involvement and motivation when it educated its managers about the Baldrige criteria. As its English managers showed, the process engages people's minds, inviting them to think about what they do—individually and as part of a group, department, and division—to meet and exceed customers' expectations.

"It's a rallying process," says Tom Kennedy, Solectron's vice-president of quality and technical operations. "Many leaders of U.S. companies understand what quality is when they see it, but they don't necessarily know the process. The Baldrige criteria aren't a prescription, but as you ask each question, up pops the recipe you can use. You can't take the position that you don't know what to do anymore. The Baldrige criteria turned what tended to be a prescription into more of a process of discovery of where you are."

Until the Baldrige criteria came along, the knowledge of quality was something a company acquired from outside experts; they were the starting point for improving quality. With the Baldrige criteria, the starting point is your *internal* experts—everyone in your company.

"The application process helps you see yourself for what you are," says John Cox, quality director for Shipley, a manufacturer of specialty chemicals for printed wire boards. "It gives you a nonamplified, nonexaggerated view of yourself. And one of the neatest things is that you can do it yourself."

Do it yourself quality is nothing new. Every quality leader, including the Baldrige Award winners, has its own "house brand" of quality. What the Baldrige criteria provide is a blueprint for what a quality system should include and a process for assessing what needs to be done to improve that system. The application process is a do-it-yourself kit for transforming your organization.

Steve Detter, director of total quality management for McDonnell Douglas, agrees. "Some of the people we take through [Baldrige criteria] training say, 'I understand total quality management for the first time. I understand how the pieces fit together. I understand what we need to improve.' We're getting comments from senior executives like, 'We can begin to tie total quality management back to financial results to help drive those results and our competitiveness.'"

Wherever your company is along the quality continuum, you can use the application process to involve your people in improving quality. Companies just getting into quality can use it to broaden understanding of what their quality systems include and to prioritize their improvement activities. Companies involved in improving quality can use the process to regenerate excitement and instill a process of continuous improvement. Quality leaders can use the process to fine-tune their quality systems by comparing them to a nationally recognized standard.

Achieving these benefits is no simple task. The application process demands significant time and energy—far more than winning an award justifies. Given a choice, most people will choose to ignore the process and hope it goes away.

"I don't think it would have been a natural thing for us to do," says Maureen Steinwall, president of Steinwall, Inc., a small thermoplastics manufacturer. "You wouldn't put yourself through writing answers to those tough questions. I don't think I would have known how to ask those particular questions myself, and I know I wouldn't have taken the time to answer them in writing."

The application process requires enormous self-discipline because it usually proceeds parallel to normal business activities, which people tend to take care of first. And last. And all the rest of the time. That is why few people or companies are able to do a proper assessment without a deadline. The deadline can be the due date for a Baldrige application, state quality award application, internal award application, senior management review, or quality team review, as long as it gives people no alternative but to meet their responsibilities in the application process.

"The process the criteria take you through focuses on defining your strategy, how do you go about doing it, and how do you know you're doing it well," says Steinwall. "In the past, the only way a business could answer that last question was, if you still have repeat orders, you've obviously been making customers happy. The criteria don't make those assumptions. You have to prove customers have been receiving quality."

THE APPLICATION PROCESS PROVIDES
A PROVEN QUALITY SYSTEM

The Baldrige criteria have been designed and are being continuously improved by leading quality and business experts. Thousands of companies have used and are using the criteria to improve quality, and their experiences both test the validity of the criteria and make them better.

"The Baldrige criteria are helping us isolate where we need additional tools," says Mary Lo Sardo, assistant vice-president of corporate quality for MetLife. "It helps because this is what recognized experts and companies we admire are doing."

Even the experts value the quality system defined by the criteria. Charles Aubrey, vice-president and chief quality officer for Banc One and president-elect of ASQC, likes the holistic view of quality contained in the Baldrige criteria.

"In 1979, I was given an assignment to find out about 'this quality stuff,'" says Aubrey. "When the Baldrige criteria came out, they brought all 'this quality stuff' into a cohesive picture. They gave me something to point to to help me sell quality, which made my job easier."

Selling quality has, until quite recently, been a frustrating task. Throw 10 quality professionals into a room and ask them what frustrates them most and 8 or 9 of them will grouse about gaining senior management commitment to the quality improvement process. The Baldrige criteria give these professionals a tool for wedging quality into their leaders' agendas.

"There's a benefit to having one assessment tool that has been widely adopted," says Scott Pfotenhauer, total quality manager for Intel's Semiconductor Product Group. "We have a supplier tool we've been using for four years. Now we're telling suppliers that we're migrating to the Baldrige criteria. And we're working with customers on a common quality language and tool. That's a great benefit."

THE APPLICATION PROCESS
FOCUSES ON THE CUSTOMER

The Baldrige criteria focus on customer satisfaction. It is the largest category in the criteria, accounting for 30 percent of the examination's possible points. You cannot go through the application process without feeling the importance of meeting and exceeding customer expectations.

"The biggest change since we applied for the Baldrige Award is that now we truly know the value of doing what customers want us to do," says G. Robert Lea, vice-president of quality for Paul Revere Insurance Group. The application process helps you home in on your reason for existence. That can be a valuable benefit for companies that have lost their focus.

THE APPLICATION PROCESS ASSESSES QUALITY

A. Blanton Godfrey, chairman of the Juran Institute, has said that the Baldrige criteria give companies what they need most: a *mirror* to look at the quality of their processes and a *window* to discover quality outside their own little world. Many are surprised by what they see in the mirror.

"The criteria reassured us that we are going down the right path, but they also earmarked areas where we need to make more progress," says

Shipley's John Cox. "You can't go through the application process and not come face-to-face with that. It's a very humbling experience. You can become convinced that you're better than you are. The Baldrige criteria help you see yourself for what you are."

This is not all bad. As Cox said, the criteria also told Shipley that it was on the right path. Many companies seem just as surprised at the strength of their strengths as they are at the existence of their weaknesses. Even Baldrige winners have remarked that they didn't know just how good they were until they completed their Baldrige applications—which is why some of them didn't decide to submit those applications until the last minute.

Quality leaders are, without exception, their own harshest critics. At Intel's first Baldrige site visit, Scott Pfotenhauer remembers the visiting examiners trying to convince Intel employees that the company really was better than the employees made it out to be. Quality leaders look in the mirror and see gray hair, wrinkles, and flab. The application process compels employees to see the good as well.

"The Baldrige criteria validated our quality process," says Tom Bloomer at Corning, "which is important because you hate to do something unless you understand its value. We never had a mirror before the Baldrige criteria came along."

The mirror reveals good that was overlooked—and bad that was ignored. When people work in a company for any length of time, they develop blind spots. You look at the same face in the mirror day after day and you stop seeing the whole face. You focus on the whiskers when you shave or the eyes when you apply makeup, but the rest of the face is neglected. The Baldrige criteria force you to study the company's entire quality system.

"As a caution I would say that the application process is like birth: there's anguish, but what you get out of it is worth it," says Joe Rocca, program manager in market-driven quality for IBM Rochester. "We thought we had a good quality program, and now we've got one that's ten times better for having gone through the application process. We can now set goals reasonable people wouldn't think possible—and surpass them. The benefit we've derived is not measurable. But it is very large."

THE APPLICATION PROCESS DEMANDS DATA

One of the reasons that the application process promotes dramatic improvements is its emphasis on data, which some people call "quality metrics." Ask most companies about quality in their operations and you are likely to get stories about a particular team or improvement, assumptions about just how good they are, and opinions about how well they are meeting customer needs. The Baldrige criteria frown on stories, assumptions, and opinions.

"The application requires proof, not perceptions," says Gary Floss, senior Baldrige examiner and a vice-president of quality at Control Data. "If you just read the criteria and make informal assessments, you are not basing those assessments on proof."

You cannot score well on a Baldrige application without data. Data tell you what your customers need and want and how well you and your competitors are providing it. Data detail the involvement of all employees in your quality improvement process. And data describe the effectiveness of your processes. "I don't know how many times I had a conversation with another Shipley employee and one of us said, 'Wouldn't it be nice if we had this data?'" says Cox.

"The Baldrige process allows you to start measuring your quality program," says Tom Kennedy of Solectron. "Once you're measuring, you can identify areas of improvement and go to work on them. It's not anything earthshaking."

Well, maybe not for a Baldrige Award winner. And maybe not even for most manufacturing companies. But it often feels earthshaking for service companies and small businesses.

"Service companies aren't good on the measurement side. There's a lot of subjectivity in what we do," says Guy Schoenecker, president and chief quality officer at Business Incentives, a Baldrige Award applicant in 1991. "Yet there is no shortage of things to measure. Last year we brought in consultants to familiarize our people with what and how to measure. Now, I think 90 percent of us have put aside the threat of measurements and are looking for ways to improve."

THE APPLICATION PROCESS PROVIDES FEEDBACK

The application process also provides a measure of its own: how your quality system compares to those considered world-class. This comparison takes the form of your own internal evaluation of, or examiner feedback to, your application, and the benchmarking and sharing you do with quality leaders.

In most cases, the feedback doesn't tell you anything you didn't discover while you were writing the application, but it is a major benefit because it confirms your findings and fuels quality improvements. Senior managers who casually ignore internal advice are often inspired by the recommendations of outside experts. And if the managers' company is committed to winning the Baldrige Award, the examiners' feedback will be treated like the path to heaven.

However, the feedback is rarely surprising, and a company's own report on strengths, weaknesses, and possible actions can have just as much impact.

"After finishing our application, we listed our areas for improvement in a document which we took to senior management," says Sherry Michael-Kenny, quality coordinator for Bank One Milwaukee. "We told them, 'This is where we had difficulty answering the application. If we want to capitalize on the process, here are our opportunities to improve.' Their reaction was very positive."

Xerox knew the reaction of its leadership even before it wrote its application. Throughout the application process, the team assembled to create the application kept a list of opportunities for improvement, which it called the "Wart List." The Wart List was the main reason Xerox went through the application process and the main "product" they wanted the process to produce. As Xerox CEO David Kearns told the team, "The assessment report should poke us in the eye."

The Xerox Baldrige team ended up with 500 items on their list, which they used to develop 51 problem sets—areas most in need of improvement. Senior management wrestled with the problem sets, prioritized them, and developed a 5-year intensification effort.

Cadillac called its warts "holes." After completing its application, Cadillac developed a "Holes Report" identifying areas for improvement. This report became an element in the situational analysis part of Cadillac's planning process.

Small businesses benefit from the internal evaluation as well. "After writing our application [for the Minnesota Quality Award], we had 30-some projects we needed to work on," says David Mitchell, president of David Mitchell & Associates. "We prioritized them and started assigning teams. We're probably good for a year or two."

THE APPLICATION PROCESS ENCOURAGES SHARING

An assessment report based on your application holds up a mirror to your operation. The application process also opens a window to benchmarking and sharing with other companies. The following comments reflect the variety of collaboration between businesses of all kinds:

> "Our award application has opened us up to more sharing," says Mark Votel, technical training manager for Hartzell Manufacturing. "In 1989, we couldn't say anything about what we were doing to get the quality message out. Now we can. I've sent many copies of our application out, and in sharing always learn what others are doing."

> "We've visited Milliken and Disney, and Xerox has been here. We've benchmarked Spiegel's—and all of that is Baldrige inspired," says Business Incentive's Schoenecker.

> "We're learning from the winners, Xerox and IBM in particular," says Dan Whelan of Ford's corporate quality office. "We had been doing extensive benchmarking but now we're doing more."

No matter what their business or size, companies that use the Baldrige criteria to improve tend to find each other.

"One of the objectives of the Baldrige program was to promote awareness of quality," says Aubrey. "It's accomplished that, especially with winning companies spreading awareness of their quality processes."

It is hard to find quality-hungry companies that haven't benchmarked Xerox, IBM, Motorola, Milliken, and Federal Express. They and the other Baldrige Award winners have become role models for quality in America, responding to a goal of the Baldrige program.

The program has also sparked an explosion of sharing as quality seekers track down quality leaders from whom they can "steal shamelessly."

"The Baldrige program has resulted in great collaboration," says Digital's Frank McCabe. "For example, we're collaborating with Motorola, Boeing, and Xerox, and Baldrige has been a major stimulus. We're also collaborating with other leaders in New England and with competitors in nonproduct areas."

THE APPLICATION PROCESS STIMULATES CHANGE

All of this collaboration, sharing, and benchmarking, together with the internal assessments and external feedback, stimulates change. After all, if you do not expect and want to improve quality—to change—why go through the process in the first place?

Xerox won the Baldrige Award with the same application that exposed 51 different problem sets. It did not write the application to win the award; it went through the application process to improve quality.

Federal Express started working on its areas for improvement after it finished the application process. Major areas, such as benchmarking and improving the use of statistical process control, are being addressed at the corporate level, whereas specific findings in the self-assessment are addressed by divisions. "At the same time, we're developing a formal action plan that will cover every area of improvement the Baldrige examiners noted," says John West, manager of corporate quality improvement. "The Executive Quality Board has been reviewing and improving drafts of the plan, which assigns responsibility and sets deadlines. When it's ready, the plan will be sent out to everybody."

Ford Motor Company provides another example, as Dan Whelan describes:

> "The application process caused a number of changes to be initiated. A lot of people were surprised by our inability to answer questions. The advantage of going through the process is that you have to address all of your business processes. Our people now think in terms of processes, and you'll see approach/deployment/results as a discipline in our business plan."

> "The battles we had over our application helped change the culture. It did a lot to open this company up. Also, there hasn't been a deemphasis on quality because of the current recession. That's another positive change."

For companies serious about capitalizing on the application process, the potential for change is unlimited. Changes in attitudes, products, services, processes, data collection, planning, leadership, and customer "delight" can all be inspired by the Baldrige criteria.

The change is often rapid and revolutionary. Joe Rocca talks about the application process improving IBM Rochester's quality program by a magnitude of 10 in one year. Motorola requested Baldrige applications from each of its business units as another avenue to Six Sigma quality. Companies that commit to the process also commit to the change it provokes.

THE APPLICATION PROCESS
BUILDS FINANCIAL SUCCESS

"We've had things happening the last few months that we would've waited years for," says Jean Otte, corporate vice-president of quality management for National Car Rental. "And they're happening because it makes business sense."

There it is. The bottom line. If senior management remains unconvinced about the benefits of involving and motivating people, improving your entire quality system, focusing on the customer, assessing quality, relying on data instead of opinions, getting specific feedback on the status of quality in your company, sharing with quality leaders, and stimulating change, only one source of inspiration remains: financial success.

Improving quality as a result of the application process can improve financial performance by increasing business, establishing your image as a quality leader, reducing your cost of poor quality, and improving critical financial measures.

For many smaller businesses, using the Baldrige criteria signals to customers that they are serious about quality. As companies insist on high-quality parts to feed their just-in-time manufacturing processes, and as they shrink their supplier bases, the suppliers that "walk the quality talk" will gain a valuable edge.

Hartzell Manufacturing is a small company that supplies parts to Motorola. When Motorola asked its suppliers to apply for the Baldrige Award, Hartzell took the directive as encouragement to improve, and they applied. They did not get a site visit, but they are using the application process to realize many of the benefits described in this chapter, including increasing their business.

"All of our customers are very interested when we tell them we applied for the Baldrige Award," says Mark Votel. "We recently won a large contract from IBM based almost solely on the fact that we had applied for the award. It's a Six Sigma project. Our competitors couldn't demonstrate they were serious about measuring their quality improvement processes. To IBM, our Baldrige application indicated quite a level of commitment to quality."

Hartzell Manufacturing and other small companies are boosting their business by showing tangible proof of their commitment to quality. That commitment is a differentiator for larger companies seeking partners in their own efforts to improve quality. If all other factors are equal, companies will choose the supplier that can prove it has assessed its quality system and acted to improve it.

Larger companies are boosting their business by enhancing their image as quality leaders. Applying for the Baldrige Award, receiving a site visit, and/or winning the award help image-conscious companies promote their quality credentials.

No company promoted those credentials harder than Cadillac—for which it has been soundly criticized. Yet Cadillac cannot attribute the sale of a single car to their winning the Baldrige Award. What it can attribute to winning is a shinier image as a quality leader. As Cadillac's Bill Lesner says, "it's part of a world-class image mosaic Cadillac is creating." That image will help sell cars.

Like Cadillac, Intel applied for the Baldrige Award in part to make its customers more aware of the company's quality excellence. "When you say the word 'Intel,' 99 out of 100 people who know us think 'high-tech,' 'innovative,' and 'profitable.' That's been our calling card," says Scott Pfotenhauer of Intel's Semiconductor Product Group. "Now our customers will realize that we are proud of our technology accomplishments *and* our quality improvements, as shown in our application."

"When our customers choose a supplier it's for five to seven years, so it's important that they trust their supplier's ability to improve quality," Pfotenhauer says. "What this process has helped our customers understand is that our commitment to excellence is across the board."

As quality leaders like Intel and Cadillac know, customer perceptions of quality excellence translate into more business and higher profits. Quality leaders use the application process to improve quality and enhance their image, and they also use it to help them improve their critical financial measures.

"We believe that our quality indicators will be leading indicators of future financial performance," says Tom Bloomer of Corning. "We can't imagine, if we're getting better at customer satisfaction, that financial performance won't go along with it."

Although the correlation between quality improvement and financial improvement has yet to be fully explored, a May 1991 study released by the General Accounting Office (GAO) suggests a strong relationship.

The GAO reviewed 20 top scorers in Baldrige competition in 1988 and 1989. Its report confirmed that *"companies that used total quality management (TQM) practices achieved better employee relations, higher productivity, greater customer satisfaction, increased market share, and improved profitability."*

Specifically, the report noted that the 20 quality leaders had increased job satisfaction, improved attendance, decreased employee turnover, improved quality, lowered costs, increased the reliability and on-time delivery of their products and services, reduced errors, reduced lead time, reduced their cost of quality, achieved greater customer satisfaction, improved market share, and improved profitability.

As the report concluded, "As measured by several ratios widely used in financial analysis, the impact of an organization's quality management practices was improved profitability."

The report estimated the following averages for the companies surveyed:

- The annual average increase in market share was 13.7 percent.

- The annual average increase in sales per employee was 8.6 percent.

- The average annual increase in return on assets was 1.3 percent.

The GAO identified some common features that contributed to this improved performance. Notice that these are attributes of the quality system described by the Baldrige criteria:

- Corporate attention was focused on meeting customer quality requirements.

- Management led the way in disseminating TQM values throughout the organization.

- Employees were asked and empowered to continuously improve all key business processes.

- Management nurtured a flexible and responsive corporate culture.

- Management systems supported fact-based decision making.

- Partnerships with suppliers improved product or service quality.

The report concludes that "these companies improved their performance on average in about $2\frac{1}{2}$ years. Management allowed enough time for results to be achieved rather than emphasizing short-term gains." In other words, senior managers took a "leap of faith" and it paid off.

Your leap of faith can begin with an assessment of your quality system using the Baldrige criteria. Although that assessment does not have to produce a written application, companies have discovered that the absence of an "end product" and an immovable deadline significantly weaken the assessment.

In the next chapter, we will look at why companies have applied for the Baldrige Award, what that process has cost them, and what happens to an application once it is submitted.

CHAPTER 12

Applying to Improve

According to some Baldrige bashers, David Mitchell's company had two strikes against it when it stepped to the quality award "plate."

Strike One: David Mitchell & Associates is a service company. Located in a suburb of St. Paul, Minnesota, the 7-year-old company provides professional computer software design, programming, and consulting services to local and international clients.

Strike Two: David Mitchell & Associates is a small business, with 100 employees and 1991 revenues of $7 million.

In 1991, Mitchell decided to apply for the Minnesota Quality Award. The Minnesota award program is patterned after the Baldrige program, including the criteria, application process, evaluation process, and categories and numbers of awards. The major difference for Mitchell was that they had 35 pages to describe their quality strategy instead of the 50 pages (now 60) allotted for small businesses applying for the Baldrige Award.

A company applying for the Minnesota Quality Award and a company applying for the Baldrige Award go through the same application process. In Minnesota, the quality of the feedback and of the competition is similar to that of the Baldrige Award. In 1991, Zytec won the first Minnesota Quality Award presented—the only award presented that year—and two weeks later, it won the Malcolm Baldrige National Quality Award.

David Mitchell, like Brian Harper, catcher of the 1991 world-champion Minnesota Twins, is a good two-strike hitter. His company rapped a solid double off the wall, earning a site visit for their application.

"We felt the best way to do an assessment was to apply for the award," Mitchell says. "We didn't have a problem applying the criteria to our business. In my mind, they fit well. Sometimes you have to interpret them differently, but everything fits, from planning to human resources to customer satisfaction."

To prepare for the process, Mitchell and others in his company attended Baldrige self-assessment workshops and read books. They hired a consultant to review their early drafts. "It's one thing to do things right and another to explain them right," says Mitchell. "It would be a shame to get a low score because you don't know how to communicate what you're doing."

The purpose of writing an application is to assess your quality system. The process forces you to evaluate your system according to the criteria, to examine its every facet, to agree on your responses, and to communicate in writing how your company addresses each area. This last requirement cannot be overemphasized.

"We applied because we wanted to breathe air into our quality improvement process," says Jean Otte, director of quality for National Car Rental. "When we got the criteria we thought we should wait a while before applying, but then we decided that going for the gold was the only way to make us run fast."

CREATING A BALDRIGE APPLICATION

Using the criteria as an assessment without creating an application is like practicing with no intention of competing; the effort lacks focus and enthusiasm. It is doomed to low priority and even lower expectations. Buried in the jobs they are paid to do, employees weasel their way out of the hard work demanded by a true assessment by producing the bare minimum required to identify a few bullet points or make a short presentation.

"When we knew it was for real it became a whole different ball game," says Chris Witzke, COO for Marlow Industries. "Writing the final draft made us get to a depth we weren't conscious of before."

Such depths are possible because a written application brings discipline to the assessment process. You cannot write your company's response to a specific item without thinking through what the criteria are asking and how that applies to your company. You cannot write a complete response without digging for information, talking with other employees, and debating the shape of your response. The process demands a disciplined approach, the result of which is a thorough—and invaluable—self-assessment.

"The Baldrige criteria gave us a solid road map," says Tom Kennedy, Solectron's vice-president of quality and technical operations, "not only in product quality and customer satisfaction, but in a broad-based focus on world-class business management. When we first went through the criteria in 1989, we knew we had shortcomings but we decided to apply anyway. We didn't get a site visit, but our own self-assessment and the Baldrige examiners' feedback gave us more enthusiasm for becoming better. As we've improved our processes, we've become more productive and profitable."

The improvements also earned Solectron a Baldrige Award in 1991.

Solectron, like National Car, David Mitchell & Associates, and others, applied because of the discipline imposed by the application process. The Baldrige Award and state quality awards like those in Minnesota and North Carolina provide companies of all sizes with a disciplined process of self-assessment (see Chapter 17 for more on state quality awards). For large companies, internal quality awards based on the Baldrige criteria demand the same disciplined assessment.

One of the goals of the process is to produce a written application that responds to the criteria completely and accurately. That goal can be achieved *without* submitting the application, and many companies enter the process with the intention of evaluating their application internally before deciding whether or not to submit it.

"It was never a given that we would submit an application," says Sam Malone, one of the coordinators of Xerox's 1989 Baldrige Award-winning application. "It wasn't until we'd written our third draft in early April that management decided to go forward."

The goal is the application, not the submission. Companies hold out the possibility of submitting to motivate people to give the application their best effort. And people need motivating because producing a Baldrige application is hard work. The following overview identifies the major tasks in the application process:

Assessment

- Familiarizing senior management and other key decision makers and participants with the Baldrige criteria and application process

- Making a preliminary assessment of what the Baldrige examination requests and what your company does

- Identifying the benefits and costs of applying

- Assessing top management's commitment to the application process

Organization

- Training key participants in interpreting the criteria

- Identifying the tasks involved in completing the application

- Assigning responsibility for pieces of the application

- Securing top management's support and participation

- Developing avenues of communication among teams, leaders, category heads, senior management, and so on

- Scheduling the application process

- Evaluating the use of outside assistance

Interpretation

- Reaching consensus on what the criteria are asking for

- Getting clarification on the criteria from NIST and consultants when necessary

- Communicating a common understanding of what is asked for and where to find the answers

- Establishing a core group to keep the application process on track

- Creating and updating a list of areas for quality improvement, as identified throughout the application process.

Collection

- Creating and implementing a data collection system

- Organizing a file system

- Identifying expert sources of information and data

- Conducting interviews with expert sources

- Securing the types of documentation required

Application

- Organizing to write the application, including assigning responsibility for writing each category

- Establishing levels of approval as drafts are written

- Scheduling the completion of each draft and review

- Developing a layout, including generating ideas for graphs and a common graphic design

- Writing the application

- Evaluating and scoring the application, both internally and externally

- Coordinating the completion of the final draft

- Printing

- Delivering the application

Most companies try to pack all this into a three-month period, which is the primary reason that people who have been "Baldriging" get wild-eyed at the thought of repeating the process. They begin with the naive notion that all they are doing is writing a 60- or 75-page report. How hard can that be?

Halfway through the application process, however, they realize how much they still have to do and how little time they have to do it, and those twin towers of stress—urgency and exhaustion—appear. As Cadillac's Bill Lesner says, "We didn't have anybody assigned to our application full-time. What we had were people with two full-time jobs."

Most people who have been through the application process once would rather not go through it again, especially if they were responsible for writing any of the application. The process is strenuous even when it is handled properly. Few companies do it right the first time.

Fortunately, you can learn from their experiences. Chapters 13 and 14 describe how companies of all sizes have gone through the application process and what they would do differently—or have done differently—the second time.

Two issues need to be addressed before diving into the application process: the cost of applying and the Baldrige evaluation process. Both have been easy targets for critics.

According to critics, Xerox "bought the Baldrige" when it spent nearly a million dollars on its 1989 application—not counting the salaries of the 20 full-time and 8 part-time people devoted to the project. What the critics choose to overlook are the complete mission of the project and its results.

A steering committee of key executives and quality officers guided Xerox's application process. The goal of the Baldrige team—to help Xerox improve its quality—translated into three objectives: to produce an application; to prepare Xerox for a site visit; and to deliver an assessment report based on the team's findings to senior management. Team members formed project teams, each of which was responsible for a Baldrige category and for one of eight major projects: planning and scheduling; communications; training; integration; production; site visit logistics; information management; and functional focus.

The team initially concentrated on its most immediate objective: producing the application. Team members tracked down data and interviewed hundreds of employees to create their first 350-page draft in less than two months. The data and information they gathered later helped to fill 300 three-inch binders cross-referenced to Xerox's application. The binders provided valuable documentation during the site visit and continue to be used as a reference within Xerox.

Team members also began identifying possible areas for improvement, "warts" which they added to their Wart List. This list would later be used to generate the assessment report.

As the application neared completion, the team turned its attention toward a possible site visit. More than 3,700 copies of the application were distributed to middle managers, and every facility was informed that it could be visited. During the actual site visit, examiners talked to more than 400 Xerox employees at five different locations. The preparation for the site visit and the visit itself, then, riveted Xerox employees' attention on quality and helped to accelerate the quality improvement process.

After the site visit, the team analyzed the areas for improvement it had listed, narrowed the list, and reviewed each item with the necessary people. It then wrote its assessment report and presented it to senior management, which initiated a five-year intensification effort to improve quality in every vital area.

The money and time Xerox spent on its application was part of an overall investment in quality improvement. David Kearns, CEO at Xerox when it applied, has said that the assessment report alone was worth millions. John Cooney, one of the team members, says that the application process moved quality at Xerox ahead two years. Is a million dollars too much to spend for these results? Xerox doesn't think so.

Of course, it would be nice to get all of this for nothing, which is close to what some companies have spent. Zytec spent less than $9,000 on its Baldrige Award-winning application. Federal Express, Cadillac, Globe, Solectron, IBM, and Motorola also claim to have spent far less than Xerox.

"The cost to apply for the Baldrige Award is a hoax," says Paul Noakes, Motorola's vice-president and director of exterior quality programs. "If you have the data, if you've worked the process, it's not a big deal. We spent 20 man-months of effort on our application and site visit. The most valable result of that was our own self-assessment because of the areas for improvement we identified."

SEEKING OUTSIDE HELP

Few critics begrudge a company's diverting employees to the Baldrige application process. What sets off their alarms are companies that hire consultants to help them with the process.

A company uses a consultant for one or more of the following reasons:

1. To educate people about what the criteria mean.

2. To act as a project manager, driving the data and information collection and the writing processes.

3. To write the application.

4. To design charts and graphs and lay out the application.

5. To evaluate early drafts of the application.

6. To edit the application.

7. To assist in identifying and implementing quality improvements.

8. To help the company prepare for a site visit.

The most common call is for help in evaluating an application. Companies that don't have employees who are Baldrige examiners (and even some that do) frequently hire quality consultants, particularly if they are Baldrige examiners, to read an early draft and tell them what fits and what doesn't, what is clear and what isn't, and what needs to be improved. An objective, expert opinion at this stage can improve the application significantly.

The evaluation should not cost much. Anyone who knows the criteria and has read applications can thoroughly assess an application in 15 to 25 hours. Depending on the consultant's rates, you should be able to get an evaluation for around $2,000. Costs start to climb, however, when companies hire consultants to do their applications for them. This ranges from bringing in a writer to handle part (or all) of the application to hiring an outside team to take over the process for you.

Writing a Baldrige application is time-consuming, which means that it can get expensive when an outside person does it. When I worked with Thermo King on their 1990 application, I wrote the first draft of categories 5.0, 6.0, and 7.0. That took about 120 hours, and subsequent edits of categories 5.0 and 6.0 took nearly 90 hours. Based on these amounts, producing the entire application would have involved roughly 500 hours of writing and rewriting. The decision applicants must make is whether they can absorb that 500+ hours internally or whether they must pay to have all or part of it done externally.

What about companies that begin the application process only to find that they cannot put in the time required to complete it? Some abandon the process for another year. Others hire an outside team to step in and manage the process to completion, including some or all of the interviewing, data collection, writing, editing, and graphic design.

This is an expensive alternative that diminishes one of the strengths of the process: employees exploring their processes in search of strengths and opportunities for improvement. Companies can avoid having to "buy an application" by having realistic expectations of the effort involved, and by planning the process using the ideas outlined in this book.

Critics imply that consultants should not be needed for a company to apply for the Baldrige Award, and the truth is, they are not. For some tasks, such as evaluating a draft of an application, they add value to the process. Is this necessary? No. Is it valuable? Definitely. Should a company shun consultants because critics say they should? Federal Express says absolutely, positively not.

"A lot of negative things had been said about using consultants for your Baldrige application," says John West, manager of corporate quality improvement. "We wanted to avoid that perception, but we bent over too far backward. We should have used them sooner, not to do it for us, but to guide us. We wasted time by letting divisions go without knowing what to do."

I have talked to other Baldrige applicants who were quick to tell me that they never used consultants or, if they did, they only used them to evaluate their applications. They, too, are sensitive to the critics who chastise companies for bringing in quality consultants. Such criticism can be lumped into two simple-minded statements: (1) if a company cannot do this itself, something is wrong with it—or with the Baldrige process; and (2) hiring a consultant is a way of "buying the Baldrige."

In a perfect world, any company could stop at any moment, turn its full attention toward its quality system, assess every aspect of that system, write down what was discovered, match those discoveries exactly to a nationally recognized framework, communicate the description of its quality system clearly and succinctly, and transform the assessment into a tool for improving quality. Most companies can do most of these steps, especially if they are seasoned quality veterans. But many choose to make their application process smoother, smarter, or faster by seeking outside help. For any other kind of process anywhere else in the organization, this desire to be better or faster would be commended. Here, it is scorned.

The goals of the application process are to produce a written application that responds to the criteria completely and accurately, and to use the process to assess and improve your company's quality system. You get no points for working toward these goals all by yourself. True, there is value in doing it yourself, just as there is value in soliciting outside assistance with interpreting the criteria or evaluating early applications, but quality leaders may certainly bring in quality experts as needed to improve the process.

Under no circumstances does a company *have* to hire consultants to apply for the award. Interpreting the criteria, gathering information, and writing an application may be difficult, time-consuming tasks, but they can all be done internally, as Cadillac and others have proved.

In the Preface, I quoted Baldrige director Curt Reimann, who believes "that 99.9 percent of all companies have within their ranks the people who could pick the criteria apart and say, 'Here's what it means, boss. Let's go through it. Here are some things we can do now, some things we can do six months from now, and some things we can do a year from now.' "

"My feeling is that the Baldrige criteria are more of a do-it-yourself kit than anything that's been on the market," Reimann says. "And it's free. So there's a certain irony in the claim that this is something you need a bona fide Baldrige consultant for."

Some critics would argue that companies do not hire consultants to improve quality but to help them "buy the Baldrige." While this makes for good copy, it is a weak argument. The Baldrige examination process thoroughly assesses an applicant's quality system. If that system is world-class, the applicant may win a Baldrige Award. If it isn't, the company won't. While you may be able to find a consultant who can make your quality system sound world-class in an application, no consultant is good enough to fake a quality system when examiners show up for the site visit. In other words, you may be able to "buy" a site visit, but you cannot buy the Baldrige.

A few companies have tried. They have bragged about being Baldrige "finalists," then looked sheepish when the site visit examiners found that their applications played loose with reality. While they may believe their dishonesty was worth it, I would think that deceiving Baldrige judges is probably not a smart long-term strategy.

THE EXAMINATION PROCESS

Judges are at the end of the Board of Examiners' "food chain." Early in the evaluation process, examiners and senior examiners feed raw scores to the Panel of Judges, which eliminates the lowest scoring companies from the list of manufacturing, service, and small business applicants. Teams of examiners and senior examiners then hold consensus reviews of the remaining companies, during which each team agrees on one score for the application it is assessing. Once again, the scores are fed to the judges, who select the companies to receive site visits.

Following the site visits, the examiner/senior examiner teams serve the main course—their scorebooks and site visit reports— to the Judges, who spend three days feasting on the feedback before recommending any award winners.

The entire evaluation process takes about six months. A closer look at this process reveals the thoroughness of the evaluations and the objectivity of the judging.

It begins when the National Institute of Standards and Technology (NIST) and the Panel of Judges select the members of the Board of Examiners. The members are chosen based on expertise, experience, and peer recognition, and do not represent companies or organizations. The number of members has climbed to more than 200 quality experts (nine judges, about 30 senior examiners, and the rest examiners) from business, professional and trade organizations, accrediting bodies, universities, and government.

NIST trains all members of the board in understanding the criteria and scoring process and in making fair and consistent evaluations. In April, after the applications have been received, NIST's Baldrige office assigns each application to at least three examiners and one senior examiner. The Baldrige people get to know each company by reading the first pages of its application, particularly the description of its products and services and the overview to the application. They then match the company to examiners based on such factors as the examiner's expertise, experience, background, personality, and "fit" with the company. As much as possible, applications from manufacturing companies are assigned to board members with manufacturing expertise and service company applications to board members with service expertise. *No examiner is allowed to evaluate the application of a competitor, a company he or she has consulted with, or any other application that poses a conflict of interest or jeopardizes the integrity of the evaluation process.*

Examiners and senior examiners typically get three or four applications to score. Their job, for each item in the application, is to identify strengths, areas for improvement, and site visit issues, and to assign a score. Most of the board members I have interviewed read the whole application first, then go back for more details.

"When I get an application I read it front to back, making notes about strengths and weaknesses and pieces that fit better somewhere else," says Cliff Moore, a senior examiner, quality consultant, and trainer of Baldrige examiners. "The second time I read it I score it. I set it down to let it cool off, then read it once more before sending it in."

It is an examiner's responsibility to evaluate a company's complete answer to an item, even if parts of that answer are scattered throughout the application. For example, if you included a trend in item 5.4 to demonstrate the quality of your suppliers, but did not put that trend in item 6.4, an examiner would evaluate the trend as part of his or her score for 6.4, where it belongs, and not for 5.4. Examiners are also told to accept all data in the application as true unless they have good reason to believe otherwise.

"I read the whole application first," says Bob McGrath, quality consultant and instructor for the ASQC's Baldrige self-assessment course. "I take a few notes—the reports are often not as well-organized as they could be. With this first reading I get a feel for the company, its driving force, customer base, etc. The next read-through is area by area, identifying strengths, weaknesses, and site visit issues. Then I score it."

Scores are assigned in increments of 10 percent. The scoring guidelines included in the Baldrige criteria outline what these percentages mean. Chapter 3 explains approach/deployment/results and provides a matrix that examiners use to help them assign scores (page 47).

Board members are instructed to first determine whether an applicant's response is equal to, better than, or worse than the 50 percent mark. "My greatest challenge is to figure out how an item scores relative to 50, how far up or down it is," says senior examiner Gary Floss.

Once they have made this decision, they enter the percent score for an item into their scorebooks. The percent score times the point value for that

Table 12.1 Baldrige Examiner Scoring

		Possible Points	Percent Score	Total Score
1.17	Senior Executive Leadership	45	80	36
1.2	Management for Quality	25	60	15
1.3	Public Responsibility	20	70	14
1.0	**Leadership**	**90**		**65**

item produces an item-by-item score for the application. Table 12.1 shows an example of one examiner's scoring for category 1.0.

In addition to scoring, examiners write comments for each item, identifying both strengths and areas for improvement. The examiners use a + for strengths and a − for areas for improvement (+ + or − − means it is very significant). The comments reflect the examiner's judgment of the approach, deployment, and/or results in the item, and should be consistent with the score for that item. The examiner's last job is to identify any site visit issues that will need to be addressed.

The examiners and senior examiners I interviewed take anywhere from 12 to 30 hours to evaluate an application. Most are skilled at tracing the connections in an application, at seeing how one part of the quality system relates to others.

"I want to see good connections in an application," says McGrath. "7.1 and 5.1., 7.0 and 3.0. If you're bragging about being close to customers in category 1.0 and I don't see that in 7.0..."

The most notable connections within the criteria have been described in Chapters 4 through 9. The structure of the criteria by category makes these connections difficult to trace unless you know the criteria intimately. NIST has begun to clarify the connections in its 1992 Criteria booklet, but you will still need to rely on the information in this book, your own knowledge of the criteria, or the insights of a consultant trained as a Baldrige board member.

Examiners send their scores to the award program administrators, the American Society for Quality Control (ASQC). ASQC tabulates the scores by category and item for each examiner on each application. The scores for all applicants, which are identified by an ID number only—not the company's name—are forwarded to the Panel of Judges.

"The first stage cut is based on numbers only," says Kent Sterett, a Baldrige judge for four years. "We start at the bottom and work up until there is some reasonable doubt about whether a company should receive further consideration. When that happens, that company and every other company above it qualify for the second stage. There's a very strong bias to pushing potentially undeserving companies to the next highest level."

"It would be impossible to show preferential treatment," Sterett says. "We don't have applications or scorebooks. We don't know who the companies are. We just have the numbers."

EXAMINER CONSENSUS

In 1991, 28 of 106 applicants made it to the second stage, a consensus review of the application. This is usually done by the examiners and senior examiner that scored it initially. Conducted by the senior examiner via telephone conference, a consensus review can take as long as eight hours to complete.

"Since the examiners don't know each other, we introduce ourselves first, then go through the items one by one," says Moore. "Each examiner has all the other examiners' scorebooks before we start. First, we agree on what the item is asking for. Then we agree on what the applicant does. It's usually pretty easy to agree. The only reasons to disagree are when you saw something I didn't, we look at the response through different 'lenses,' or we have different experiences, such as knowledge of the applicant's industry."

After reaching consensus, the senior examiner writes the senior consensus report with consolidated strengths and weaknesses and the consensus score. NIST then provides the Panel of Judges with these reports and data spreads, showing by examiner the scores of each company on each item in both graph and table forms.

"The judges evaluate each company beginning with the lowest," says Baldrige program manager Kathy Leedy, "asking themselves if they would like to see this company at the winning stage. If not, they go to the next one. When they can say, 'Yes, if everything goes in their favor I'd like to see them at the winning stage,' the cut line goes below this company and every company above it gets a site visit."

The Panel of Judges does not know who these companies are until after the decision has been made. "At the end of that meeting we know who we have selected," says Sterett, "and then we explore conflicts of interest in great detail." A judge is not allowed to vote on an applicant if he or she has a conflict in any *one* of four areas: (1) direct linkage, such as current or recent employment or client relationship; (2) significant ownership; (3) business competitors of companies for which direct linkages or ownership exists; or (4) award category conflict (the company the judge works for is competing in the same category).

SITE VISITS

In 1991, 20 of the 28 applicants that received consensus reviews passed to the site visit stage. Each company that receives a site visit, whether it had the highest or lowest score or scored somewhere in between, is a candidate for the Baldrige Award. The scores are no longer a factor in the judging process. "There is a gradation throughout the evaluation process from being based solely on numbers to being based solely on the subjective opinion of the judges," Leedy says.

If possible, the same examiner team that participated in the consensus review performs the site visit. According to the 1992 Baldrige Application Forms and Instructions, "the primary objectives of the site visits are to verify the information provided in the application report and to clarify issues and questions raised during review of the report."

The senior examiner on the site visit team coordinates a site visit plan with the applicant. The team meets for the first time the day before the site visit to discuss key information to be verified, issues to be clarified, and questions to be answered, and to assign responsibilities for each.

A site visit takes three to four days depending on the size and complexity of the company (Chapter 15 looks at the site visit from the applicant's viewpoint). The examiner team meets nightly to compare notes and modify the agenda for the next day. The day after the site visit ends, the team completes its work by meeting off-site to reach consensus on its findings, which are listed in the site visit report. The team's overall conclusions focus on whether the applicant was stronger, weaker, or the same as its application described.

"All the effort up to and including the site visit is to provide information in writing to the judges," says senior examiner Frank Caplan. "To do that, we have to document everything we find very thoroughly."

RECOMMENDING THE WINNERS

For each applicant, ASQC packages the consensus report and site visit report and sends copies with the examiners' scorebooks and the application to all nine judges. The judges rely primarily on the site visit report for their evaluation, using the application as a reference document for understanding the site visit report.

Each judge has two levels of responsibility: to review the materials for each company that received a site visit, and to lead or help lead the discussion of several of the applications.

A site visit company's application has a lead Judge and a back up judge. When the panel convenes to choose winners, the lead and back up judges present the application to their peers and guide the discussion of it.

"I spent 15 hours on each one I presented this year," says Sterett. "You have to become intimately familiar with them, not to quote chapter and verse, but in a position to say what was covered where, this is what they said, let's look in the application, this is how I interpret it."

For the rest of the applicants, the judges must be familiar enough with their applications to participate in discussions. Sterett's description of the process he uses to accomplish this suggests the connections discussed earlier:

> I look at the pattern of the scoring to see if the applicant has any spectacularly weak areas, then verify active leadership and a strategic quality plan based on a logical evaluation of the company's competitive environment. Then I look back at category 2.0 for sources of data. What I'm looking for is, if the company has a plan based on a good analysis of the things they are trying to improve, that ought to be in their results. If it isn't, maybe they just got lucky. Finally, I look at category 7.0 to determine if all this had an impact in the marketplace.

The Panel of Judges meets for three days to decide which companies, if any, it will recommend for the Baldrige Award in each of the three categories. The judges begin their discussion in each category by considering the site visit company that had the lowest score, then work their way to the highest. If a judge has any conflict of interest with a company, he is not present for the discussion of that company.

The discussions may involve immediate phone calls to the senior examiners responsible for the site visit companies to ask about evidence or clarify something in the application. The judges must decide if they wish to recommend any company for a Baldrige Award; there is a limit of two per category.

"When you get to the end where you're trying to select two when three are qualified, that can take five or six hours," says Sterett. "The discussion is tense at four, intense at three, and it stays that way until we reach a decision."

In these situations, the final distinction becomes which companies will be the best role models for quality in the United States. Through 1991, this distinction was only necessary in the manufacturing category, because service and small business have never had more than one award winner in a year. You would think that would make the judging process simpler for these two categories, but it doesn't.

"The problem in the service industry is that, as you begin to narrow it down, if there isn't a three-way competition there is competition to standards," Sterett says. "Is it over or under the bar? It's easier to rank companies against each other, to talk about specifics and differences. The standards are a little fuzzier. I struggle a lot more comparing to standards than comparing to alternatives."

The companies that the panel recommends to be Baldrige Award winners are documented by NIST and communicated to the Secretary of Commerce, who makes the final decision. The Secretary can decline a recommendation (if, for example, a recommended company has criminal charges pending against it that the judges would not know about), but cannot substitute or add award winners.

INTEGRITY IN THE PROCESS

The question more than one site visit company has asked itself is whether the judges are influenced by anything other than the reports and applications they receive. Do politics figure into their decisions? Are they "encouraged" by the Secretary of Commerce to pass over one company or give another the benefit of the doubt because of size or industry or the personality of its CEO? Are they pressured by the site visit companies, either by direct lobbying or by public statements and advertisements?

No, no, and no.

The Secretary of Commerce and NIST have never advised, suggested, recommended, or demanded the consideration of any applicant in any year. They have no input into the judge's decisions.

As for the site visit companies: "No one to my knowledge has ever approached a judge," says Sterett. "I think that's a combination of respect for the process and good sense. Judges would react very negatively if they were approached, which would not be in the applicant's best interests."

Can a company "buy the Baldrige"? Only by spending the time and money necessary to create a world-class quality system.

Can it hire a host of Baldrige examiners to write its application, collect its data, and prepare its employees for a site visit? Yes, but if the company does not have a world-class quality system, it is still not going to win.

Companies that think they should win but don't are eager to believe that the application review process has been corrupted, but I have found nothing to suggest that this is true. In fact, every member of the Board of Examiners I have interviewed has emphasized and exemplified the integrity of the process.

One reason for this record is the caliber of quality professionals chosen to be judges and senior examiners. Another reason is that the process itself minimizes the influence of any single board member. If one examiner, for dishonest reasons, scored an application very high or very low, his or her scores would stand out against—and their impact would be diminished by—the scores of the other examiners. If the applicant then reached the second review stage, the examiner would face the daunting task of having to justify those scores.

The Panel of Judges is also ruled by consensus. No single judge in a group of nine of our country's finest quality leaders can push through his own agenda, not in the face of extremely strict conflict-of-interest rules and even stricter peer pressure.

Companies that apply for the Baldrige Award can feel confident that their quality systems will be fairly assessed. They can also feel confident of the objectivity and thoroughness of the feedback they receive.

In 1991, all applicants could expect their applications to be reviewed by quality professionals for at least 100 hours. If their applications made it to the second stage, another 50 hours were spent evaluating each application. For site visit companies, board members invested nearly 350 hours in evaluating a small business and more than 600 hours studying a large company with many sites.

The feedback report generated by these evaluations can be a driving force for quality improvement. And for companies concerned more with improving quality than with winning the Baldrige Award, expert feedback is a nice payoff for an intense application effort. I will explain what to expect in a feedback report, but first you need to know how to get one of your own. The next two chapters guide you through the application process.

PART FOUR

$\leftarrow \leftarrow \leftarrow$

The Baldrige Application Process

CHAPTER 13

Organizing to Apply

The first time Advance Circuits, a small manufacturer of printed circuit boards, applied for the Baldrige Award, president and CEO Robert Heller wrote the entire application. He interpreted the criteria, gathered the information, and wrote and rewrote the application. The whole thing.

The day after express mailing it to Baldrige administrators, Heller received a phone call. "The Baldrige person told me our application was six pages too long," says Heller, "and he asked me which six pages they should remove. It was a humbling experience." Heller realized what many applicants have discovered the hard way: the more people you involve in the application process, the better your chances of submitting a complete and accurate application.

"The second time around we took a totally different approach," Heller says. "We assigned each category to a different team, led by members of senior management. We met as a group to discuss the criteria and our responses to the entire application. We didn't rely on one person's memory or interpretation, and that made our second application much stronger."

For small businesses, senior management ownership of the application process is no problem because the senior manager either handles or is actively involved in the whole process.

David Mitchell, president of a small computer consulting company, believed the best way to assess quality at his company was to apply for a quality award. "I had one key person that I delegated some of the sections to," he says. "We solicited input and ideas from department managers, then I and another person wrote it."

Maureen Steinwall, president of a small thermoplastics manufacturer, researched and wrote her company's state quality award application over a two-month period. "I was the project coordinator and the author," she says. "I was the one who did most of the interviewing, involving as many people internally as possible who had the information and insight I needed.

The first write was extremely powerful, in part because I was able to see the holes in our process. I'm delighted I did it."

Many of the people I have interviewed who were heavily involved in the application process look back on it as a rewarding experience. However, that is *not* how they felt during the process. Most would compare it to hitting yourself on the head with a hammer: it is very unpleasant while it is happening but it feels great when you stop.

The leaders of small businesses often beat themselves to exhaustion when they heap the entire application process on top of running a business. Most, like Mitchell, intend to delegate more of the work the second time around.

Sharing the workload is what large companies usually do best. When Ford's North American Automotive Operations decided to apply in 1989, the vice-president of North American Quality and the directors of quality at Ford's other offices formed a seven-person team to lead the process.

"We went through the criteria first, then took what Ford was doing and fit it to the criteria," says Dan Whelan of Ford's corporate quality office. "It didn't work. We ended up with a camel."

Whelan and another person took over the process, establishing their Baldrige headquarters in a conference room at a nearby hotel. "We involved a few hundred people in putting together responses to the criteria," he says. "People would come over and we'd chat for hours. We ended up with a 150-page first draft, which we presented to top executives. For the first time we had, in one place, an integrated picture of quality at North American Automotive Operations."

KEY STEPS IN THE APPLICATION PROCESS

To get that priceless picture, applicants must proceed from ignorance to knowledge, from knowing little about what the Baldrige criteria have to do with their quality systems to explaining their quality systems through the criteria. While every company approaches this task differently, these key steps are common to most:

1. Involve senior management

2. Establish Baldrige teams

3. Train team members

4. Assign responsibilities

5. Collect data and information

6. Identify areas for improvement

7. Communicate needs, ideas, and information

8. Write the first draft

9. Begin the layout, including graphics

10. Evaluate the first draft

11. Write subsequent drafts

12. Coordinate writing and graphics

13. Produce the final draft

14. Print and deliver the application

This chapter covers the steps up to writing the first draft. Chapter 14 describes the last seven steps.

STEP 1: INVOLVE SENIOR MANAGEMENT

For many companies, the desire to involve senior management in the application process is one of those "be careful what you want because you might get it" situations. The only thing worse than executives declining to participate is executives who agree to participate, then drop the ball.

A typical scenario begins with the president or CEO and his staff "owning" Baldrige categories. Usually, the president or CEO takes category 1.0 (Leadership), the Human Resources V.P. gets category 4.0 (Human Resource Utilization), the Marketing V.P. gets category 7.0 (Customer Satisfaction), and the rest are assigned or chosen. At the kickoff meeting, the president or CEO gives a stirring speech about the company's commitment to quality and to winning the Baldrige Award by 1995, then sends the troops on their way. After the meeting, he delegates his category to the company's quality expert and returns to more important business, and his vice-presidents find people on their staffs to take over.

The troops, who believe that nothing truly important gets delegated, resent their new, additional responsibilities— especially once they realize how much work is involved. They stumble along, unsure of exactly what the criteria are asking or where to look for answers.

A month passes. Category team meetings have been held. The criteria have been discussed. Possible responses have been suggested, but nothing has been written. Top management pokes its collective head in the door and asks for an outline in a couple weeks.

Two weeks later the category teams, which have just finished their rough outlines the day before, meet with their executive "owners" to review their responses. Senior managers realize their application is in trouble. Most responses are too general, too anecdotal, lacking documentation, and/or too far off the mark. With the application due in two months, the executives panic.

The panic usually leads to one of four courses of action:

1. One or more of the senior executives takes over the process and drives it to completion. This option is the least popular.

2. The executives name a core team of one to three upper managers to write the application. This is the most popular option.

3. The executives hire an outside consultant or consulting group to write the application. These consultants can gather data, interview key people, write the application, design the graphics, and complete the project. This is the most expensive option.

4. The executives decide to postpone their application until next year. At this point, this is probably the smartest option—unless senior management repeats the same mistakes next year.

I know companies in which senior management, after trying to lead the effort without doing much work, ended up facing these options.

I know other companies in which senior management promoted applying for the Baldrige Award but did not participate in the process except to comment on what was being written. Those companies produced applications with a lot of grumbling but few mid-course adjustments. They also missed an opportunity for their leaders to learn firsthand about the company's quality system. It's like sending a surrogate to take a college class for you. You may get a good grade, but what have you learned?

I know companies in which senior management contributed to the process without driving it. Xerox's senior executives visited the company's National Quality Award office to meet with writers and participate in groups.

"We told senior management we wanted four hours of their time per week devoted to the award effort, to learning the criteria and helping us develop the answers," says John Cooney, who helped lead Xerox's effort. When you consider that some executives only manage eight hours a week with their families, this was a major commitment.

I also know companies in which senior management's commitment meant "putting their bodies into the process": gathering data, interviewing key people, and writing the application. Those companies delivered quality documents that spurred quality improvements.

When IBM Rochester first applied for the Baldrige Award in 1989, the executive owners of the categories delegated their responsibilities to others. Lori Kirkland remembers how she got involved: "I had section 6.0. It was originally given to the plant manager, who delegated it to one of his managers, who delegated it to someone else, who delegated it to me."

The delegatees started working on the application in November 1988. By the end of February it still wasn't coming together. Four internal leaders met with the teams to present their views on an overall strategy for the application. "Of course, the obvious question was, 'What are we doing having an overall strategy session now?'" Kirkland says.

One of the four leaders was put in charge of the effort, which eventually produced an application worthy of a site visit. However, continuing senior management's hands-off approach to the Baldrige Award, no corporate executives were present at the site visit. It was no surprise, then, that the feedback IBM Rochester received noted that management's commitment to quality was not as strong as it could have been.

Management took the feedback to heart. For their 1990 application, the plant manager and his direct reports gathered the data and did the writing. "The person responsible for a category worked with a team of his choice to go where he needed to go across the site to get whatever information he needed," says Joe Rocca, one of the leaders of IBM's application effort. "Senior executives think they know how their business is running, but at the end they sit down and say, 'I learned everything.'"

As Kirkland learned, "A lot of people think it's an exercise in writing. It's really an exercise in explaining what you do—and it's very eye-opening."

Senior managers who plunge into the application process find themselves immersed in their company's quality system, and this experience frequently changes them. For the first time, they understand what world-class quality means and how close their company is to achieving it. They discover the impact of quality through the eyes of employees who are active in quality improvement. And they confront the weaknesses in their system as they struggle to write a response that they know will earn few points.

When Digital applied for the Baldrige Award, Frank McCabe, vice-president of quality, and five other people put their application together in a month, and "had a lot of fun doing it." Still, the next time he will do it differently.

"The next time we apply we'll get all the senior managers involved directly in preparing the application because of what they can learn from it," McCabe says.

The Baldrige application process demands a relentless factual assessment of a company's entire quality system. To the degree that senior managers are involved in the process, their understanding of the system and how to improve it will increase.

STEP 2: ESTABLISH BALDRIGE TEAMS

Unless your company is small enough for one person to do your application, you will need to establish Baldrige teams. In fact, you may want to create a Baldrige team even if your company is small.

Teams share the workload while bringing individual insights and ideas to the process. Smaller companies often form a single team to handle the application process, whereas larger companies may have an overall steering committee to guide the process and several teams organized to produce the application.

Hartzell Manufacturing is a small plastic molding supplier whose customers include Motorola. In 1989, when Motorola "encouraged" its suppliers to apply for the Baldrige, Hartzell decided to do it right away.

"We formed a three-person team," says Mark Votel, technical training manager, "myself, the vice-president of sales, and the vice-president of manufacturing at one of our plants. By area to address, we assigned people to gather data, address specific issues, and write responses. The first time we had any knowledge of the total was when we brought all 144 areas to address to an all-day meeting of our executive steering committee."

Hartzell's approach is unique because of the way it broke down the criteria. Most companies form seven working teams, one for each Baldrige category. Team members then take items within their category. Very few make assignments at the area to address level.

The Shipley Company, a small manufacturer of specialty chemistry for printed wire boards, started the process by forming teams to focus first on the categories, then on Shipley's four principal areas: customer satisfaction, quality planning, education and training, and new product introduction. A vice-president led each of these teams.

"Before deciding to apply, we were identifying systems we had that related to the criteria," says quality director John Cox. "What do we have, what might we want to put into place, what might these look like."

At the 1990 Quest for Excellence conference, Cox heard David Kearns, head of Baldrige Award-winning Xerox, say that a company thinking about applying should do it because it would improve the company. He brought that message back to Shipley.

"I didn't think we were ever going to carve out a space when we had nothing better to do than apply for the award," Cox says. "We had to allocate resources to it. I proposed that I and two colleagues write the application, and management agreed."

The three-person team wrote Shipley's application over a six-week period, devoting one-half to two-thirds of their time to it. They brought between 50 and 75 people into the process—a significant number of their 550 U.S. employees.

For its award-winning 1991 application, Zytec had one Baldrige team, its senior management staff. One senior manager was responsible for each category. Most category "owners" updated the company's 1990 application, although a few sections had to be substantially rewritten. The staff members gathered the data and wrote the responses themselves, then met as a team to review each other's efforts and suggest improvements. In addition to writing category 1.0, the CEO edited the entire application, modifying or removing any statement that could not be documented. This personal knowledge of and involvement in the company's quality system by senior management created a complete and accurate application, impressed the site visit team, and contributed greatly to Zytec's winning the Baldrige Award.

Another 1991 award winner, Solectron, brought together people from a cross-section of groups—finance, human resources, operations, and others—for its application team. The cross-functional team made it easier to get the data needed to respond to the criteria.

National Car Rental formed teams around the categories, pairing up senior executives for all but one of the categories. "We put executives together who aren't normally," says Jean Otte, who directed the application effort, "and that was a big plus." The executives appointed task force leaders responsible for gathering the information, and two members of the quality department managed the process and helped teams interpret the criteria.

Companies like National Car form teams around the categories because it is logical. Each category is a tidy package easily separated from the rest. In addition, several categories seem tailor-made for specific departments, such as "Leadership" for senior management, "Human Resource Utilization" for human resources, and "Customer Satisfaction" for sales and marketing. This "smokestack" approach seems like the best way to break the criteria into manageable pieces, and it usually is, but it is not without problems.

The most difficult problem is communication among teams, as each team naturally focuses all of its attention on its own category to the exclusion of all others:

- Connections between categories are missed.

- Teams responsible for describing an approach fail to inform the team responsible for presenting the results of that approach.

- Vital information, such as key product or service features and short- and long-term goals, are written differently from category to category.

- Other vital information never makes the application because each team assumed another would use it.

- The same process can be hard to recognize from one category to the next.

- One category uses bullets for its key points; another is all narrative; another weaves in a lot of charts and graphs.

Each category becomes an island, and each team is isolated from the others. The result, to borrow Dan Whelan's description, is a camel.

The second most difficult problem is the unfairness of it all; the seven categories are not equal. The person or team assigned to category 7.0 is responsible for more points than the teams for categories 2.0, 3.0, and 4.0 combined. As points should roughly translate into pages, the category 7.0 team must produce 22 pages compared to 7 pages for category 1.0, 6 pages for category 2.0, 5 pages for category 3.0, and 11 pages for categories 4.0 and 5.0. Only category 6.0 comes close with 13 pages, but it is all charts and graphs, whereas more than half of 7.0 must describe approach and deployment.

To be fair, the 7.0 team should have two to three times more members than the other teams, including two or three senior managers leading it.

Instead, all categories are treated as equals, all team leaders must achieve the same goals in the same time frame, and the 2.0 and 3.0 teams wonder what all the fuss is about.

Although I have not heard of any company doing it, I believe that one solution to these problems would be to assign two types of teams, one to coordinate work within the categories and another to gather data and write the responses for linked items.

For example, you could form a small "supplier" team responsible for item 5.4 (approach to and deployment of supplier quality) and item 6.4 (supplier quality results). If the team has two members, one of them could also be a member of the category 5.0 team and the other a member of the 6.0 team. In addition to gathering data and writing the responses for items 5.4 and 6.4, the "supplier" team would also communicate with other category and link-it ("linked item") teams having supplier connections, such as item 2.2 (competitive and benchmark data for suppliers), item 3.1 (supplier capabilities as a factor in planning), and so on. The "supplier" team would be the supplier experts for all other Baldrige teams.

Other link-it teams might include the "customer requirements" team, primarily responsible for items 7.1, 7.6, and 5.1; the "support services" team, responsible for items 5.3 and 6.3; and the "product/service quality" team, responsible for items 5.2, 5.5, and 6.1.

Some link it teams could be within categories. The "customer service" team would handle items 7.1 and 7.2, and the "customer satisfaction" team would be responsible for items 7.3, 7.4, and 7.5.

The primary roles of the category teams would be to support the link-it teams, to gather data and write responses for unlinked items (such as item 1.3, "Public Responsibility," or item 4.3, "Employee Education and Training"), and to make sure that the responses to all items within their category are properly connected.

Organizing your Baldrige application process this way would require a working knowledge of the criteria and the ability to plan the entire process up front. The payoff, I believe, would be a deeper understanding of the connections within your quality system, a more complete and sophisticated application, and improved communication during and after the application process.

IBM Rochester solved the communication problem by establishing weekly checkpoints for the four months of its application process. Four internal quality experts, some of whom had Baldrige experience, read and scored drafts as they were written, advising the writers on how to improve.

The checkpoints and reviews by a core team improved communication while keeping the process on track.

"You have to recognize it's a process and we didn't realize that for the first month-and-a-half in 1989," says Rocca. "Then it dawned on us that this is supposed to be a learning experience."

STEP 3: TRAIN TEAM MEMBERS

Training is the forgotten step for the reason that Rocca describes: companies don't realize that this is a learning process. To make it a successful learning experience, people need to be trained.

When Federal Express got serious about applying in mid-1989, it handed the criteria to each of its 11 divisions and asked them to use the criteria as a self-assessment. No 75-page requirement. No specific process they had to follow. No imminent deadline to meet. Just the freedom to invent your own. A few months later, the most frequently heard response to this directive was, "Huh?" Federal Express decided that some training was in order.

"We arranged to have an outside Baldrige examiner conduct a workshop for people from all our divisions on how to write an application," says John West, manager of corporate quality improvement. "The most common question was about how you weave approach, deployment, and results into the fabric of the application. Another common question was on the scoring, on what examiners look for. We found we were off-track enough to extend the deadline to the end of January."

Many companies swerve off-track from the start when they overlook the need for training on how to write an application and how to use the application process to assess and improve quality. The people you haul into the process have never done anything like a Baldrige application. The criteria are complex. The process is confusing. Sources for data are hard to identify. Writing is difficult. Documentation is frustrating. Communication is overlooked. Knowing this, you can expect trouble if you hand the beginners on your Baldrige teams copies of the criteria with no more than a deadline and a pat on the back. The preventive approach is to train people in the criteria and the application process.

When Intel's ECMG division decided to apply for the Baldrige Award in 1990, it trained all key people within a week of making the decision, bringing in a Baldrige examiner to provide examples and direction.

"Since the beginning of the award program in 1990, training has been a key factor," said Roy Sanford, director of corporate quality programs. In 1992, Baxter Healthcare trained 250 of its management personnel to understand the criteria and serve on its Board of Examiners. Baxter also conducted a variety of Baxter Quality Award workshops throughout the company worldwide.

Training for the application process need not be an expensive or time-consuming activity. Sources of information include books such as this, customers and suppliers who have been through the process, Baldrige Award winners, internal and external experts (Baldrige or state quality award examiners), and self-assessment training courses. The case studies used to train Baldrige examiners, available from ASQC, can help people see what an application looks like and how it would be scored. Most self-assessment courses train participants in three days or less; your internal training could take as little as three half-days, with homework between sessions.

Baldrige team meetings early in the process provide an excellent training opportunity. "If possible, the whole application team should meet to clarify the criteria and brainstorm sources of data," says Robert McGrath, an instructor for the ASQC Baldrige self-assessment course. "And use case studies. Assess them as individuals, then reach a consensus as teams."

The first time Xerox's National Quality Award team met it discussed the criteria and brainstormed potential responses. Then it assigned responsibilities.

STEP 4: ASSIGN RESPONSIBILITIES

Xerox had 20 full-time people on eight teams assigned to gather data and write responses. IBM Rochester had category owners and developers that chose teams and directed them to gather information across the site. At Bank One Milwaukee, the quality staff was responsible for interviewing key sources and gathering data. At Zytec, the key sources themselves—the senior managers—gathered data and wrote responses.

Whatever approach a company chooses, responsibilities must be defined clearly and taken seriously. Zytec developed a process flow analysis that identified every major step in the application process, from "define format" on December 1, 1990, to "implement corrective actions from feedback" on December 1, 1991. The senior managers who owned the process and the application referred to this document repeatedly in order to keep the process on track.

Key responsibilities that need to be assigned include:

- *One person to lead the application effort.* This is typically the head of quality at larger companies and the president or CEO at smaller companies. In addition to managing the process to completion, this person (and his or her team) oversees criteria interpretation, assists in identifying sources of information, edits the written responses, and makes sure that the entire application is cohesive and consistent.

- *People responsible for the final written responses to each category.* These people can then assign responsibilities for data gathering and writing to their category team members, but the category leaders have ultimate responsibility for the completion of their categories. Team members may also be part of link-it teams, but they are responsible to the category leaders for their written responses.

- *A person or team in charge of layout and graphics.* The person or team designs the layout and the format for charts and graphs, then creates the charts and graphs and lays out the application as sections become available. Cadillac had a "chart czar" responsible for making sure that all charts and graphs throughout their application were consistent.

In a small company, all of these responsibilities could conceivably be handled by one person, although two is the fewest I have seen (one does all the data gathering and writing, the other all the layout and graphics). Larger companies, such as Xerox, may dedicate people full-time to each of these tasks.

The key is not how many people are given responsibility; it is the *reliability* of the people with the responsibility. Producing an application in three months demands devotion to a strict timetable. Team members who fail to meet their responsibilities burden the rest of the team and weaken the application, and that includes senior executives who offer to participate, are penciled into the lineup, then never show up for the game. The beginning of the process is the time to honestly determine how much you can contribute, not later when it hurts the team.

STEP 5: COLLECT DATA AND INFORMATION

"The two hardest parts of the application process are getting data and organizing it," says McGrath. "You get data by talking to people. The first step is to identify who these people are, all at once. Then cross-integrate."

When applicants talk about "pulling people into the process," most of those people are subject experts. As McGrath says, "you get data by talking to people," and the people you talk to are the ones who have the answers.

If you need to know about quality training for employees, you talk to the head of human resources, who may refer you to someone else in the department for more details. If you want to understand your company's process for designing a new product, you talk to the head engineer. If you want to know about customer-contact personnel, you go to the head of marketing or sales.

What is so hard about that? Well, for one thing, these are busy people with lots of responsibilities. You may spend some time just arranging the interview, and then discover when you get it that the person knows what *should* be going on but is not the best person to talk about what *is* going on. And then you may be referred to someone else. "Our executives gave us input," says Sherry Michael-Kenney, quality coordinator for Bank One Milwaukee, "but we often had to go further down in the organization because they didn't have all the details."

So you arrange another interview and discover that, yes, this is the right person, but the kinds of data you seek are not readily available and there is yet another person you should talk to anyway. And on it goes. You can burn up a lot of time trying to nail down good data.

Another problem occurs when the teams are poorly coordinated. There are only a few top-level subject experts in any organization, and if the category teams do not "cross-integrate"—find out how many team members will need to talk to a particular subject expert, then assign two people to talk to the expert about all their concerns— the expert will be deluged with requests for interviews and data. Many people will have to wait their turn to get at an expert, who rapidly grows weary of the process.

A third problem is finding nothing at the end of the rainbow. "First you have to understand why they're asking that question," says Rocca, "then you understand it and go to find the data and you can't find it because it doesn't exist." This discovery provides you with an excellent addition to your areas for improvement list, but it does nothing for your answer.

The fourth problem is finding something at the end of the rainbow, but you are not quite sure what it is. If you are looking for a pot of gold but find a pot of silver instead, you have to decide whether to take a pot of anything or keep looking for the gold.

Much of the application process involves making what you do fit what the criteria seem to want. That's why it is so important for you to understand the criteria, and why you need to talk to experts who know their part of your quality system well enough to fit it to the criteria.

The solution to these problems is to organize your data collection efforts. Consider the following steps:

1. Identify what you need to find out.

   Each category team or link-it team can do this. One way is to break down each area to address into statements or questions. (To see how this can be done, refer to Chapter 10.)

   Another approach is to expand the questions beyond the specific areas to address. This approach asks more questions and more detailed questions, which makes it a good choice for teams that are having trouble interpreting the criteria themselves and for companies that are using outside writers. As an outside writer myself, I prefer jobs in which I must distill a lot of information to jobs that make me stretch the information I have. An example of this approach for 1.1(a)(2) might be: "Who created our quality mission, objectives, and goals?"; "How were they created, and how are they evaluated and improved?"; "What role do our quality mission, objectives, and goals play in the leadership of our company?"; and so forth.

   The advantages of translating the areas to address into questions are that it is easier to ask an expert a question than it is to explain a statement, and the more questions you create the more connections you see and the better you understand the criteria. The disadvantages are that you can create the wrong questions (in other words, you have to be able to speak "Baldrige" to translate properly), and the more questions you create the more time it takes. Roger Kane, director of quality for Thermo King, a 1990 site visit company, believes detailed questions "were a good way of collecting a lot of data and ideas to dump into the system. They stimulated input, especially from other locations."

2. Identify who has the data/information you need.

   At the Baldrige self-assessment training conducted by ASQC, they recommend using a matrix to identify the primary source of data for each area to address. For example, item 1.1 might look like this:

Item 1.1	CEO	V.P. Finance	V.P. Sales	V.P. Mfg.	Etc....
(a)	X	X	X	X	
(b)					
(c)					
(d)					

3. Interview subject experts.

Two-person teams are then assigned one or more subject experts to interview. Team members should be familiar with the topics without being part of the expert's group. One team interviews a subject expert about every area to address that is "X-ed" on the matrix, for all seven categories. The interview team talks to as many people as necessary to respond to its assigned statements or questions, then distributes what it learns to the appropriate category or link-it teams.

An alternative is for each category and/or link-it team to conduct its own interviews of the primary sources of data. This method requires less communication, but it is much harder on the experts.

Whichever interview method is chosen, the interviewers must pursue specific answers relentlessly. As noted in the previous chapter, anecdotal responses earn no points. A story about exceptional service, a testimonial from a delighted customer, a promise to implement a better process this year: these are typical responses to the criteria, especially by senior executives (and in particular, by vice-presidents of sales and marketing). But the interviewers must politely ask for more. How do we do this? Where do we do it? What is the process? How do we improve it? What are the results? How do they compare to our competitors and to the best in the world? The responses demand evidence, proof that you are doing what you say you are doing. Not unsubstantiated statements. Not good intentions. And not wishful thinking. Evidence. You must be tenacious about getting it.

You must also ask for data for charts and graphs and documentation that supports what the expert has said. You probably won't get it for awhile, but now is the time to ask. "We didn't document as we were going," IBM's Lori Kirkland remembers. "We found out that substantiating after the fact is very hard."

When you ask for data, be clear about what form you want that data to be in. "We really didn't give clear direction to our contributors about how to turn data in," says Roger Kane, quality director at Thermo King. "Some turned in line charts, some bar graphs, some generated computer graphs, but what we needed were data points, the exact numbers." *Tell people exactly what data you need, and ask them to keep copies of everything they provide you.* The copies will be a handy reference if you call with questions or if your company receives a site visit.

4. Organize data.

The first part of this step actually begins during the interviews, with taking good notes and requesting documentation. I will talk about documentation more in the next chapter.

"Key all information into word processing," McGrath says. "Put a pedigree on everything—1.1(a) from John Smith, February 5. Start collecting data right away, and don't throw away anything."

By entering the results of all interviews into word processing, the data becomes available to all teams through your computer network. This is valuable for cross-referencing and hunting down information on specific topics.

The pedigree reflects a filing system based on the Baldrige criteria. As data is collected, through either interviews or the documents supporting the interviews (manuals, procedures, charts, graphs, meeting minutes, executive calendars, sales literature, and so on), it is identified by category, item, and area to address, if appropriate.

STEP 6: IDENTIFY AREAS FOR IMPROVEMENT

As Baldrige team members search for data, they are actually exploring their company's quality system. Their exploration will lead them through lush meadows and barren plains, glittering avenues and dark alleys. These are places most people have never seen and few even know exist, so you would be wise to keep a diary of your travels.

Every time the Xerox Baldrige team discovered an area for improvement, they added it to their Wart List. Nasty warts got quick attention. The final Wart List fueled Xerox's quality improvement process.

Identifying areas for improvement is one of the most valuable products of the application process. It begins as you collect data, continues while you write the application, and concludes when you document your statements or prepare for a site visit.

According to William Lesner, one of three people responsible for Cadillac's award-winning application, when Cadillac finished its application it had 15 pages of "holes," its term for areas for improvement. Asked to identify the benefits of applying for the Baldrige Award, the first thing Lesner said was, "Holes."

Whether you call them warts or holes or OFIs (Milliken's term, meaning "Opportunities For Improvement"), they alone can justify your application effort. As Xerox CEO David Kearns told his Baldrige team, "Poke us in the eye." They gave him warts instead. He has since said that the warts were worth millions to Xerox.

STEP 7: COMMUNICATE NEEDS, IDEAS, AND INFORMATION

The common smokestack approach—addressing the criteria by category— is an obstacle to communication. Interviewers hot on the trail of vital information may pause to tell their category cohorts what they are doing, but the news rarely travels to other category teams. The results are redundant research, conflicting ideas, and an inconsistent application.

The solution lies in how you organize the application process. Link-it teams and/or two-person interview teams that ask a subject expert relevant questions for all the criteria help to connect the smokestacks. These teams report to or contain members from more than one category.

Frequent scheduled meetings of Baldrige team members are invaluable, because the entire team is then able to track progress toward completing the application. Team members share their ideas on interpreting the criteria, identifying other sources of data, and evaluating what has been collected so far. They support and inspire each other.

These meetings typically focus on category reports and the discussion of major problems or issues, and include category leaders and all other significant contributors. A well-organized meeting should take no longer than an hour, which gives each category 5 to 10 minutes for its report. Larger companies may need more time; IBM Rochester's Baldrige team met three or four times a week. The goals are to eliminate redundant research, resolve conflicting ideas, and produce a cohesive and consistent application.

A predictable snag to achieving this goal is the explanation of major processes and themes. Every quality system features a few key processes that reach across category lines. At Cadillac it was simultaneous engineering and its business planning model. Zytec's long-range strategic planning process appeared in several categories. Federal Express had its service quality index and Wallace its focus on training. Other major themes have included leadership through quality (Xerox), pursuit of excellence (Milliken), and market-driven quality (IBM).

Snags also occur when more than one category relies on the same major process for the bulk of its response, when categories interpret the same process or theme differently, and when major processes or themes are missed or underutilized. All of these can be avoided by identifying your major processes and themes early in the application process, deciding in which category or item they will be explained and in which categories or items they will be referenced, and communicating these decisions to all Baldrige team members.

"We put together a matrix identifying our major themes, where they were defined, and where they were referenced," says IBM's Kirkland.

The goal of matrices and frequent meetings is the best possible application with the least possible work. This goal cannot be achieved without continuous formal and informal communication, from the initial meeting of the Baldrige teams, to training team members, to gathering and sharing information, to the next stage in the process: writing the application.

CHAPTER 14

Creating the Application

"It sounds like creative writing but it really isn't." Joe Rocca should know. He helped write IBM Rochester's Baldrige Award-winning application and was one of a few people who reviewed, scored, and suggested improvements in other people's writing.

"Most everyone figures they can answer this in a couple weeks and be done," Rocca says. "Then you call them into a room and dump all over them and tell them they're not done. It's a very anguished situation because you thought you had it down pat, but often you didn't even understand the question. We went through four or five drafts before we really felt we had our act together."

The process of creating an application is not for the faint of heart or fragile of ego. It requires enough confidence to write what you know, enough humility to accept constructive criticism, and enough determination to incorporate suggestions into a second draft, a third draft, a fourth draft, and so on. Sections you love will be coldly removed. Sections you struggled to explain will be condensed or replaced by a graph. Sections that reflected every scrap of information you had will somehow need to be expanded. And this will all happen more than once, justified by your company's desire to submit a complete and accurate application.

Do not despair. Writing is like any other process: you decide what you want to do, you figure out the best way to do it, you do it, you evaluate what you have done, then you make improvements. PDCA writing: plan-do-check-act. Think of it as a learning process and the criticism will not feel so personal. You can also soften the blows by improving your writing; I will suggest ways to do that in this chapter.

Writing, however, is only part of creating an application. Many applicants rely heavily on graphics (charts and graphs) to communicate key information. Xerox wanted to have one graphic per page and they almost did. Cadillac's 1990 application featured 115 charts and graphs, including a lot of process models. I will describe how to create graphics and show examples in this chapter.

The coordination of writing and graphics probably causes more heartburn than any other part of the application process. It is common for companies to underestimate how much time this will take, wait too long to start, then work around the clock to get it done. I will discuss strategies that have worked for other companies later in the chapter.

Writing the first draft may be the eighth step in the application process, but it is usually the first time that Baldrige team members feel as though they are making real progress.

STEP 8: WRITE THE FIRST DRAFT

You can assign this task in one of several ways. Some companies have only one writer. Ken Leach, for example wrote Globe Metallurgical's Baldrige Award-winning application by himself. Maureen Steinwall wrote her company's Minnesota Quality Award application. It requires complete knowledge of your organization and a working knowledge of the criteria, but it can be done.

Some companies have two writers. Bank One Milwaukee had two internal writers, one who had been dedicated to the application process from the start and a technical writer familiar with the bank's quality improvement process. Thermo King hired two outside writers to produce a first draft, one for categories 1.0 through 4.0 and another for categories 5.0 through 7.0. Two members of Ford's quality department wrote the first draft of their application.

Some companies have three writers. Three people wrote Shipley's application in six weeks, working one-half to two-thirds time on it, and Cadillac had three team leaders who coordinated the writing of its item leaders.

Some companies have seven writers, one for each category. Zytec had seven writers responsible for their first draft, although others contributed. Other companies have many writers. Solectron's first draft was written by its cross-functional application team. Intel had the people on its category teams write responses to the areas to address, and 14 coordinators used these responses to write the application. Federal Express took the applications from its 11 divisions and aggregated them by category. Category teams then wrote the responses for their categories, often with one writer per item.

All of these methods work, and none is necessarily better than the others. You would think that the larger the company, the more writers that would be needed, but Ford disproves that theory. The key seems to be to choose writers based on availability and knowledge of the subject, whether that means one writer or 30. And don't worry about different writing styles at this point. You can fix that with later drafts.

Once you have identified your writers, what do you tell them? Chris Witzke, Marlow's COO, says simply, "I would make sure people did the first draft with data, not stories."

Robert McGrath managed the process that produced Westinghouse Commercial Nuclear Fuel's Baldrige Award-winning application, has since become a quality consultant, and is the primary instructor for ASQC's Baldrige self-assessment course. He advises would-be writers to "describe the system or process, then tell where it is used—who, how often, etc. It's nice to understand deployment after the process. Then put an example—last, not first. Otherwise, the example becomes the answer."

That is sound advice. By describing a system or process, you are providing information about your *approach*. When you continue with who is using the approach and how often, you are providing information about *deployment*. These are two of the dimensions upon which the evaluation of your application will be based.

The third dimension, *results*, almost always implies trends. No wordy descriptions here, just graphs and charts that show quality improvement and how it compares to competitors and world-class quality leaders.

Figuring out which dimensions to reflect in your answer is part of your first job as a writer, and one of eight tasks required to produce a first draft.

Writer's Job #1: Understand What Is Being Asked

This is harder than it sounds. Rocca's description of what happened at IBM Rochester could fit any company that has applied for the Baldrige Award or a state or corporate quality award. People read through an item and its areas to address, assume they know what it means, then start writing. For example, Zytec's senior managers wrote their 1990 Baldrige application, and used that experience when they wrote their 1991 application. Yet they still interpreted some areas to address incorrectly, causing those initial answers to miss the mark.

Whether you are responsible for writing one area to address or an entire category, you must be clear about what is being asked and how that relates to the rest of the criteria. Good training at the beginning of the process helps, as does the availability of expert assistance throughout the process.

The expert may be part of the Baldrige team, a local Baldrige examiner, or NIST, which will answer questions about the criteria for any caller. Or it may be an "associate" expert. Cadillac, for instance, relied on a senior executive who worked in another part of General Motors.

The easiest task is determining which dimensions to include in your response. The Criteria booklet tells you what types of information each item requests. If an area to address asks "how" or for "approaches," "strategies," "key indicators," "principal types," or any other process or system, you will want to describe your company's approach and how well that approach has been deployed. If an area to address asks for trends, you will want to show results.

As you read the areas to address, you will see the words "such as" followed by a laundry list of examples. The examples define the previous phrase but are not meant to be the only possibilities. Before you proceed to the answer, think about which examples are appropriate for your company and which are missing. Another frequently used term is "key." In the criteria, "key" means the vital few, major, or most important.

Finally, make sure that you read and understand the "Notes" that follow several of the items. They explain terms in the item, clarify what is being requested, and make distinctions and connections between one item and another.

Writer's Job #2: Have Enough Data and Information Available

The quality of your data and information determines the quality of your response. Once you understand the criteria, determine if you or other members of your team have gathered enough data and information for you to write a decent response. The data collectors might not have dug into the criteria as deeply as you are now, which means that you may not have what you really need. Don't start writing until you are confident that you do.

Writer's Job #3: Write a Positive, Honest Response

"Positive" and "honest" can be hard to achieve. I have had to write and edit responses that we knew would score poorly. When that happens, it is tempting to imply that you are doing more than you really are, or to contrive a response that might be true by someone's convoluted reasoning, but is misleading by intent. Resist the temptation. Deceit to gain points will be exposed eventually, sending a message to the examiner (and to employees who read the application) that dishonesty is acceptable and that other parts of the application may be less than truthful as well. If the exposure occurs during your site visit, your company will lose credibility that will be hard to recapture. Take your lumps, improve your system, and score better the next time.

As Zytec's application neared final draft form, CEO Ron Schmidt read every line one last time. If he was not absolutely sure that a statement could be supported, he revised it or took it out. The integrity of Zytec's application contributed to an exceptional site visit.

If you have little positive to say, say little. You get no sympathy points just because your response is longer.

Writer's Job #4: Write a Complete Response

As any editor will tell you, it is much easier to reduce than it is to expand. Don't worry about length as you write the first draft. Cadillac's first draft in 1989 exceeded 400 pages; the next year, it was "only" 250 pages. Xerox's first draft totaled 175 pages, and Ford started with 150 pages.

For those items requesting approach and deployment, the writer's job is to describe them clearly and accurately and to provide one or more examples, if appropriate. For those that require results, the writer's job is to include all trends that he or she thinks might be relevant, with necessary explanations. At this stage, you should never cut any response short unless you have nothing valuable left to say.

Writer's Job #5: Write a Factual Response

Thermo King sent the first draft of its application, which I helped write, to a Baldrige examiner. The examiner leaped on every grand statement I made. For example, when I quoted Thermo King's slogan, "serving customer needs better than anyone else," the examiner scrawled, "Says who!" I called one process a "world-class approach," which the examiner questioned: "Are you sure?" When I claimed that another process was measured "against world standards of excellence," the examiner asked, "Do you demonstrate this elsewhere?"

If you make bold statements, be prepared to prove them. Examiners evaluate evidence, not grandiose claims. And don't tell stories. The difference between an example and an anecdote is that the example illustrates your answer and the anecdote *is* your answer. Use examples to illustrate the processes, and lose the anecdotes.

Writer's Job #6: Write in English

As you write about your company's quality system, it is easy to forget that the eventual readers know little about your company except what they read in this application. Keep in mind that you are communicating to a quality expert in a totally different industry, and you won't assume a level of knowledge that does not exist.

You cannot escape your company's acronyms and jargon, but you can explain them in your response and in a glossary. If some terms are overused, the people who edit this and subsequent drafts will correct the problem. If your company is large enough, or if you have several writers, you may want to create a style sheet for uniformity.

The style sheet should be developed before any writing is done by the Baldrige team or leader or by an internal writer or editor. It should tell everyone who will be writing or editing the application how to refer to specific style issues, such as how to use variations of the company name (American National Manufacturing Company, American National Mfg. Co., American National, or American?), how to write titles (Vice-President, Quality; vice-president of quality; or quality v.p.?), how to write department names (Manufacturing Department, Manufacturing department, manufacturing department, or manufacturing?), how to refer to major processes and programs (Corrective Action Report, corrective action report, or CAR?), how to label charts and graphs (Figure 1-1, 1-a, or 1-i?), and how to refer to other sections of the application [*always* in this format: 1.1(a)]. Clarifying these issues before the writing begins can save a lot of confusion and correction later.

Writer's Job #7: Note Data and/or Graphic Needs and Connections

Writing tends to generate as many questions as answers. If you feel that more data are needed to support a statement or if you believe that data exist that could improve your response, identify the need and communicate it to your Baldrige team.

You may also discover a place where a chart or graph would explain something better than words. Cadillac relied heavily on process models to visually portray key processes (such as its business planning process model on page 85). If you identify such a need, sketch what the chart or graph would look like or write down what you imagine and pass it along to the Baldrige team.

As you immerse yourself in the writing, you may find your subject matter spilling over into other items and categories that are another writer's responsibility. You will want to communicate with the other writer, either directly or through your team, to make sure that your responses are not redundant or that the other writer is not missing an important part of his or her answer.

Writer's Job #8: Meet the Deadline

This is no time to delay the schedule. You will need every day from the completion of the first draft to the day the application is due to turn a bunch of rough drafts into a cohesive, polished, illustrated, high-quality application.

STEP 9: BEGIN THE LAYOUT, INCLUDING GRAPHICS

As with the writing, the first question to answer here is who will do the layout. This involves entering and/or organizing the written responses, creating charts and graphs, matching the charts and graphs to the narrative, making changes, and producing a final, print-ready copy of the application.

Many choose to do this internally. At Zytec, one person did all the layout and graphics using desktop publishing software. She succeeded because she was very good with the software and very dedicated to getting it done right. Of the companies I talked to about their applications, Ford, Federal Express, Cadillac, and Xerox, among others, handled all graphic work internally, although their reasons sometimes differed. Some did it because they felt the information was too confidential. Others did it because they wanted to utilize their in-house graphic design capabilities. All seemed happy with the results.

A few companies had the layout and graphics done by an outside firm. Thermo King, for example, hired a graphic design company to develop a layout and coordinate the charts and graphs. Two graphic artists worked on-site with the writing team to create the charts and graphs as the narrative neared final form. Intel also used an external printing firm to design its application. "We had a theme and we wanted that carried through," says Scott Pfotenhauer, who managed the application process. "We wanted to make it as easy as possible for readers to get information. We created the graphs and the printers loaded them up so that they had one consistent style."

Whichever route you choose, make sure that the graphics people know what they are in for. As the deadline nears, creating graphs and organizing graphic elements tend to gobble up nights and weekends.

The nature of an application's layout and graphics is largely defined by the Application Forms and Instructions, which state the following:

- Identify each Category, Item, and Area to Address by its proper designation. The proper format (1.1a, etc.) should be used at the beginning of the response to each Area to Address and when referring to another Area in the application. At the beginning of an Area, the designation should also be underlined (1.1a).

- Print the application on standard $8\frac{1}{2}$ by 11-inch paper using a fixed pitch font of 12 or fewer characters per inch, or a proportional spacing font that's 10 points or larger. Helvetica or Times, or equivalents, are preferred. Leading should equal two points (that's the space between the lines). These requirements apply to all type (narrative, charts, data tables, etc.).

- Use no more than 60 lines per page, including page headings and page numbers. A two-column format is preferred. Pages may be printed on both sides.

- The page limit is 75 single-sided pages for the manufacturing and service categories, 60 pages for small businesses. This page limit includes pictures, graphs, figures, data tables, and appendices. It does not include the Overview, dividers, covers, tab separators, glossaries, title pages, and tables of contents. Labeled section tabs and a glossary of terms and abbreviations are appreciated; heavy covers and bulky binders are discouraged. The application should be securely fastened together to prevent separation during handling.

- Supplemental Sections are required if units of your company are in different businesses (two or more diverse product or service lines and/or dissimilar quality systems). Supplemental Sections can be no longer than 50 pages and must adhere to the same formatting guidelines as the application.

- The Overview is a four-page summary that introduces your company to the Examiners. According to the Application Forms and Instructions booklet, it should include types of major products and services, key quality requirements for products and services, nature of major markets, description of principal customers, competitive environment, your position in your industry, major equipment and facilities used, types of technologies used, general description of your employee base, importance of and types of suppliers of goods and services, occupational health and safety and other regulatory considerations, and other factors you consider important. The Overview is not counted as part of the page limit.

- A complete application package includes, in this order:
  - Title Page
  - Eligibility Determination Form*
  - Application Form*
  - Site Listing and Descriptors Form(s)*
  - Table of Contents
  - Overview
  - Organization Chart
  - Summary of Supplemental Sections, if applicable
  - Your responses to the Categories/Items/Areas to Address (presented in the Criteria booklet, available from NIST)

* These forms are included in the Application Forms and Instructions booklet, also available from NIST

Your layout/graphics people will need to be familiar with these requirements before they develop a layout or begin to design charts and graphs. They will also want to take some time to decide what software to use. Zytec's use of desktop publishing software meant that the layout person had to rekey all text into the software. You might want to start with a common word-processing software, at least until the first drafts are done. This should reduce the amount of rekeying that is necessary, and will make it possible to give disks to editors for editing by computer instead of by hand.

With few exceptions, companies struggle with the page limit. Imagine Cadillac's task of slimming 400 pages down to 75. Graphics people can help make it fit, but their mobility is restricted by the layout requirements. The sooner they can give your Baldrige team some sense of how many pages need to be cut, the easier it will be to edit your application.

I have not noticed any bias toward companies that submit fewer pages than the limit, that print on both sides instead of one side, or that print in black instead of adding one or more colors. *The purpose of the layout and graphics is to present your responses clearly.* Four colors and classy design do not seem to buy much.

Figure 14.1 A trend chart showing Supplier Percentage of On-Time Delivery.

Graphics range from simple trend charts to more complex process models. For items 6.1, 6.2, 6.3, 7.7, and 7.8, trend charts *are* the response. These five items are worth 320 points, which makes the trend charts extremely valuable.

To give you an idea of what these trend charts might look like, consider the examples shown in Figures 14.1 and 14.2, taken from a Baldrige application.

A matrix is a good way to display lists of items, as shown in Figure 14.3, also taken from a Baldrige application.

Process models can save a lot of words. By its nature, a process is easier to visualize than it is to explain. A good example is the model of Cadillac's business planning process. Another example is from Zytec's Baldrige application, shown in Figure 14.4.

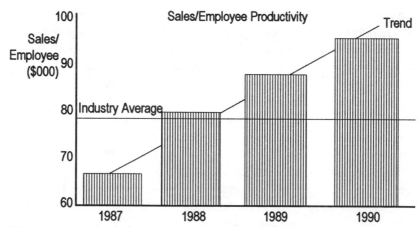

Figure 14.2 A trend chart showing "Improve Profitability."

Mandatory Training

Legend: M—Mandatory (1) Mandatory—New Hires Only (2) Annual Refresher Required

Table: Zytec Mandatory Courses — WHO TRAINS (X) and WHO ATTENDS (M)

Zytec Mandatory Course	Class No.	Hours	Qualified Personnel	Sales	Senior Staff	Training Technicians	Quality Director	Statistician	Facility Engineer	Manager	Sales and Marketing	Engineers	Technicians	Managers	Program Writers	Office Clerical	Production-MFE Employees	Materials	Accounting	Personnel	Executives
New Hire Orientation (1)	351	16.0				X					M	M	M	M	M	M	M	M	M	M	M
Basic Statistical Process Control (SPC)	300	8.0	X			X	X	X				M	M				M				
Intermediate Statistical Process Control	301	40.0					X	X			M	M	M	M	M	M	M	M	M	M	M
Quality Control (QC) Story	302	1.5									M	M	M	M	M	M	M	M	M	M	M
Just-in-Time Manufacturing (JIT)	305	4.0	X		X	X	X				M	M	M	M	M	M	M	M	M	M	M
Zytec Involved People I (ZIP I)	328	16.0	X			X				X	M	M	M	M	M	M	M	M	M	M	M
Right to Know (2)	337	1.5							X		M	M	M	M	M	M	M	M	M	M	M
Six Sigma Basic	348	2.0	X		X	X	X					M	M				M				
Six Sigma Advanced	349	4.0					X				M	M	M	M	M	M		M	M	M	M
Electrostatic Discharge (ESD) (2)	335	1.0	X			X					M	M	M	M	M	M	M	M	M	M	M
Service America	030	4.0		X							M	M	M	M	M	M	M	M	M	M	M
Seven New Planning Tools	935	4.0			X		X			X	M	M	M	M	M	M		M	M	M	M
FOCUS	2	2.0	X		X						M	M	M	M	M	M	M	M	M	M	M
Sexual Harassment	359	1.5	X			X					M	M	M	M	M	M	M	M	M	M	M

Figure 14.3 A matrix showing Zytec's Mandatory Training. (Courtesy of Zytec)

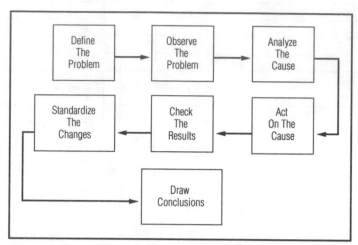

Figure 14.4 A chart of Zytec's problem-solving process.

When I worked with Thermo King and Zytec on their Baldrige applications, we welcomed the chance to see how other companies presented data. The examples I have provided are intended to fill similar cravings, not to prescribe a "best way" or to dictate how you should design your graphics.

Companies also wonder how many charts and graphs they should include. There is no magic number, although examiners, like the rest of us, are attracted to and probably learn more from charts and graphs than from verbal descriptions. By coincidence, Cadillac and Zytec each had 115 charts and graphs in their award-winning applications. Intel had 60 in an application that earned it a site visit in 1991.

STEP 10: EVALUATE THE FIRST DRAFT

Toward the end of January 1991, ten of Zytec's senior executives and I assembled to review the first draft of the company's Baldrige application. Most had written their categories during the Christmas holidays.

The employee responsible for the layout had entered all the responses into her computer, then printed them out double-spaced with wide margins for comments. A few charts and graphs were included—most from the previous year's application—and others were noted. We received copies of the first draft a few days before the meeting.

The meeting started at 8 A.M. with the largest category by point value, 7.0, and proceeded through the categories to the one worth the fewest points, 3.0. This ended up taking 15 hours over a one-and-a-half day period, with little time spent on category 4.0, which was not yet completed.

We reviewed each category by area to address. Anyone could ask questions or make suggestions, with the comments directed to the person responsible for the category. The discussion frequently focused on interpretation of the criteria, relevance of the response, and completeness of the response. Consensus was not always possible, so the final decision was left to the author. The group was very supportive, but also very direct. This was a broad discussion; grammar, spelling, and even the clarity of responses were ignored at this stage. The focus was: "Do we answer the question?"

The process was long and mind-numbing, but it did lead to a significant refinement of the first draft. It would have been more beneficial if every participant had dug into the first draft, compared the responses to the criteria, and come prepared to discuss it. As it was, three people tended to carry the debate.

I cannot imagine this review process going any faster, but I can sure see it going slower if the quality of the writing is poor or if the group has not applied the previous year. I would improve the process by splitting it up into as many half-days as necessary, because people wore down quickly in the afternoon. Otherwise, I thought it was an excellent way to share the entire document and begin to develop a cohesive application.

Of course, this is not the only way to review a first draft. Ford's first draft went to its senior executives, not for close review, but to determine whether to proceed to a second draft. Bank One Milwaukee's Baldrige team also gave its first draft to senior management for their input. Federal Express and others used Baldrige examiners, internal and external, for scoring and feedback.

The advantages of having outside experts read the first draft are the diligence, expertise, and objectivity they provide. It is hard to get employees to (1) read the first draft and (2) determine if it responds to the criteria, because it is time-consuming and they have other things to do. A lack of expertise can make the job even more difficult, and a lack of objectivity can lead to inaccurate conclusions. Therefore, an outside expert paid to assess the first draft provides a valuable perspective.

"I say take somebody with skill and have them look at the requirements and ask, 'Is this a good approach?'" says McGrath. "The person can't be so inside that he or she can read between the lines. I would get as many people as are willing to do this."

STEP 11: WRITE SUBSEQUENT DRAFTS

Write, review, write, review, over and over until the deadline comes.

The major problem during this phase of the process is burnout. After two or three months of Baldriging on top of their regular jobs, people get tired. The deadline may still be a month away, the next revision does not look a whole lot different than the current draft, and who cares whether the response is completely accurate or clear, anyway?

It is time for the leaders to lead. If you have got a second team on the bench, now is the time to bring them in. If you don't, now is the time to fire up the first team. Throw a party. Buy everybody who participated a hat or a T-shirt to show your appreciation. Praise profusely. Remind them how far you have come, help them see the finish line, then spur them on.

One way to relieve the strain is to turn some of the editing over to professional writers. As their applications neared the final draft, Xerox, Cadillac, IBM Rochester, Solectron, Zytec, and others each had a writer edit the entire application to give it one cohesive style. In addition to providing uniformity, a professional writer makes sure that your responses are on target and understandable.

The burnout problem is caused, in part, by the ongoing pursuit of data. It would be nice to have all the data in hand before the writing starts, but that is not realistic. You would be asking some people to provide data that does not exist in the form you require. "The data problems we had were measuring effort," says Roger Kane, quality director at Thermo King, "like the number of people participating on quality improvement teams, the percentage of hourly employees on these teams, senior management's contact with customers and suppliers, training given and received, etc. We did it; we just didn't keep records of it." As you search for data, you may be surprised at what is not readily available but can be generated. But don't be surprised by how long it can take.

Another cause of burnout is fitting your quality system to the criteria. Several categories will claim legitimate rights to explaining your best processes, but pleasing them all would be redundant. You will have to decide who is responsible for explaining each key process, then refer to that explanation wherever the process appears in the rest of the application.

Cadillac used these "REF SECs" heavily throughout its application, and also tried a creative approach to explaining issues that did not mesh well with the criteria. "We wrestled with, 'Where do we put dealers? Are they customers? Are they suppliers? Are they part of Cadillac?'" says William Lesner, one of the leaders of Cadillac's application process. "We decided to spend one-half page at the beginning of category 5.0 to say, 'This is how we're going to cover the next three sections.' I think that really helped the examiners clarify our approach."

In the crush to condense, clarity often suffers. A less detailed explanation that is clearly presented is better than a more detailed explanation that nobody can understand.

At some point in the writing process you may want to score your application. This is not necessary and may not even be advisable, as the goal is to improve quality and not to "get good grades," but few companies can resist the temptation of "the number." Some companies have outside experts score their applications as part of their critique. Others ask a few internal experts to score it. Some, like Zytec's senior managers, wait until the application is done before scoring it themselves. If you ask for a score, be prepared for the number you get.

"In the Baldrige scoring system, if you come in at 500 points you're a good company," says Frank Caplan, quality consultant and senior Baldrige examiner. "Anything over 500 and you're beginning to move ahead of the pack toward excellence. Most American companies would score 100 or 200 or lower if they applied."

While the scores for award-winning companies are not revealed, most experts assume that those scores are in the 700 to 800 point range. Adjust your expectations accordingly.

As you approach the final draft, make sure the other pieces of the application package are being handled. Someone must write the overview and create the glossary, both of which are important because examiners read and refer to them, and someone must gather and complete the necessary forms. Assign these tasks and track progress toward their completion with the same diligence that you devote to your application.

STEP 12: COORDINATE WRITING AND GRAPHICS

This should probably be Step 11-B. Initially, your layout/graphics people will spend their time entering text, printing draft copies for review, and creating charts and graphs. As the deadline nears, however, they will face a rush of charts and graphs. As early as possible before the final draft, then (but not until you are relatively close to final draft text and know what charts and graphs will go where), you will need a properly formatted copy of your application to see how close you are to fitting the page limits. Chances are you will be long. It's important for your editors to know that.

In addition to assessing overall length, look at the length of each category. It makes sense to allocate pages according to the value of the categories, as follows:

		Approximate # of Pages	
Category	**Total Points**	**Small Business**	**Mfg/ Service**
1.0	90	5	7
2.0	80	5	6
3.0	60	4	5
4.0	150	9	11
5.0	140	8	11
6.0	180	11	13
7.0	300	18	22

A page or two more or less per category, especially for the larger categories, is no big deal, but significant disparities should be studied closely. For example, I have seen applications in which category 5.0 was 20 or more pages and category 7.0 came in around a dozen pages. Think of it this way: that is 20 pages devoted to earning 140 points and only 12 focused on 300 points. Not a good strategy.

Your layout/graphics people will spend the last three or four weeks adjusting pages to categories, adding charts and graphs, cutting, pasting, juggling, and swearing, all with an immovable deadline looming. As much as possible, the charts and graphs should appear on the same page as the text that refers to them. This gets harder, however, as the text is revised and graphs and charts are added or deleted.

Down the home stretch, formatting the application can feel like a 300-pound jockey on your layout/graphics "horse." The more time you can give them to carry that load to the finish line, the better your finished product will be.

STEP 13: PRODUCE THE FINAL DRAFT

Before you produce your final draft, print a few copies for proofreading. Distribute them to team leaders and to people who are good at proofreading—either employees, consultants, or both.

Proofreading gets rid of mistakes that can tarnish the quality of your application, such as misspellings, grammatical errors, punctuation mistakes, incomplete charts and graphs, misnamed or misnumbered charts and graphs, misplaced charts and graphs, missing data or text, and inconsistent references to titles, departments, processes, and programs. Cadillac estimates that its proofreaders found 100 such errors per page. That may seem high—until you see what proofreaders mark on your application.

After the proofreaders' corrections have been made, you are ready to print the final draft.

STEP 14: PRINT AND DELIVER THE APPLICATION

You must submit 20 copies of your complete application package (see Step 9), along with your fee payment, postmarked on or before the due date. The due date and mailing address can be found in the Application Forms and Instructions booklet.

Many companies go outside for printing and binding, depending on their internal printing capabilities. Intel, for instance, used an outside printer because it wanted four-color printing on its cover and tabs. Ford used color to show its Concept to Customer process, but printed its application internally. (By the way, color is certainly not required or necessarily preferred. The only color other than black in Zytec's award-winning application was on the cover.)

At this point you may also want to decide how you will distribute your application, both internally and externally. Some companies print thousands of copies for their managers. Some companies send copies to their major customers and suppliers. And some companies print a few copies, number them, distribute them to their senior executives, and lock any extras in the company vault. I will talk more about getting the most out of your application in the next chapter, and about the ultimate good news/bad news announcement:

We're getting a site visit!

CHAPTER 15

Acting on the Application

To most companies that apply for the Baldrige Award, the application process is much like the regular season for a professional basketball team. You begin with enthusiasm and hope, but halfway through the season, your expectations and your energy are starting to droop. The last few weeks you push your tired mind and body to their limits, with the final week an exhausting blur.

And then, for some, come the playoffs. Or in this case, a site visit. You are not done yet, not even close, but now the prize is within reach. Now, as Wallace's Michael Spiess said, "you want everybody playing above the rim for four days."

A site visit is an exhilarating opportunity to "strut your stuff." Those who have had to perform under expert scrutiny emerge with a new respect for their fellow workers and a renewed pride in their work. "The process of being judged was valuable because a lot of people were put on a stage and they had to perform," says Motorola chairman Robert Galvin. "Someone came looking at us and we weren't found wanting."

For those companies that have not applied for the award yet or that have applied but not scored well, the obvious question is: Why should I care about a site visit? The best answer is: Because once you know what they are about, you will want to get one.

Consider receiving a site visit an interim goal to winning the Baldrige Award. Some companies commit to it on paper: "Receive a site visit by Baldrige examiners by 1993," and "Win the Baldrige Award by 1994."

The value of a site visit as an interim goal is that it is quicker and easier to achieve than the actual award. In 1991, 20 of 106 applicants earned site visits, but only three won awards.

In the next chapter I will talk about what winning the Baldrige Award has meant to the winners. To summarize, it has meant more work and more rewards. The same can be said for a site visit. If 30 people are involved in creating the application, the entire company gets involved in the site visit.

THE BENEFITS OF A SITE VISIT

People who have been through a site visit—especially leaders—are often changed by the experience. They "witness the miracles." Witness William Lesner's reflections on Cadillac's site visit:

> Part of the problem in the day-to-day operation of a business is that you see and respond to problems. You ask yourself, "Are we that bad?" "Do we have that far to go?" The site visit shows you what's positive.

> At one plant they talked to the man who was the bumper polisher, maybe the worst job in the plant. An examiner asked him who his customer is, and he said, "Do you want to know about my internal customer or my external customer?"

> Over and over, people amazed me with the consistency of their responses. People understand.

People do understand. They are listening when you preach quality, and they are practicing what they learn. They are involved. They care. The site visit illuminates the breadth and depth of your quality system, and that may be its greatest gift.

But there is more. A site visit is an opportunity for employees to tell people who truly care what they do and how they do it. Doug Tersteeg, Zytec's quality director, equates it with being stranded on a deserted island: You anticipate the day you will be able to share all you have learned and done with someone else.

At world-class companies, people tell their stories with excitement and pride, and they feel recognized for their contributions. Listen to Tom Kennedy talk about the site visit at Solectron:

> Everyone wanted to talk to the Baldrige examiners. At lunch, one examiner had 13 people around him and they were all trying to talk to him. We estimate they talked to 500 of our 2,000 employees, and they spent quality time with each of them.

> We knew the examiners were taught to be receiving and they did that well, except when they would talk to our people to assess the deployment of our quality concepts. Then the examiners would get enthusiastic.

We were surprised at how positive an experience the site visit was. It was a huge, positive recognition of everyone's efforts through the years.

Not every company is as pleased with their site visits as Cadillac, Zytec, and Solectron, especially when questions are asked that can't be answered or data requested that doesn't exist, but most enjoy its benefits: a personal assessment by quality experts; an opportunity for employees to perform; an exceptional form of recognition; an inspirational goal to work toward; and the experience of putting people and processes to the test and watching them respond.

COMMUNICATING YOUR APPLICATION

Whether or not you expect to receive a site visit, sending in your application does not finish your Baldrige business. You have your self-assessment and, later, the feedback from examiners to incorporate into your quality improvement plans. You may also want to communicate your application, in its entirety and/or in an abridged version, to employees.

Xerox sent 3,700 copies of its application to its managers. "The people at Xerox tend to see the glass as half-empty," says Sam Malone, a member of Xerox's NQA team. "You get an entirely different view of your company when you read the application. I don't think any executive or senior manager knew the impact it would have on employee morale."

The biggest problem that companies have with mass distribution of an application is the proprietary information it contains. Most companies only give copies to senior executives, then keep a few in the company library or by the corporate quality department if other managers or employees want to read them. They fear that competitors will get the application and take advantage of any confidential information it contains. Ford and Thermo King, for example, removed numbers from particularly sensitive graphs, thereby showing a positive trend without revealing private data. These same companies also guarded the distribution of their applications closely.

Other companies have been very open with their applications. Intel's Scott Pfotenhauer sent me a copy of its application for my files, with no apparent concern for confidentiality. Such openness was refreshing. Zytec created a fairly long abstract of its application that covered every major point, including important trends and survey data, and sent it to all of its customers and suppliers.

My sense is that a lot of the secrecy that companies exhibit is a knee-jerk reaction to a history of isolationism, a reaction that will not serve them well in the current climate of benchmarking and sharing quality ideas and successes. Some data may need to be protected and can be, as Ford and Thermo King showed, but keeping applications from your own managers or employees inhibits continuous improvement. The application documents the condition of your quality system in a way that has probably never been done before, and you can extend its value by communicating it to the people who make that system work.

Companies communicate their applications in a variety of ways. When Cadillac first applied in 1989, "we communicated our application through a series of videotapes," says Lesner. "The second year we couldn't spend that much so we gave complete copies of the application, together with the guidelines, to 150 top executives and encouraged them to read them and share them with employees. We gave sections of the report to people who needed them. And we had complete copies available in our training department for anyone to read."

Thermo King condensed each category of its application into four- to six-page weekly reports, then employees added the reports to a special binder they had received for this purpose. The binder included tabs for each category, on which were printed a synopsis of the criteria for that category. The report format was also used to inform employees about issues related to its impending site visit.

"We created the Baldrige Report as a communication vehicle to let people know what was going on," says the report's editor, Hope Scamehorn. "We've continued to add to it since our site visit with newsletters describing the results of our Baldrige feedback report and the action plans based on that feedback."

IBM Rochester sent 4,500 copies of its 1989 application to all of its departments. In 1990, "we passed copies out to all managers and asked them to communicate key points to their people," says Lori Kirkland, quality consultant. "Two weeks before our site visit, every day, a category owner got on the intercom and reviewed the world-class indicators for their categories. We had meetings with second-line managers and above about the information in the application and suggested that they take this information to their people. We created sample questions and asked how they would answer them, such as 'How do you define quality?'"

PREPARING FOR THE SITE VISIT

Companies that think they may get a site visit usually spend more time communicating their application to employees. For example, Federal Express talked to employees about the Baldrige Award, the criteria, and its application periodically on 5-minute closed-circuit broadcasts. It prepared a packet for managers that reviewed the company's quality improvement process, provided background on the Baldrige Award and criteria, and posed typical questions that visiting examiners might ask. Three weeks before the site visit, when the company learned which three cities the examiner team would visit, it sent people to those cities to prep management there, "but that had limited benefit since we have so many facilities in those three cities," says John West, manager of corporate quality improvement.

Wallace wanted its employees to have the mindset of selling something to their largest client. "We had meetings twice a week, for one hour after work, to go over basic things like how to answer questions," Spiess says.

Intel held one meeting for its employees. "I didn't want to go overboard in preparing employees for our site visit," says Pfotenhauer. "We gave them a 60- to 90-minute overview of the Baldrige program and our quality process, plus time for questions and answers. We wanted them to feel comfortable in providing open, honest, and natural answers in an abnormal situation."

The fact that a site visit is an abnormal situation causes many companies to counsel employees about how to relate to examiners.

"In 1989, we told our employees that the examiners liked to eat with employees in the cafeteria," says Kirkland. "For the three days the examiners were here, the cafeteria was empty. In 1990, we *prepared* our site for the visit. We let people know what to expect so that we would have greater participation from them."

Every company prepares its employees differently, but most convey these messages:

- Expect to be interviewed. Examiners will conduct random interviews.

- Be prepared to talk about what quality means to you. What is your job? Who are your customers? How do you know you are meeting your customers' expectations?

- When you answer, think in terms of approach/deployment/results. What is the process? How widely is it being used? What are the results? How is the process improved? Examiners will pick a topic and "follow the thread" to see how well an approach is deployed in the activities it affects, and what results it has achieved. Marlow's Chris Witzke remembers examiners asking him about issues in category 3.0 or 6.0, asking to see supporting data, then cross-checking what he said during interviews with others on unrelated subjects or categories.

- If you don't know an answer, admit it and point the examiner in the direction of someone who does.

- Be courteous, honest, open, and positive. For self-critical companies, which most quality leaders are, honesty and openness are easy compared to being positive. "We had to give ourselves permission to say we're good," Pfotenhauer says.

Another way companies prepare is through mock site visits. At least one month before its site visit, Cadillac did mock site visits at its plants and for all staff functions. Cadillac's Baldrige team developed a list of 15 areas they thought the examiners would focus on. However, the list had limited value. "There were areas in every category that the examiners focused on that we didn't expect," says Lesner. "There were surprises throughout the whole thing."

Thermo King had three Westinghouse people, two of whom had Baldrige examiner training, conduct a mini-audit of its operations. The Westinghouse team spent two days evaluating Thermo King's application and identifying site visit issues and another two days conducting the mini-audit on site. In its report to Thermo King's senior managers, the team described what it learned and suggested issues that the Baldrige site visit team might explore.

I realize that preparing sites for examination rankles some people in the same way that hiring consultants to help with the application does. Ideally, all employees would be eager to tell examiners all they know about quality at their company and in their jobs, and they would have a lot to tell. And in fact, many companies "play above the rim" more consistently than they ever expected. But they only do that well when they make it possible for employees to excel by clearing away their concerns, misconceptions, and fears. And the only way that is possible is through preparation.

During the site visit, the examiners will spend their time either talking to people or analyzing data. You must be prepared for both.

If you started gathering documents while you were writing your application, you are more efficient than most. Cadillac did. It also had one of the most imposing databases I have come across.

"To prepare for our site visit, the Baldrige team went through the application line by line," says Lesner. "Every claim needed supporting data and was assigned an owner within the team. The claims made up a 20-page, small print list. For every example of a process in the application, we found others. Every chart or graph had someone who was able to explain it, update it, and explain adverse trends. We had 20 rolling file cabinets of documentation, organized by plant and staff, then by category. We had documentation czars in charge of the documents, plus each plant had copies of its own documents."

When companies find out they are getting a site visit, one of the first things they do is call other companies that have had site visits to find out what to do. Those who call Cadillac must hang up the phone with deep despair in their hearts. If they then call Xerox, their despair blossoms into severe depression, because Xerox assembled 300 three-inch binders cross referenced to every statement made in its application.

Smaller companies are not spared because of their size. After talking to previous winners, Solectron identified the data it needed to back up the information in each sentence, then assembled a huge cross-functional team to pull together the data for each division.

Wallace Company documented anything that looked like it needed documenting, then labeled each file by section and paragraph. "The examiners went through every document we had," says Spiess. "They didn't accept anything we said unless we could prove it. They went through our surveys for three straight days, probing and probing."

Wallace also operated under a "three-minute rule." "Anything they wanted we could produce in less than three minutes," Spiess says. "Our documentation was so thorough they only needed one other document, which we produced in one minute."

While such efficiency is admirable, it comes at a high price. Locating, collecting, and cataloging documentation that supports every sentence in an application takes an enormous amount of time. Not everyone thinks it is necessary.

"There's no 'three-minute rule,'" says Pfotenhauer. "The examiners are very accommodating when they ask for something—you've got at least until the end of the day. It's not necessary to have all the data there."

Senior Baldrige examiner Charles Aubrey agrees. "Examiners request information in writing. We would like to have it the next day, sooner better than later, but it's not necessary to have notebooks or files all on hand."

Asked what he tells banks in the Banc One system, he says, "My recommendation to Banc One applicants who get a site visit is to ask anyone who contributed to identify the documentation supporting what they wrote. Not to pull it together into one place. And they're not to verify the entire application."

It is natural for a company preparing for a site visit to want to do everything possible to make that visit a success. Now that precedent exists for documenting every sentence and organizing that documentation in a central location, future site visit companies may feel compelled to follow suit. According to others, though, that degree of preparation is not necessary.

One unexpected benefit to consider is the value of the documentation *after* the site visit. More than one company has told me that its managers continue to use their Baldrige database as a source of information.

THE SITE VISIT

As mentioned in Chapter 12, the site visit begins when the examiners arrive at the company's main office, armed with their list of site visit issues. The site visit team includes a senior examiner, who manages the team and writes the report to the judges and the feedback report to the company, four to six other examiners, and an overseer from NIST.

"The day before the actual visit we spend six or seven hours meeting to decide who will pursue what," says Robert McGrath, a Baldrige examiner from 1988 to 1990. "During the site visit days we're going from 6:30 A.M. to midnight. Every day we share what we learned that day. It's a lot of fun."

More than one examiner has told me that being on a site visit is fun. These are quality professionals, leaders in their field. The opportunity to dig into a world-class company's quality system challenges and intrigues them.

The first day the site visit team arrives on the site, it meets with company personnel. The company decides who should be at that meeting, but it usually includes all senior management and all key contact people for each category or section of the application. The senior examiner introduces the team, provides an overview of how the site visit will proceed, then answers any questions.

The company then has 30 minutes or so to introduce itself. A typical introduction starts with a welcome by the CEO, a presentation of the corporate overview videotape, a summary by the CEO or another senior executive of the company's attributes that make it a quality leader, and an introduction of every employee in the room.

Once the formalities are concluded, the site visit team gets busy. They work in two-person teams, each with its own areas to cover.

"The leadership section is critical," says Spiess. "It was the first one our team got into. Two examiners had our CEO for five hours. They want to know if you are truly driving the quality process and that you are knowledgeable of your application and can defend it."

The teams talk to a lot of people: 200 people at IBM, 425 at Xerox, 450 at Intel, 600 at Cadillac. They talk to people eating lunch with them in the cafeteria, people riding with them in the elevators, people driving them to other locations—any employee, in any situation.

On one site visit, Charles Aubrey and another examiner were talking to some of the company's mechanics. The other examiner asked a few of them, "What are you guys doing in quality improvement?" They looked at each other, then one of them said, 'Quite frankly, we were trying to avoid you guys.'" I'm sure that is not the answer their company was hoping for, but it wasn't all the mechanics' fault.

"It turns out they weren't sure how to answer the question," Aubrey says, "so we got more specific with our questions, focusing on their jobs, and it quickly became apparent that they were actively measuring quality, preventing defects, and more."

The Examiners' goals are to verify the application through the date it was submitted and up to the time of the site visit, clarify the application, answer questions they had while reading it, and investigate areas they don't understand. To achieve these goals they will review documentation and talk to people, but they will *not* trick, badger, scold, pressure, or criticize.

"My expectations are that the applicant will be able to support the statements in the application," says senior examiner Cliff Moore. "But this isn't an IRS audit."

Although the people being interviewed are spared harsh treatment, they are also deprived of positive feedback. Examiners are instructed to be as noncommittal as possible. "Examiners have to exhibit unnatural behavior during the site visit," Moore says. "They're supposed to have poker faces and not ask leading questions."

"These people are trained to give blank stares," Spiess says. "You can't read them. So we coached people to expect this."

A few weeks before the site visit, the team leader works out a tentative schedule with the company. If the company has several sites, the team leader identifies two or three sites in addition to the main office that members of the team will visit. If the company has several sites in each city, as Federal Express did, all they know is which cities the team will visit, not which sites.

The following site visit stories convey the spontaneity that is characteristic of these events.

Xerox, John Cooney

The site visit involved five sites: three in Rochester, one in Denver, and one in El Segundo. We tried not to overmanage the examiners. For example, after our opening remarks on the 29th floor of our office building in downtown Rochester, the examiners said they wanted to talk to employees. We got in the elevator and asked them to push a button. When we got off on that floor, we followed their lead as to which direction to go.

Intel ECMG, Scott Pfotenhauer

The examiners met people at five sites. One day an examiner who focused on human resources asked if he could see a business support area, so I brought him up to business planning and finance. He walked around for two hours and just stopped by people's cubicles.

Marlow Industries, Chris Witzke

About two years ago I took all the test and inspection people away from the quality department and gave them to the manufacturing department, since it's responsible for quality. Our quality department went from 25 people to 5. A Baldrige examiner asked one of our quality engineers how many people were in the quality assurance department. The quality engineer said, "160" (the number of people working at Marlow). The examiner smiled and said, "Good answer."

Wallace, Michael Spiess

In the examination sessions, we told everybody to answer the question thoroughly, then shut up. Sonny Wallace, the president of the company, and I were meeting with examiners about section 7.2, the toughest area of the application because it was the hardest to defend. We finished discussing it and the examiners had closed the book but Sonny wanted them to reopen it. So I kicked him in the knee under the table.

Ford, Dan Whelan

The examiners decided where they wanted to go. They even changed their location selections during the site visit. It was the first time in their history with Ford that our plant managers didn't have complete control of outsiders. The plants have always been sacred ground. The site visit made us open up.

IBM Rochester, Lori Kirkland

The Examiners told us they wanted to see a branch office but wouldn't tell us when or where. One night, when they were here, they told us they wanted to visit a branch office at six o'clock the next morning. We offered the Rochester branch but they declined because it was too close. They chose our Twin Cities branch and had a great visit. They said the linkage was excellent.

Cadillac, William Lesner

At the Cadillac plant, one examiner team went to the plant to talk about human resources. When they got there they were told they could talk to anyone on the floor—human resources was this plant's strength. The examiner team caucused, then emerged with their agenda crossed out. Instead, they wanted to talk to union leadership, then get into the data for category 2.0, which the Cadillac people could assemble while the examiners were talking to the union people. The plant manager still remembers the anxiety that caused.

Through all the little surprises, the sudden changes in schedule, the planned and impromptu interviews, and the diligent review of documents, the business of verifying and clarifying gets done. Site visit issues identified by the team and duly recorded on site visit worksheets are now completed with the findings of the examiners. The site visit team meets with company leadership one final time to thank them and answer any last questions.

The site visit is finished for the company; many have parties that very night to celebrate. For the site visit team, however, there is more work to be done. The next day they meet, usually in their hotel, to review their findings and arrive at consensus findings and scores. The team lists significant strengths and areas for improvement for each category on a site visit conclusion worksheet—one category per page. These consolidated worksheets support the team's final recommendation: Did the site visit confirm the written application score or would it have raised or lowered the score? The answer to that question, along with an explanation of the team's recommendation, is entered on the recommendation worksheet. This worksheet, along with the team's findings on the site visit issues, are then forwarded to the Panel of Judges, which completes the judging process by choosing that year's Baldrige Award winners.

The team does not, however, complete the evaluation process. That is done by the team leader. He or she takes all the strengths and areas for improvement noted by all the team members when they reviewed the application, plus the findings from the site visit, and writes the feedback report.

THE FEEDBACK REPORT

This 16- to 24-page report begins with boiler plate information about how the application is reviewed, the distribution of written scores, and the scoring system. The rest of the report is devoted to specific feedback on the company, beginning with a one-page summary and an item-by-item list of the most common strengths and areas for improvement.

The comments are painfully nonprescriptive. Companies hungry for advice on ways to improve quality will not find them here, and with good reason: the Baldrige people have no intention of promoting a path to total quality. They will tell you where you are strong and what might need to be fixed, but they will not tell you how to do it.

The following are actual examples of comments from feedback reports:

+   Senior executives are easily accessible, communicate freely, and are visible throughout the company.

−   There was little evidence of involvement in quality by all management levels.

+   The benchmark process of gathering information is broad-based to provide adequate information for planning quality goals.

−   No information was provided on how the quality plan or process will result in a competitive position change.

+   Warranty expense trends are down and are forecast to go lower.

−   The application did not contain data from any independent external surveys.

Most companies admit that their feedback reports provided few surprises, if any. The assessment they conducted to write their applications and their site visit experiences revealed most of their strengths and weaknesses.

However, the feedback report does validate their own findings and stimulate change. As many who work within company cubicles know, those who ignore the observations of internal experts often drool over the same observations by outside experts. Quality professionals use the feedback to help senior management focus on the company's most serious quality problems.

"The result of the Telephone Operations division's application and feedback was that 19 areas came out that we could do better in," says D. Otis Wolkins, vice president of quality services for GTE. "The Baldrige criteria set in motion a mechanism to measure and improve. TelOps formed 19 teams to address the gaps. They're doing this on their own. The leaders of all 19 teams get together monthly to review where they're going. For example, the Employee Ownership Team identified actions to improve involvement, such as setting up a new suggestion system and developing a new customer satisfaction survey, then developed a timeline for each. It's a formal process. In addition, the division is using the criteria annually to benchmark its progress."

The division plans to reapply for the Baldrige Award sometime in the future. What it will find, as other applicants have found, is that winning the Award is getting harder. "The bar has been raised," says G. Robert Lea, vice president of quality for Paul Revere. "To win now you must be a whole lot better than you had to be in 1988."

Companies apply for the award to learn how high the bar is and whether or not they can clear it. Most can't, so they watch how the winners do it, then go back and perfect their techniques in preparation for the next big competition. It is a closed loop process: assessing, applying, improving, and assessing again. Companies strive for continuous improvement, with the goal of meeting and exceeding customer expectations.

And maybe, someday, joining an elite group of companies that have won the Malcolm Baldrige National Quality Award.

CHAPTER 16

Winning the Baldrige Award

T he date of the Baldrige Award ceremony is set according to when the President of the United States will be in Washington. In 1991, the date was October 29. That morning, the president flew to Madrid to meet with the head of the Soviet Union, leaving the vice president to handle the presentation. So much for planning.

The ceremony, conducted by the Secretary of Commerce, takes place in Malcolm Baldrige Hall at the Herbert C. Hoover building, home of the Commerce Department and the National Aquarium. It is a brief ceremony, during which the president or CEO of each winning company speaks and is presented with a red leather folder bearing a photograph of the award and a congratulatory note from the secretary. The award itself, one of which is on display during the ceremony, is too fragile to pick up. It is the answer to a question posed by Ron Zemke in *Training* magazine, "What's made of crystal and slate, weighs 20 pounds, stands 14 inches high, and can make a gray-haired CEO as giddy as a teenage nerd on a date with the prom queen?"

They are giddy with good reason, because there have only been a dozen prom queens in the country in the first four years of the award. That is a tough date to get and the envy of the also-rans.

Do they want to win because they want the trophy or because they want the benefits of the trophy? In a word, yes. Americans love to compete. Encourage us with beneficial, but intangible, goals, and our attention wanders. Stick a prize in front of us and we will hurt each other to get it.

American business leaders live to compete. They operate in an extremely competitive environment in which success is measured by comparisons: how well you did compared to last quarter, compared to your competitors, compared to your objectives, compared to your peers.

THE BENEFITS OF WINNING

Would CEOs do anything for a Baldrige Award? Would they, as some journalists have suggested, tell their staffs to "get me one of those Baldrige Awards?" Well, because they cannot buy one or get one by deception, their only avenue to winning the award is to build a world-class quality system. That seems like a lot of work just to appease an ego, even if it does belong to a CEO.

Therefore, there have to be some major benefits involved to justify the effort. I have outlined the benefits of using the criteria to improve in Chapter 1, and there are additional benefits to be gained from winning the award. In his excellent book, *Managing the Total Quality Transformation*, Thomas Berry writes:

> A company that wins the Baldrige Award and receives the recognition related to this remarkable achievement will be viewed by its current and potential customers as one of the very best in the country when it comes to quality and customer satisfaction. A company that makes the consumer public aware of this achievement will find its customer ranks swelling with more and more delighted customers.

Early numbers seem to confirm Berry's conclusion. In June 1990, *Business America* published the results of a survey of 550 executives from 1,000 top U.S. corporations, conducted by Opinion Research Corporation. According to the survey, 87 percent of the executives said that a firm's winning an award for quality, such as the Baldrige Award, would increase their desire to do business with that company, and 38 percent said it would increase their desire a great deal.

Xerox's John Cooney calls this "marketing through quality." One of Xerox's demands when it is asked to give a quality presentation to a company is that the company's senior executive must be present. One reason is that, because the senior executive can have the most impact on the company's quality system, he or she needs to hear the presentation. A second reason is that the presentation sells senior executives on the quality of Xerox products and services.

"As a result of insisting that the senior executive be present, we've had CEOs who have said they want Xerox products in their offices," says Cooney. "Our marketing people can cite specific sales due to our award-winning image and presentations. They now have access to the highest levels in major corporations."

IBM Rochester notices the same benefit. "I got a call from a large company in Houston asking if I would talk to their senior executives about quality at Rochester," says Lori Kirkland. "I went there and spent a day talking to a small group of executives. One of the things I told them was that their information systems were outdated and ineffective."

"When I returned I called our marketing people and told them about this opportunity. They asked me who I had talked to. I told them the names of the people and they were amazed; they had been trying to set meetings with these people for months. They now had a foot in the door at a level marketing hadn't been able to reach before."

Carl Arendt, a public relations executive for Westinghouse Corporate Productivity and Quality, is quoted in *Industry Week* as saying, "We can absolutely demonstrate [that the Award has brought in business]. We have letters from customers and prospective customers saying they're interested in doing business with us since we won the Baldrige."

Zytec learned that it had won the award on October 10, 1991. It proceeded to have its best fourth quarter ever. Globe Metallurgical's business increased 10 percent after it won the award. At Federal Express, John West says that winning the award had no measurable impact on business, "even though we feel it has had an impact. For one thing, interest in partnerships is much greater."

Many point to the internal benefits of winning. "Winning made us a storyteller," says Motorola chairman Robert Galvin, "and that's an exceptional benefit to us. You learn by teaching."

"To me, winning the Baldrige Award is characterized by a conversation I overheard in an elevator," Galvin says. "Two Motorola people were talking to each other. One said, 'Isn't it great that we won the Baldrige Award?' The other replied, 'Yeah, now we're going to have to earn it.'"

Galvin continues, "Winning has been a wonderful result for us for substantial reasons. We have people who want to live up to other people's expectations. They'd like to believe in their heart that it's true. It's been a fine motivator."

The companies that win the Baldrige Award value motivation because they want to continue to improve. Winning the award is a milestone in their quality journey, but it does not mark the end or even a resting point in that journey. The award validates that the right path has been chosen, that the efforts of people have been valuable, and that the company has a world-class quality system. It recognizes the winners as role models for quality in the United States.

Throughout this book I have used the Baldrige Award winners to illustrate important points. In thinking and talking about them there is a tendency to lump them together, to forget the distinctions in their cultures and in the paths they are taking to total quality. Yet those distinctions are what make them so valuable as models and resources.

One area that the Baldrige process has elevated to a major means of improving quality is benchmarking. Before 1989, if companies did benchmarking at all, it was usually limited to product comparisons with competitors. Baldrige Award winners such as Xerox and Motorola showed people how processes could be improved by learning from those who excelled at the process, regardless of their business. Because the Baldrige Award winners excel at many quality processes, some of which are described in Chapters 4 through 9, and because they are compelled to share what they have learned, they offer benchmarking opportunities for any size company in any business.

Appendix B provides the addresses and phone numbers of the Baldrige Award winners. To give you some idea of what they do and in what areas they excel, I have summarized their summaries, beginning with the small business winners.

SMALL BUSINESSES

1988: Globe Metallurgical, Inc.

Globe, which manufactures silicon metal and ferrosilicon products, has over 200 employees at two plants, one in Selma, Alabama, and the other at its headquarters in Beverly, Ohio. Its primary market is the automotive industry. In addition to the Baldrige Award, Globe has won several quality awards: it was the only ferroalloy supplier to win the Ford Q-1 Preferred Quality Award; it won five Mark of Excellence Awards from General Motors for quality, cost, technology, delivery, and management; it received the Certified Quality Supplier Award from Intermet Foundries, the largest independent producer of automotive castings in the United States; and it won the first Shigeo Shingo Prize for Manufacturing Excellence.

The foundation of Globe's quality system is its QEC (Quality, Efficiency, and Cost) program. Goals for quality improvement are integrated into strategic planning and research and development activities. Quality committees exist at every level within the company, including senior management, which makes up the QEC steering committee. The committees meet weekly. At each plant a QEC committee, composed of the plant manager and department heads, assembles each morning to review the previous day's performance. Improvements, many of them originating with workers, are tracked and the results, both successes and failures, are published monthly.

Globe utilizes computer-controlled systems to monitor important processing variables, and color control charts document each product's processing history. Workers trained in statistical process control use the charts to appraise performance, and customers use the information for their manufacturing processes.

The computer-controlled systems have contributed to significant improvements in achieving the targeted grade of metal and in reducing scrap, and a more consistent operation has increased the production rates of the furnaces and reduced energy consumption. At the same time, Globe has improved manpower efficiency by more than 50 percent.

Customer service is a Globe strength. All employees meet with customers, including visiting their facilities. Customer complaints dropped 91 percent from 1985 to 1988. In 1987, no products were returned for replacement.

Such performance has earned Globe a reputation for excellent quality. When many European traders order magnesium ferrosilicon alloy, they specify that the material must be "Globe quality," a standard that other suppliers must match.

1990: Wallace Co., Inc.

Wallace is a family-owned distributor, primarily of pipe, valves, and fittings, to the chemical and petrochemical industries. Its ten offices in Texas, Louisiana, and Alabama distribute directly in the Gulf Coast area, and also serve international markets. The company, headquartered in Houston, has nearly 300 employees it refers to as "associates."

Wallace initiated a three-phase quality program in 1985. Its top five leaders each took more than 200 hours of quality training, which they put to use by participating in all of the company's quality activities. Leadership drafted a mission statement, which committed the company to continuous quality improvement, and 16 quality strategic objectives to guide business decision making. Business and quality goals are united in Wallace's quality business plan.

Wallace has identified and measures 72 discrete processes that contribute to on-time delivery and accurate invoicing. Customers receive computer-generated reports that document how well the company has been servicing its accounts. Wallace also uses electronic data interchange to improve inventory management, save time, reduce errors, and produce more accurate data.

Wallace was the first in its industry to provide training for suppliers in continuous quality improvement. In less than two years, the company cut its supplier base from more than 2,000 to 325. Its sales increased 69 percent from 1987 to 1990; on-time deliveries increased from 75 percent to 92 percent; and market share rose from 10 percent to 18 percent. All of this helped Wallace to win the Baldrige Award.

Unfortunately, however, the effort may have contributed to Wallace's financial problems in 1991. Wallace spent a great deal of money to improve quality, a cost it offset by increasing its prices. When the company was also hit by an industrywide slump, sales started to fall off, and in 1990, the company lost nearly $700,000 on revenue of $88 million.

Wallace has had to act quickly to remain in business, including severely limiting its responses to requests for information. Some have been quick to blame the Baldrige process for Wallace's problems. Its CEO, John Wallace, does not. In a story in *Newsweek* about Wallace's difficulties, he said, "Without the quality program we wouldn't have made it this far."

1991: Marlow Industries

Marlow makes small thermoelectric coolers that cool, heat, or stabilize the temperature of electronic components in products ranging from medical diagnostic equipment to missile guidance systems. It has 160 employees at its plant in Dallas.

When Marlow initiated its quality improvement process in 1987, its share of the world market already exceeded 50 percent. It chose to embrace total quality management to maintain that leadership position, and the strategy has worked: since 1987, Marlow Industries' world market share has continued to grow—even against local competition in Japan.

CEO and President Ray Marlow chairs the TQM Council, which develops the company's strategic business plan. He oversees efforts to achieve short- and long-term goals and has daily responsibility for quality-related matters. In addition, worker representatives participate in weekly TQM Council sessions. In 1990, 88 percent of all personnel—compared to 44 percent in 1988—participated on teams organized to reach corporate and departmental goals or to prevent potential problems. All of the teams make regular, formal presentations to the TQM Council.

Training averages 32 hours per employee per year. All workers, including temporary employees, receive quality awareness training, and the entire work force has taken statistical problem solving courses.

Suppliers are part of Marlow's TQM system. The company considers the technological expertise of its suppliers at the start of product and process improvement efforts, because suppliers often provide design and analytical expertise that is not available in-house. Nearly 75 percent of Marlow's key suppliers are certified to "ship to stock" without inspection.

Marlow focuses on building long-term relationships with its customers. More than 90 percent of its products are custom designed to meet customers' requirements. To understand these requirements and how satisfied customers are with Marlow's ability to meet them, the company has developed many different feedback mechanisms, including surveys and direct customer contact.

Since 1988, Marlow has won six major quality awards from customers and has passed on first inspection all 30 audits of its quality assurance system by defense industry customers. The company has not lost a major customer in ten years, and in 1990, its top ten customers rated the quality of Marlow TE coolers at 100 percent.

MANUFACTURING COMPANIES

Of the eight manufacturing companies that have won Baldrige Awards, five are tied to the electronics industry, including the most recent winners, Zytec and Solectron.

1991: Zytec Corporation

Zytec's 750+ employees design and manufacture electronic power supplies for domestic original equipment manufacturers who integrate Zytec's products into their systems, which range from computers to peripheral, medical, office products, and test equipment. The company also repairs power supplies and CRT monitors. Zytec has two facilities: its headquarters in Eden Prairie, Minnesota, and its manufacturing plant in Redwood Falls, Minnesota.

Zytec's founders embraced Dr. W. Edwards Deming's 14 Points for Management as the cornerstone of the company's quality improvement culture. Deming's 14 Points continue to guide Zytec's actions, from long-range strategic planning to employee empowerment to leadership.

The company's management by planning (MBP) process has become a major driver of quality values. Senior executives set corporate objectives to guide the process, then lead six cross-functional teams that review and develop individual plans for presentation to employees. Each department develops a supporting objective for each of the corporate objectives, thus converting major strategies into measurable goals. Every employee is on an MBP team working on at least one supporting objective, and senior management reviews progress on these corporate objectives monthly.

Employee involvement in the planning process is one example of how Zytec empowers its employees. Another is that any employee can spend up to $1,000 to resolve a customer complaint without prior authority. Zytec's multifunctional employee (MFE) system was designed by production workers for production workers. They identified tasks that, when mastered, would make the employee more flexible and increase his or her pay. An employee group monitors and improves the MFE system.

Zytec relies on 18 different processes to gather data and information from and about customers and 9 sources to determine customer satisfaction. The data from these sources are reviewed and compared, and changes in customer needs and trends in customer satisfaction are tracked.

In an independent survey of power supply manufacturers, Zytec ranked first against its competitors and exceeded the industry average in 21 of 22 attributes deemed important to customers. Since 1987, Zytec has received nine awards from customers for supplier excellence.

1991: Solectron Corporation

Founded in 1977, Solectron has 2,300 employees at five sites in San Jose and Milpitas, California. The company manufactures and assembles electronic equipment and systems designed by its customers, including complex printed circuit boards for computers and telecommunications and medical equipment.

Solectron competes on service, quality, and cost, and excels at determining how customers define superior performance. It calls each of its 60 customers weekly to see if they received products on time and are satisfied with Solectron. The results are compiled in a customer satisfaction index, which is reviewed weekly by senior management and is used to evaluate performance at the work group, department, and division levels.

As a result of this focus on customer service, major computer firms known for manufacturing efficiency have closed their internal assembly operations and outsourced the work to Solectron because they can lower their costs and improve quality.

Solectron's multilingual work force includes workers from more than 20 different cultures. The barriers this creates have been overcome through a team-focused approach to employee involvement that promotes training and mentorship.

Workers use statistical process control regularly in all departments; division quality managers and the corporate quality director track and review results daily. In addition, assembly line workers are empowered to stop the line if they notice something wrong.

As a result of developing a highly committed work force, working with suppliers as partners in pursuing Six Sigma quality, and investing in advanced technology, its defect rates have fallen to within the five sigma range (233 parts per million), and it has achieved an on-time delivery rate of 97.7 percent over the last two years. Solectron has won 37 superior performance awards in the last ten years—ten of those in 1990.

1990: IBM Rochester

IBM Rochester manufactures intermediate computer systems for the Application Business Systems product line and hard disk drives for the Enterprise Systems product line. More than 8,000 employees work at the 3.6 million-square-foot Rochester site. Two-thirds of the work force is comprised of engineers, programmers, and other professionals.

The concept of quality is linked directly to the customer. At each step from design to delivery, customers are involved in every aspect of the product through advisory councils, global information systems, prototype trials, and other feedback mechanisms.

Improvement plans are based on six critical success factors: improved product and service requirements definition; an enhanced product strategy; a Six Sigma defect elimination strategy; further cycle time reductions; improved education; and increased employee involvement and ownership. Each senior manager owns one of the six factors and assumes responsibility for plans and implementations. Progress is monitored.

Support processes are continuously improved through aggressive worldwide benchmarking involving more than 350 teams. Cross-functional teams also develop plans for achieving quality objectives and identify needs for equipment, staffing, education, and process development.

IBM Rochester invests the equivalent of 5 percent of its payroll in education and training. In 1989, about one-third of the work force moved into new positions and 13 percent were promoted. The company also supports employees with the tools and information they need to achieve quality and customer satisfaction goals.

Suppliers are trained, audited, and certified, and they are required to submit quality plans. IBM Rochester and its suppliers also share expertise and technology. From 1984 to 1989, IBM Rochester employees trained more than 1,000 supplier employees on continuous flow manufacturing, statistical process control, and design of experiments.

From 1986 to 1989, IBM Rochester improved productivity by 30 percent. Product development time for new computer systems was cut by more than half, and the manufacturing cycle was trimmed by 60 percent since 1983. Its share of the world market for intermediate computers increased one full percentage point in both 1988 and 1989, and revenue growth in 1989 was double the industry rate.

1989: Xerox Business Products and Systems

One of two Xerox Corporation businesses, Business Products and Systems (BP&S) employs more than 50,000 people at 83 U.S. locations. BP&S makes more than 250 types of document-processing equipment, with copiers and other duplicating equipment accounting for nearly 70 percent of its revenues.

Senior management recognized the need for a quality effort at Xerox, developed the plans, benchmarked Xerox performance against other world-class companies, and created the quality environment that enabled Xerox to reverse its loss of world market share.

Xerox is now a leader in benchmarking, an area it pushed to the forefront when it won the Baldrige Award, and its benchmarking system has become a model for other companies. The company measures its performance in about 240 key areas of product, service, and business performance. The ultimate target for each attribute is the level of performance achieved by the world leader, regardless of industry.

The phrase "Team Xerox," reflects the company's approach to tackling quality issues. BP&S estimates that 75 percent of its workers are on one or more of its 7,000 quality improvement teams, and every employee has received at least 28 hours of quality training.

The Xerox Delivery Process is a world-class process for ensuring the quality of new hardware, software, systems, supplies, and customer support products. It has evolved through 20 years of development, benchmarking, and improvement.

Information about customer requirements is collected in a number of ways, including the customer satisfaction measurement system. Each month, more than 45,000 surveys are mailed to customers, asking them to rate Xerox equipment, sales, service, and customer administration performance. The results are segmented, analyzed, and used to plan for improvements.

In 1984, the machines of Xerox's competitors ranked highest in customer satisfaction in all six product categories. By 1990, Xerox copiers had taken the lead in five of the six categories.

1988: Motorola Inc.

With more than 100,000 employees, Motorola is the largest company to win the Baldrige Award. As one of the first, it set high standards of quality for all that follow.

Headquartered in Schaumburg, Illinois, Motorola produces a variety of products. It is the world leader in two-way radio communications, radio paging communications systems and pagers, car telephone systems and telephones, modems, and many parts of the semiconductor industry.

Quality at Motorola is driven by senior management, which believes that the responsibility for quality rests not on the plant floor, but with management. Building on leapfrog goals of 10 times improvement and then 100 times improvement, both of which were achieved, Motorola charted a course to Six Sigma quality, the equivalent of 3.4 defects per million for every process, product, and service. In some areas, Six Sigma quality has already been achieved.

Motorola ties error-free production to total customer satisfaction, the company's overall corporate objective. Six Sigma quality is one of five key operations initiatives, the others being total cycle time reduction, product and manufacturing leadership, profit improvement, and participative management within and cooperation among organizations.

To carry out these initiatives, Motorola has established Motorola University, an education and training center with more than 100 full-time and 300 part-time staff people. Motorola invests nearly $120 million a year in education, nearly 40 percent of it in quality-related training.

Motorola's quality improvement process has yielded impressive results. Motorola has received more than 50 awards and citations from customers for delivering certifiable product quality. In ten years, Motorola's annual sales grew from $3 billion to more than $10 billion.

Although five of the eight Baldrige Award winners in the manufacturing category have been in one industry, the other three represent three very different industries: nuclear power, textiles, and automobiles.

1988: Westinghouse Commercial Nuclear Fuel Division

The Westinghouse Commercial Nuclear Fuel Division (CNFD) employs approximately 2,000 people at three sites in Pennsylvania and South Carolina. CNFD supplies about 40 percent of the U.S. market and about 20 percent of the world market for fuel rod assemblies used in nuclear power plants.

CNFD tracks progress toward total quality by a unique system called "pulse points." The system tracks improvements in more than 60 key performance areas identified with statistical techniques and other tools and helps to set measurable goals at every level of the division.

In strategic planning, senior management develops formal quality initiatives and pulse points considered most critical to improving performance and customer satisfaction. Supporting goals aimed at accomplishing the division's objectives are developed for each department and then for each worker. Pulse point trends are reviewed each month during a teleconference involving top management at each site.

CNFD maintains close contact with its utility customers and regularly collects technical data to evaluate the performance of its fuel assemblies. Consistently high scores in surveys and customer-conducted audits reflect high levels of satisfaction, trends supported by CNFD's repeat business, which accounted for 90 percent of its orders in 1987.

1989: Milliken & Company

Headquartered in Spartanburg, South Carolina, Milliken has 13,000 "associates" employed at 47 plants in the United States. It produces more than 45,000 textile and chemical products ranging from apparel fabrics and automotive fabrics to specialty chemicals and floor coverings.

Milliken's quality improvement process is driven by its Pursuit of Excellence (POE), a commitment to customer satisfaction that pervades all company levels at all locations. Milliken's senior executives devote more than half their time to the POE process.

Milliken has a flat management structure in which associates, working primarily in self-managed teams, exercise considerable authority and autonomy. The company currently has 17 plants that are being run by self-directed teams, not by managers. Any associate can halt a production process if that person detects a quality or safety problem. From 1977 to 1988, Milliken increased the ratio of production to management associates by 77 percent.

Milliken promotes teams. In 1988, 1,600 corrective action teams were formed to address specific manufacturing or other internal challenges, about 200 supplier action teams worked with suppliers, and another 500 customer action teams were formed to respond to customer needs.

Milliken invests in training. The company spent $1,300 per associate in 1988. The company also actively solicits ideas from its associates. Its Opportunities for Improvement (OFI) process encourages, evaluates, and implements ideas without bestowing any financial rewards for them. The company practices a 24/72 philosophy: a supervisor must acknowledge receipt of an OFI within 24 hours and come back with a plan to act on the idea within 72 hours. In 1991, 663,000 ideas were submitted, an average of 52 ideas per associate.

Milliken received 41 major customer quality awards from 1984 to 1988, and was voted the outstanding residential carpet manufacturer in the United States in 1988. In independently conducted surveys, Milliken tops the competition in all 15 measures of customer satisfaction.

1990: Cadillac Motor Car Company

Cadillac employs about 10,000 people at its Detroit-area headquarters, four Michigan-based manufacturing plants, and ten sales and service zone offices in the United States. In the domestic market, cars are sold through a network of 1,600 franchised dealerships.

Cadillac's turnaround can be traced to senior management's implementation of simultaneous engineering (SE). SE contrasts sharply with the traditional approach to building cars. Product design and development begin with an integrated knowledge of all essential elements that will go into production, including performance targets, product features, systems and parts, processes, and maintenance requirements. SE anticipates how changes in one functional area will affect others, making it easier to prevent problems, control processes, and identify opportunities to improve quality.

More than 700 employees and supplier representatives participate on SE teams responsible for defining, engineering, marketing, and continuously improving all products.

Cadillac's partnerships with the United Auto Workers have also been a catalyst in the company's quality transformation. Cadillac executives and plant managers and union leaders serve together on the divisional quality council.

Cadillac solicits the views of all employee teams during the preparation of its annual business plans, which include short- and long-term quality improvement goals. Its people strategy, designed to create a trusting, empowered work force, was responsible for increasing the number of hourly and salaried employees on teams by 600 percent from 1985 to 1989, improving injury rates by more than 33 percent, reducing workers compensation cases by half, and setting an employee turnover rate that is one of the lowest in the industry at 0.3 percent per year.

Leadership and employee involvement have translated into increased customer satisfaction. For example, customers' rating of overall satisfaction with the car after one to five years of ownership improved 17 percentage points in four years, and satisfaction with service improved 19 percentage points. In 1989, for the fourth year in a row, Cadillac ranked as the number one domestic make on the independent J.D. Power and Associates Customer Satisfaction Index, improving 42 percent since 1986.

SERVICE COMPANIES

The only service company to win the Baldrige Award in the first four years it was presented was Federal Express.

1990: Federal Express

Federal Express has over 84,000 employees at more than 1,650 sites tracking 1.5 million shipments daily, sorting at facilities in Memphis, Indianapolis, Newark, Oakland, Los Angeles, Anchorage, and Brussels, and shipping by land and through the largest air cargo fleet in the world. In 1989, Federal Express had 43 percent of the domestic delivery market, compared to 26 percent for its nearest competitor.

The company's "People-Service-Profits" philosophy guides management policies and actions. Federal Express strives to create a "power environment" through three basic quality concepts: (1) empowering its people; (2) giving them the right tools to manage and measure their performance; and (3) developing a candid, open two-way communication environment.

An example of two-way communication is the company's management evaluation system, called SFA (survey/feedback/action), which involves a survey of employees, an analysis of each work group's results by the work group's manager, and a discussion between the manager and the work group to develop written action plans for the manager to improve and become more effective. The year Federal Express instituted its formalized quality process it achieved the highest leadership score in the SFA's 10-year history.

Federal Express provides employees with the information and technology they need to continuously improve their performance. The company has a "no lay-off" philosophy and a "guaranteed fair treatment" process for handling employee grievances, a process used as a model by companies in other industries. Its quality action teams, which currently involve hundreds of teams around the world, look for the root causes of problems and suggest solutions. From 1986 to 1990, at least 91 percent of employees responded that they were "proud to work for Federal Express."

Federal Express measures quality performance through a 12-component indicator called the service quality indicator (SQI), which weights each item to reflect how significantly it affects overall customer satisfaction. SQI is a major element in Federal Express's quality system. It is used to identify problems, evaluate executive performance, and direct corporate planning. The company has one cross-functional team for each service component in the SQI, headed by a corporate officer. Two of these teams have a network of over 1,000 employees working on improvements.

Federal Express estimates that it spends millions a year to undo missorted packages, delayed airplanes, invoice adjustments, and other errors, and that does not include the cost of lost customers. The goal of its quality improvement process is 100 percent customer satisfaction.

THE MOTIVATION TO WIN

These 12 Baldrige Award winners have created their own world-class quality systems. All have learned from quality experts in this country and abroad. All have "stolen shamelessly" from each other and from other quality leaders. All have experimented, failed, improved, tried again, fallen short again, and dared to persist, to believe that the pursuit of quality was worth it.

Perhaps most importantly, all have pursued total quality not for the sake of quality, and not because it was profitable, and not because they wanted to improve customer satisfaction—although they will claim such ambitions after the fact. They pursued total quality because they *had* to pursue total quality. They would not have survived without it.

It is no accident that half the winners have been electronics companies; they have had to compete directly with Japanese quality. The other winners have had equally serious threats. Westinghouse Commercial Nuclear Fuel Division had to achieve high quality to meet government regulations and the stringent demands of nuclear power plants. Globe rode total quality out of the valley of dying steel companies. Milliken flourished in the textile industry when few others stayed in business. Cadillac lost its luster as a name synonymous with quality, and is only now regaining it. Wallace embraced total quality as the only way to make money in a depressed oil industry—and even that may not save it. Federal Express used total quality to create a service, then to hold off a host of competitors.

If your company's existence is seriously threatened, you may find hope in these Baldrige Award winners' stories. However, *you don't have to wait for a crisis to embrace total quality management*. You can realize the same benefits, achieve similar results, and even win the award without a near death experience. You just have to find the motivation from another source (quality leadership is the first place to look).

SPREADING THE QUALITY MESSAGE

The companies that have won the Baldrige Award agree to spread the quality message. As Motorola chairman Robert Galvin says, "Those of us who win the award must be an echo of quality in the United States." As U.S. role models, they make themselves accessible to companies that want to know more about how they have achieved world-class quality. And they have been deluged with requests.

In the first 18 months after it won the award, Xerox talked to nearly 900 groups totaling more than 110,000 people. They had 350 requests for information within two weeks of winning, and were still getting 20 requests a day 18 months later.

"Winning puts you in a different club," says John Cooney. "Now that we're recognized as a world-class leader in quality, we wanted to act like a world-class leader and share what we know and are learning about quality."

Xerox talks to companies and groups in all sectors, including government, services, and education. The company certified 200 executives to talk to groups about its quest for quality.

"One of the greatest benefits to Xerox is the effect these speaking engagements have on the speakers," Cooney says. "First, they must know what they're talking about to make the presentation and handle the questions that follow. Second, their enthusiasm for our quality journey is rekindled."

About twice a month Xerox conducts quest for quality sharing conferences, each a seven-hour course. Half the audiences, all of which are there by invitation, are presidents and CEOs.

In the first ten months after winning, IBM Rochester received nearly 2,200 requests for documentation, more than 100 requests for benchmarking, and thousands of inquiries. Nearly 800 speaking engagements reached more than 100,000 people worldwide.

Motorola set up a "Baldrige Desk," staffed by two full-time people, to handle requests related to its winning the Baldrige Award, and it got more than 1,000 requests for speakers in 1989 and 1990. The company also held five-hour briefings for 150 visiting executives at a time.

Westinghouse CNFD continues to get 25 to 30 requests for information each month and has hosted 3,000 international government and business executives. It holds two monthly seminars in Pittsburgh that are booked four to five months in advance.

Globe Metallurgical received up to 50 calls a day after it won the award. One person, Kenneth Leach, became the company's designated speech giver. In 1989, he gave more than 130 speeches on four continents, and he spoke 81 more times in 1990.

Wallace also received up to 50 calls a day, but it only had a half-dozen people available to speak. Its executives have admitted spending too much time traveling the "rubber chicken" circuit and giving plant tours and not enough time running their business. They have since cut back on their availability to allow them to focus on their problems.

Federal Express averaged 30 requests for information a week during the year after it won the award. Through the first nine months of 1991, it averaged nearly 55 speeches a month, a demand that required the company to create an official speakers bureau. In 1991, nearly 2,000 people attended semiweekly quality forums at Federal Express.

"We're making the resources available because, since everybody is a FedEx customer, it behooves us to take advantage of their interest in our company," says Nancy Chaffin in FedEx's public relations department. "People want to come here at their own expense, so it's a great opportunity for us."

Cadillac promoted the Baldrige program heavily through its mass advertising campaign, a move that drew heavy criticism. The criticism was justified when it ripped misleading statements tying the award to all of General Motors or exaggerations about the number of applicants.

For example, one print ad said, "So comprehensive is this process, and so high are the standards, that of the thousands of different companies that applied for consideration this year alone, fewer than 100 were judged sufficiently qualified to go on to the final round." Copywriters used to writing car ads have a tough time with reality.

When the criticism turned snobbish, however, it missed the mark. Cadillac had every right to promote winning the Baldrige Award. They have been recognized as a world-class leader in quality, even if they had their doubters. One skeptic wrote a letter to Cadillac in which he said, "I own a Ford and it's lousy and I can't believe Cadillac won the Baldrige Award."

Ford's Dan Whelan was a skeptic himself. "When Cadillac won, many here first thought they'd snowed the Baldrige people," Whelan says. "Then we visited Cadillac and realized they did it. They deserved to win."

Many thought that Cadillac's heavy promotion was exactly what the Baldrige Award needed. "I think publicizing has helped the Baldrige," says senior examiner Frank Caplan. "There's an old saying in show business, 'I don't care what you say about me as long as you spell my name right.' I used to get on an airplane and talk to people about the Baldrige Award and nobody had heard of it. Now more people have some idea what I'm talking about."

A few months after Cadillac won the award, William Lesner, who helped manage its application and site visit processes, put together a list of activities that required their attention "after the win." For those of you who aspire to win the Baldrige Award, the demands placed on previous winners and Lesner's list are fair warning of what you can expect (see "After the Win" in Appendix C).

While the demands on the winner can be a burden, they are also an opportunity. Winning the Baldrige Award puts you in a much- admired group. Potential customers, suppliers, partners, and allies seek your counsel. You find yourself at the center of the quality movement.

Winning also inspires you to live up to extremely high expectations. You ask yourself, "Is this what a Baldrige Award winner would do?" Total quality becomes an expectation more than a goal, a way of doing business rather than a future ideal.

However, winning does *not* allow you to rest. As Roger Milliken said when he accepted the Baldrige Award for his company, "In the pursuit of total quality improvement, we recognize that good is the enemy of best, and best the enemy of better."

CHAPTER 17

Baldriging Into the Future

In late 1991, the *Harvard Business Review* published an article by Harvard professor and author David Garvin on the Baldrige Award. The next issue of the magazine devoted 14 pages to reactions to Garvin's article, which ranged from high praise to harsh criticism. Most of the praise came from business leaders whose companies use the criteria to improve quality. Most of the criticism came from consultants who have their own ideas about the best way to improve quality. As Garvin noted in his own answer to the responses, "If I had any doubts that the award was a Rorschach test, the responses set my concerns to rest."

Across the country and around the world, in the business community, the education community, the government community, and the nonprofit community, people are studying the Baldrige criteria and seeking ways to apply them to their organizations.

Companies model the award with quality offspring of their own. States tinker with it, producing twins or clones that local companies just gotta have. Countries change its allegiance, enlisting modified criteria in the service of their national agendas.

The Baldrige program was born of the desire to make U.S. quality competitive worldwide. It has surpassed expectations. In less than five years it has wedged quality into the consciousness of American business, creating interest and awareness where little existed before. It has given business leaders a way to understand, promote, and implement quality. It has pulled American industry out of the death spiral of uncompetitive processes, products, and services into a slow climb to total quality.

Well, that may be a slight exaggeration. Although pockets of American industry are climbing, more are still spiraling. Many business leaders remain Neanderthals when it comes to quality, and the push to make quality visible on the American agenda is often submerged by Wall Street woes, recession fears, financial cutbacks, and layoffs.

Still, quality in the United States is significantly better than it was five years ago. Many factors have contributed to that trend, but none has helped more than the Malcolm Baldrige National Quality Award, and its effect continues to multiply.

Consider the companies that have adopted the criteria as the tool for assessing their quality systems. Motorola, 3M, Cargill, Corning, McDonnell Douglas, GTE, Baxter Healthcare, Banc One, MetLife, and many other companies of all sizes in a variety of industries use the Baldrige criteria for monthly assessments, annual audits, corporate quality awards, and performance measurement. As the number of companies using the criteria continues to grow, the Baldrige criteria will be even more firmly established as the definition of total quality management in the United States.

THE BALDRIGE AWARD AS A MODEL

The Baldrige criteria are also being localized by city, regional, and state quality efforts. Although few quality awards are in place, many are being discussed and proposed across the country.

One of the most notable city awards is in Texas: the Austin Quality Award. Members of the Austin Quality Council, which includes Dell, CompuAdd, Motorola, and IBM, worked with local and state governments to create the award, the first of which was presented in 1991.

"We modified the criteria to make them shorter and we expanded two ways from the Baldrige program," says Jim Ziaja, director of quality at CompuAdd. "We expanded to four size categories and we added awards for education, nonprofit, and government. We also have two levels of awards, one for significant progress and another for significant achievement."

Applicants for the Austin Quality Award complete a 7-page questionnaire arranged by Baldrige categories. In addition to the small amount of space provided for answers, applicants can use up to four more pages for their responses.

The questions are roughly at the Baldrige item level or more general than that. In the 1991 application, for example, category 5.0 asks only four questions on a single page:

5.1 Describe how processes are designed and implemented to meet key product and service requirements.

5.2 How does your organization bring about quality improvements in those supplying products and services?

5.3 How do you evaluate the quality of products and services of suppliers internal to your organization?

5.4 How do you evaluate the quality of products and services of suppliers external to your organization?

A Board of Examiners reviews all applications, then interviews applicants by phone or mail to determine if a site visit is in order. Examiners forward the results of any site visits to the Austin Quality Council, which chooses the winners. The Austin award is considered a forerunner for a state quality award, which Texas plans to begin handing out in 1992.

Like city quality groups, regional quality networks are fertile ground for growing quality statewide. The Seattle Quality Information Network (SEQUIN), formed in 1989, meets monthly to discuss topics of common interest. The network includes representatives from Microsoft, Weyerhauser, and Boeing. The first time they prioritized the subjects their members would most like to explore, the Baldrige program ranked number one.

"Sharing what we know about quality is one of the group's responsibilities," says Paul Steel, president of Total Quality, "In April 1990, SEQUIN sponsored a local conference that drew 500 people from many companies. Curt Reimann kicked it off. That conference has become the nucleus of a statewide effort to establish a Washington Quality Award."

One of the first community quality networks was formed in Madison, Wisconsin. The Madison Area Quality Information Network (MAQIN), formed in 1985, focuses on sharing information, learning from the experience of others, and transforming the community culture to support quality principles. It has grown to include more than 300 members, offering a variety of services including discussion groups, tutorials, videotape lending, a newsletter, and special meetings.

STATE QUALITY AWARDS

The most successful transplants of the Baldrige program have been at the state level. At least 20 states have in place or are working on establishing state quality awards. Many are aiming to present their first awards in 1992 or 1993, including New York, New Jersey, Georgia, Iowa, Arizona, Illinois, Kentucky, Michigan, Pennsylvania, and Massachusetts.

Five states—Virginia, Maryland, Alabama, Nebraska, and Nevada—give U.S. Senate Productivity Awards, which originated with a Senate resolution in 1982. The criteria differ from state to state, but they tend to cover similar issues addressed by the Baldrige criteria.

For example, the Maryland award asks applicants to describe their productivity and quality improvement efforts in five categories: Productivity and Quality Leadership (20 points); Human Resource Excellence (20 points); Productivity/Quality Results (25 points); Customer Orientation and Results (25 points); and Impact on State and Local Community (10 points). Each of these categories is defined by statements such as: "2.a: The extent to which people are viewed as a strategic resource and a source of competitive advantage." Applicants have up to 18 pages in which to respond to all categories.

A few states present quality awards based on the Baldrige criteria, including Connecticut, Maine, North Carolina, and Minnesota. People working to begin a quality award program in their state frequently benchmark North Carolina and Minnesota as models of what they hope to create.

In 1990, the governor of North Carolina signed a bill creating the North Carolina Awards Council, the certifying body that presents the awards. The award program is funded by private business and industry contributions to a nonprofit foundation, the North Carolina Quality Leadership Foundation.

"The Foundation has a multitude of activities," says Donna Rosefield, award administrator. "It sponsors a public sector panel with representatives from government agencies. It's been very active with regional panels established across the state to help business and industry implement the criteria. It's also working on a management development program, with the goal of forming an alliance of major universities in the state to establish a masters degree of quality."

Applicants for the award must respond to the Baldrige criteria within the same 60- or 75-page limit. Categories have been split into large and small manufacturing and large and small service companies. "Small is defined by meeting two of three criteria: 100 or fewer full-time employees; less than $5 million in sales; less than $7.5 million in total assets," Rosefield says.

The Minnesota Quality Award program is administered by the Minnesota Council for Quality, a nonprofit organization funded by state government and private industry. The program closely resembles the Baldrige Award program in the categories of awards presented and the judging process. It differs slightly, however, by asking applicants to respond to criteria at the item level (not by areas to address) in 35 pages or less.

"Minnesota wasn't a rush job," says Curt Reimann, director of the Baldrige Award. "They got the community built, broadened the base, gained wide acceptance, and did it right. If we had some models like that in a few states it would help, which is why we've devoted so much time to helping Minnesota."

In 1991, the program's first year, 35 companies applied for the Minnesota Quality Award. The only company to win the award was Zytec, which two weeks later won the Baldrige Award, a testament to the high standards of quality required to win the Minnesota Quality Award.

At the state level, administrators experiment with the Baldrige process. They change the categories, shorten the application report, and improve the transfer of information. In a sense, they are test sites for the Baldrige program, each developed to serve the needs of its state, yet each providing valuable data that will feed the Baldrige program's continuous improvement process

As the Board of Overseers considers expanding the program to include nonprofit organizations and possibly education and government (see Chapter 3), it will look to those states that include these categories for lessons they can learn.

States may also be leaders in broadening the transfer of information. Unlike the Baldrige program, which prohibits identifying companies that apply or receive site visits, Minnesota announced all but one of its applicants and all of its site visit companies. As soon as a state convinces applicants to share their applications, information transfer, one of the objectives of the Baldrige program, will improve significantly.

An article in *Quality Progress* noted that Corning's David Luther, a Baldrige judge, "believes the completed award applications are a national treasure that could lead to immense gains in quality improvement... because they contain the techniques, approaches, and strategies of many of the country's most advanced companies." Right now, no one sees an application without the company's permission, and very few grant permission because of proprietary information. Because most who wish to learn from the applications couldn't care less about the proprietary information, there must be a way to release the parts of the application that are not sensitive. Chances are, a state will do this first.

State quality award programs not only tinker with the process, they mess with the criteria. They add items, eliminate areas to address, and change point values, none of which go unnoticed by the criteria's caretaker, Curt Reimann.

"I feel that changes leading to fundamental differences in structure or in the purpose of what's being examined would be counterproductive to the national effort," says Reimann. "As a courtesy to applicants and those trying to learn the system, I think there should be as much registry as possible to the basic criteria. If there are criticisms of the criteria that would constructively improve them, we're glad to listen."

"I don't consider changing point values all that serious," Reimann says. "They *should* be different from company to company."

My research suggests that companies are more likely to mess with the criteria than states, and that their efforts are not always fruitful. "We had a group of 20 people working on improving the criteria for McDonnell Douglas' purposes for ten hours," says Steve Detter, director of TQM and a Baldrige examiner. "At the end of that time one person said we hadn't made it any better—in fact, we'd made it worse. So we kept the criteria as they are."

As more and more companies and states board the Baldrige bandwagon, possibilities will be explored, ideas tested, and improvements made. The Baldrige program will benefit in the process. It is a national framework, broad enough to fit any company regardless of size or business, yet specific enough to accurately assess each company's quality system. It improves as our understanding of quality improves.

That understanding, and the granting of quality awards, extends beyond our borders to countries we benchmarked during the creation of the Baldrige Award, and to countries that have benchmarked our program.

INTERNATIONAL QUALITY AWARDS

Japan has been giving the Deming Prize for quality since 1951, under the auspices of the Union of Japanese Scientists & Engineers (JUSE). The purpose of the Deming Prize is to "award prizes to those companies which are recognized as having successfully applied companywide quality control based on statistical quality control and which are likely to keep up with it in the future." Individuals, factories, company divisions, and companies can win the prize.

The Deming Prize criteria resemble a checklist divided into 10 categories: policy and objectives; organization and its operation; education and its extension; assembling and disseminating information; analysis; standardization; control (*kanri*); quality assurance; effects; and future plans. The elements measured by the Deming Prize and the Baldrige Award overlap the most in Baldrige category 5.0. But the Deming Prize criteria dig deeply into the quality assurance of products and services, whereas the Baldrige criteria have a broader scope and less depth.

Deming Prize subcategories define major areas of emphasis, in more general terms than the Baldrige items. For example, under the first category are "(1) policies pursued for management, quality, and quality control; (2) method of establishing policies; (3) justifiability and consistency of policies; (4) utilization of statistical methods; (5) transmission and diffusion of policies; (6) review of policies and the results achieved; (7) relationship between policies and long- and short- term planning."

Companies applying for the Deming Prize often spend years qualifying for it. They hire experts from JUSE as consultants to help them improve their quality systems to the point that they can meet the prize's standards. Florida Power & Light, for example, the first non-Japanese organization to win the Deming Prize, spent $855,000 on fees to Japanese consultants.

Deming Prize applications typically run about 1,000 pages. But when NEC Toho-ku Ltd. pursued the prize, its directives, plans, and reports totaled 244,000 pages.

The Baldrige Award places different demands on applicants, but that has not lessened its impact on quality in the United States. JUSE Executive Director Junji Noguchi credits the Baldrige Award with providing an important stimulus in the United States' drive to catch Japan in the 1990s.

Quality awards similar to the Baldrige Award are being given in Mexico, Australia, and Canada. In the last year, Reimann has communicated with people in Sweden, Spain, Colombia, Argentina, and the European Community about the Baldrige program. In addition, quality experts from several European countries have created the European Quality Award, which uses criteria that were obviously inspired by the Baldrige criteria.

The format of the European Award is similar to that of the Baldrige Award, although the European criteria have nine categories instead of the Baldrige Award's seven. The categories with their point values and what they measure, as described in the 1992 Assessment Criteria, are the following:

1.0 Leadership (100 points): the behavior of all managers in driving the company toward total quality.

2.0 Policy and Strategy (80 points): the company's values, vision, and strategic direction—and the manner in which it achieves them.

3.0 People Management (90 points): the management of the company's people.

4.0 Resources (90 points): the management, utilization, and preservation of resources.

5.0 Processes (140 points): the management of all the value-adding activities within the company.

6.0 Customer Satisfaction (200 points): what the perception of your external customers, direct and indirect, is of the company and of its products and services.

7.0 People Satisfaction (90 points): what your people's feelings are about your company.

8.0 Impact on Society (60 points): what the perception of your company is among the community at large. This includes views of the company's approach to quality of life, the environment, and the preservation of global resources.

9.0 Business Results (150 points): what the company is achieving in relation to its planned business performance.

For the most part, the European and Baldrige criteria measure the same elements. The major differences are in how these elements are placed and described and in the European criteria's inclusion of entire categories for corporate citizenship (8.0) and business performance. In the latter, the criteria requesn "evidence . . . of the company's continuing success in achieving its financial and other business targets and objectives, and in satisfying the needs and expectations of everyone with a financial interest in the company."

When considering international quality standards, many people wonder how ISO 9000 compares to the Baldrige Award. Established in 1988, ISO 9000 has 20 clauses that cover business processes, beginning with the initial contact with a customer and extending to servicing the product. It is primarily concerned with the quality assurance of products and services, which ties it closely with category 5.0 of the Baldrige criteria. Any relationship with other Baldrige categories is minimal.

Lessons learned from international quality standards, several national quality awards, a growing number of state quality awards, regional and city quality awards, and corporate quality awards challenge the Baldrige

Award program and criteria to improve. At the same time, these programs look to the Baldrige Award program as a leader in defining the elements of a complete quality system.

THE BALDRIGE AWARD AS A NATIONAL STANDARD

The Baldrige Award is the most visible sign of a national quality movement. Business schools, scrambling to incorporate total quality management into their curriculums, recognize the Baldrige criteria as a framework for TQM. In 1991, the annual meeting of the business school deans had managing quality as its main topic. It was the best-attended meeting in their history.

"I think a lot of business leaders are waking up to the fact that there's a body of knowledge available," says Reimann. "For the first time, business schools are showing interest."

Political leaders are also showing interest, drawn into the quality arena by proponents such as Motorola Chairman Robert Galvin. He is lobbying to make the Baldrige Award a national policy.

"The Baldrige Award criteria are a superb profile of what American industry should aspire to," he says. "If every company prepares to compete for the award through the early nineties, it will change the growth rate of the GNP by a minimum of one-half of one percent. To do that we need a catalyst, and that catalyst is to make competing for the Baldrige Award a national policy."

Galvin's voice is one of many promoting quality at the national level. Pennsylvania Congressman Donald Ritter has also been involved in the Baldrige program as a member of the Science Research and Technology subcommittee. He commissioned the GAO report that evaluated 20 Baldrige site visit companies to determine the impact of formal total quality management practices on their performance. (For the results of that study, see Chapter 11.)

"I think quality should be a national issue," Ritter says. "We're going to try to get it into the national campaign. We would like to see somebody out there on the point spreading the quality revolution."

In 1991, Ritter wrote legislation creating a national quality council, which he believes is the next step beyond the Baldrige Award. "The goal of the council will be to set quality goals, to give visibility to the revolution and the revolutionaries, and to make sure everything we do in the federal government stimulates and doesn't hold back."

According to B. Joseph White, dean of the University of Michigan's Business School, the next step beyond the Baldrige Award is a national quality index (NQI). His school is working with the American Quality Foundation to develop a set of indexes that will measure the quality of U.S. products and services. The first set of NQI results is expected in the fall of 1992.

These efforts and others serve the quality cause by keeping quality in front of people. The more it seeps into our collective consciousness, the more quality will become an expectation and a way of doing things. As the Baldrige Award program has discovered, a widespread fascination with quality already exists.

"The Baldrige program has exceeded our expectations," says Kent Sterett, a Baldrige judge and one of the people involved in establishing the award. "Most people thought the program would be evolutionary, requiring several decades to come into people's consciousness and to the forefront in this country. It was more of a long-term commitment, like a siege mentality.

"We just did not expect the kind of reaction the program's gotten here in the U.S. It took the Deming Prize 15 years to get the notoriety that the Baldrige Award has right now."

The notoriety has been achieved because many American companies stood at the doorstep of global competition and did not know the quality password needed to enter the room. They were desperate for help at the same time the Baldrige criteria arrived on the scene. The companies that embraced them praised the criteria and encouraged others to use them to improve. Many are. The number of state awards starting in 1992 and 1993, the number of companies planning to apply for the Baldrige Award in 1993 and 1994, and the number of companies who are sharing the criteria with their customers and suppliers suggest an explosion of interest in the Baldrige Award program, a transition from notoriety to paradigm.

All aboard the Baldrige bandwagon! As a first step into the new quality paradigm, consider the advice of Gary Floss, a vice-president of quality for Control Data and a senior Baldrige examiner. "For companies new to total quality management or the Baldrige criteria, I would suggest: (1) Read the criteria. Reread the criteria. Read them again. (2) Understand how the categories fit together, the driver, system, measures, and goal. (3) Visit other companies that are winners or that have used the criteria for continuous improvement."

Ken Leach, also a senior Baldrige examiner and author of Globe's Baldrige Award-winning application, wrote in the *Harvard Business*

Review, "...the most common question asked by smaller businesses is, 'Where do we begin?' The answer is clear: adopt the Baldrige criteria. Assess your business against the criteria, determine where you need to improve, and set a plan into action to get you to where you want to be."

The same advice works for all companies, regardless of their size or position on the quality continuum. As this book has shown, the companies that are using the criteria are more than willing to share their experiences. You can use those experiences, especially the wisdom of the Baldrige Award winners, to step lively on the quality path.

What is required, in the beginning, is the determination to excel. Noted author Robert Fulgham told this story in the *Star Tribune* about his experiences traveling with the Minneapolis Chamber Symphony.

> [My most memorable experience] was going with them on one of those long bus trips out to Marshall, Minnesota. We got there, and the wind was howling and the snow was coming down, and we went into the junior high and sat down with the members of the (junior high) orchestra, chair by chair, and with them played whatever they were working on. It was like something Charles Ives would have conceived, because here was this beautiful melody, and below it, this *reaching* for that same loveliness. I was profoundly moved by that outreach on their part, and by their attitude.

The Malcolm Baldrige National Quality Award and the companies that have won it offer a beautiful melody, a do-it-yourself kit for transforming your organization. All that is left is the reaching.

APPENDIX A

1992 Malcolm Baldrige
National Quality Award Criteria

T he criteria are taken from "The 1992 Award Criteria," a 34-page document available from the National Institute of Standards and Technology (see Appendix B for address and phone number). Contact NIST for a free copy of the document.

You can use these criteria to assess and improve quality at your company or organization. NIST modifies and improves the criteria every year, with the new criteria usually available around January 1. *If you are planning to apply for the Baldrige Award, be sure to use the current criteria and application forms for the year in which you are applying.*

In "The 1992 Award Criteria," a description of the criteria notes that they are directed toward dual results-oriented goals: "To project key requirements for delivering ever-improving value to customers while at the same time maximizing the overall productivity and effectiveness of the delivering organization." For examples of how companies are using the Baldrige criteria to achieve these goals, refer to Chapters 10 through 15.

1.0 LEADERSHIP (90 POINTS)

The Leadership Category examines senior executives' *personal* leadership and involvement in creating and sustaining a customer focus and clear and visible quality values. Also examined is how the quality values are integrated into the company's management system and reflected in the manner in which the company addresses its public responsibilities.

1.1 Senior Executive Leadership (45 points)

Describe the senior executives' leadership, personal involvement, and visibility in developing and maintaining a customer focus and an environment for quality excellence.

Areas to Address

a. senior executives' leadership, personal involvement, and visibility in quality-related activities of the company. Include (1) reinforcing a customer focus; (2) creating quality values and setting expectations; (3) planning and reviewing progress toward quality and performance objectives; (4) recognizing employee contributions; and (5) communicating quality values outside the company.

b. brief summary of the company's quality values and how the values serve as a basis for consistent communications within and outside the company.

c. personal actions of senior executives to regularly demonstrate, communicate, and reinforce the company's customer orientation and quality values through all levels of management and supervision.

d. how senior executives evaluate and improve the effectiveness of their personal leadership and involvement.

Notes: (1) The term "senior executive" refers to the highest-ranking official of the organization applying for the award and those reporting directly to that official.

(2) Activities of senior executives might also include leading and/or receiving training, benchmarking, customer visits, and mentoring other executives, managers, and supervisors.

(3) Communication outside the company might involve: national, state, and community groups; trade, business, and professional organizations; and education, health care, government, and standards groups. It might also involve the company's stockholders and board of directors.

1.2 Management for Quality (25 points)

Describe how the company's customer focus and quality values are integrated into day-to-day leadership, management, and supervision of all company units.

Areas to Address

a. how the company's customer focus and quality values are translated into requirements for all levels of management and supervision. Include principal roles and responsibilities of each level: (1) within their units; and (2) cooperation with other units.

b. how the company's organizational structure is analyzed to ensure that it most effectively and efficiently serves the accomplishment of the company's customer, quality, innovation, and cycle time objectives. Describe indicators, benchmarks, or other bases for evaluating and improving organizational structure.

c. types, frequency, and content of reviews of company and work unit quality plans and performance. Describe types of actions taken to assist units which are not performing according to plans.

d. key methods and key indicators the company uses to evaluate and improve awareness and integration of quality values at all levels of management and supervision.

1.3 Public Responsibility (20 points)

Describe how the company includes its responsibilities to the public for health, safety, environmental protection, and ethical business practices in its quality policies and improvement activities, and how it provides leadership in external groups.

Areas to Address

a. how the company includes its public responsibilities, such as business ethics, public health and safety, environmental protection, and waste management in its quality policies and practices. For each area *relevant and important* to the company's business, briefly summarize (1) how potential risks are identified, analyzed, and minimized; (2) principal quality improvement goals and how they are set; (3) principal improvement methods; (4) principal quality indicators used in each area; and (5) how and how often progress is reviewed.

b. how the company promotes quality awareness and sharing with external groups.

Notes: (1) Health, safety, environmental, and waste management issues addressed in this item are those associated with the company's operations. Such issues that arise in connection with the use of products and services or disposal of products are addressed in item 5.1.

(2) Health and safety of employees are not covered in this item. These are addressed in item 4.5.

(3) Trends in indicators of quality improvement in 1.3a should be reported in item 6.2.

(4) External groups may include those listed in item 1.1, note 3.

2.0 INFORMATION AND ANALYSIS (80 POINTS)

The Information and Analysis Category examines the scope, validity, analysis, management, and use of data and information to drive quality excellence and improve competitive performance. Also examined is the adequacy of the company's data, information, and analysis system to support improvement of the company's customer focus, products, services, and internal operations.

2.1 Scope and Management of Quality and Performance Data and Information (15 points)

Describe the company's base of data and information used for planning, day-to-day management, and evaluation of quality. Describe also how data and information reliability, timeliness, and access are assured.

Areas to Address

a. criteria for selecting types of data and information to be included in the quality-related data and information base. List key types included and very briefly describe how each supports quality improvement. Types of data and information should include (1) customer-related; (2) internal operations; (3) company performance; and (4) cost and financial.

b. how the company ensures reliability, consistency, standardization, review, timely update, and rapid access to data and information throughout the company. If applicable, describe how software quality is assured.

c. key methods and key indicators the company uses to evaluate and improve the scope and quality of its data and information and how it shortens the cycle from data gathering to access. Describe efforts to broaden company units' access to data and information.

Notes: (1) This item permits the applicant to demonstrate the *breadth and depth* of its quality-related data. Applicants should give brief descriptions of the data under major headings such as "company performance" and subheadings such as "product and service quality" and "cycle time." Note that information on the scope and management of competitive and benchmark data is requested in item 2.2.

(2) Actual data should not be reported in this item. Such data are requested in other items. Accordingly, all data reported in other items, such as 6.1, 6.2, 6.3, 6.4, 7.4, and 7.5, are part of the base of data and information to be described in item 2.1.

2.2 Competitive Comparisons and Benchmarks (25 points)

Describe the company's approach to selecting data and information for competitive comparisons and world-class benchmarks to support quality and performance planning, evaluation, and improvement.

Areas to Address

a. criteria the company uses for seeking competitive comparisons and benchmarks: (1) key company requirements and priorities; and (2) with whom to compare—within and outside the company's industry.

b. current scope, sources, and uses of competitive and benchmark data, including company and independent testing or evaluation: (1) product and service quality; (2) customer satisfaction and other customer data; (3) internal operations, including business processes, support services, and employee-related; and (4) supplier performance.

c. how competitive and benchmark data are used to encourage new ideas and improve understanding of processes.

d. how the company evaluates and improves the scope, sources, and uses of competitive and benchmark data.

2.3 Analysis and Uses of Company-Level Data (40 points)

Describe how quality- and performance-related data and information are analyzed and used to support the company's overall operational and planning objectives.

Areas to Address

a. how customer-related data (category 7.0) are aggregated, ana-
    lyzed, and translated into actionable information to support
    (1) developing priorities for prompt solutions to customer-related
    problems; (2) determining relationships between the company's
    product and service quality performance and key customer in-
    dicators, such as customer satisfaction, customer retention, and
    market share; and (3) developing key trends in customer-related
    performance for review and planning.

b. how company operational performance data (category 6.0) are ag-
    gregated, analyzed, and translated into actionable information to
    support (1) developing priorities for short-term improvements in
    company operations, including improved cycle time, productivity,
    and waste reduction; and (2) developing key trends in company
    operational performance for review and planning.

c. how key cost, financial, and market data are aggregated, analyzed,
    and translated into actionable information to support improved
    customer-related and company operational performance.

d. key methods and key indicators the company uses to evaluate
    and improve its analysis. Improvement should address (1) how
    the company shortens the cycle of analysis and access to results;
    and (2) how company analysis strengthens integration of cus-
    tomer, performance, financial, market, and cost data for improved
    decision making.

Notes: (1) This item focuses primarily on analysis for company-level strategies, de-
            cision making, and evaluation. Usually, data for these analyses come from
            or affect a variety of company operations. Some other items in the crite-
            ria involve analyses of specific sets of data for special purposes such as
            evaluation of training. Such special-purpose analyses should be part of
            the information base of items 2.1 and 2.3 so that this information can be
            included in larger, company-level analyses.

      (2) Analyses involving cost, financial, and market data vary widely in types
           of data used and purposes. Examples include relationships between cus-
           tomer satisfaction and market share; relationships between quality and
           costs; relationships between quality and revenues and profits; conse-
           quences and costs associated with losses of customers and diminished
           reputation resulting from dissatisfied customers; relationships between
           customer retention, costs, and profits; priorities for company resource al-

location and action based upon costs and impacts of alternative courses of action; improvements in productivity and resource use; and improvements in asset utilization.

3.0 STRATEGIC QUALITY PLANNING (60 POINTS)

The Strategic Quality Planning Category examines the company's planning process and how all key quality requirements are integrated into overall business planning. Also examined are the company's short- and longer-term plans and how quality and performance requirements are deployed to all work units.

3.1 Strategic Quality and Company Performance Planning Process (35 points)

Describe the company's strategic planning process for the short term (1 to 2 years) and longer term (3 years or more) for quality and customer satisfaction leadership. Include how this process integrates quality and company performance requirements and how plans are deployed.

Areas to Address

a. how the company develops plans and strategies for the short term and longer term. Describe data and analysis results used in developing business plans and priorities, and how they consider (1) customer requirements and the expected evolution of these requirements; (2) projections of the competitive environment; (3) risks: financial, market, and societal; (4) company capabilities, including research and development to address key new requirements or technology leadership opportunity; and (5) supplier capabilities.

b. how plans are implemented. Describe (1) the method the company uses to deploy overall plan requirements to all work units and to suppliers, and how it ensures alignment of work unit activities; and (2) how resources are committed to meet the plan requirements.

c. how the company evaluates and improves its planning process, including improvements in (1) determining company quality and overall performance requirements; (2) deployment of requirements to work units; and (3) input from all levels of the company.

Note: Review of performance relative to plans is addressed in item 1.2.

3.2 Quality and Performance Plans (25 points)

Summarize the company's quality and performance plans and goals for the short term (1 to 2 years) and the longer term (3 years or more).

Areas to Address

a. for the company's chosen directions, including planned products and services, markets, or market niches, summarize (1) key quality factors and quality requirements to achieve leadership; and (2) key company performance requirements.

b. outline of the company's principal short-term quality and company performance plans and goals: (1) summary of key requirements and key performance indicators deployed to work units and suppliers; and (2) resources committed for key requirements such as capital equipment, facilities, education and training, and personnel.

c. principal longer-term quality and company performance plans and goals, including key requirements and how they will be addressed.

d. two-to-five year projection of significant improvements using the most important quality and company performance indicators. Describe how quality and company performance might be expected to compare with competitors and key benchmarks over this time period. Briefly explain the comparison.

4.0 HUMAN RESOURCE DEVELOPMENT AND MANAGEMENT (150 POINTS)

The Human Resource Development and Management Category examines the key elements of how the company develops and realizes the full potential of the work force to pursue the company's quality and performance objectives. Also examined are the company's efforts to build and maintain an environment for quality excellence conducive to full participation and personal and organizational growth.

4.1 Human Resource Management (20 points)

Describe how the company's overall human resource development and management plans and practices support its quality and company performance plans and address all categories and types of employees.

Areas to Address

a. how human resource plans derive from quality and company performance plans (item 3.2). Briefly describe major human resource development initiatives or plans affecting (1) education, training, and related skill development; (2) recruitment; (3) involvement; (4) empowerment; and (5) recognition. Distinguish between the short-term (1 to 2 years) and the longer-term (3 years or more) plans as appropriate.

b. key quality, cycle time, and other performance goals and improvement methods for personnel practices such as recruitment, hiring, personnel actions, and services to employees. Describe key performance indicators used in the improvement of these personnel practices.

c. how the company evaluates and uses all employee-related data to improve the development and effectiveness of the entire work force. Describe how the company's evaluation and improvement processes address all types of employees.

Notes: (1) Human resource plans might include the following: mechanisms for promoting cooperation such as internal customer/supplier techniques or other internal partnerships; initiatives to promote labor-management cooperation, such as partnerships with unions; creation of modifications to recognition systems; mechanisms for increasing or broadening employee responsibilities; permitting employees to learn and use skills that go beyond current job assignments through redesign of work processes; creation of high performance work teams; and education and training initiatives. Plans might also include forming partnerships with educational institutions to develop employees or to help ensure the future supply of well-prepared employees.

(2) "Categories of employees" refers to the company's classification system used in its personnel practices and/or work assignments. "Types of employees" takes into account other factors, such as bargaining unit membership and demographic makeup. This includes gender, age, minorities, and the disabled.

(3) All employee-related data refers to data contained in personnel records as well as data described in items 4.2, 4.3, and 4.5.

4.2 Employee Involvement (40 points)

Describe the means available for all employees to contribute effectively to meeting the company's quality and performance objectives; summarize trends in involvement.

Areas to Address

a. management practices and specific mechanisms the company uses to promote employee contributions, individually and in groups, to quality and company performance objectives. Describe how and how quickly the company gives feedback to contributors.

b. company actions to increase employee empowerment, responsibility, and innovation. Briefly summarize principal goals for all categories of employees, based upon the most important requirements for each category.

c. key methods and key indicators the company uses to evaluate and improve the extent and effectiveness of involvement of all categories and types of employees.

d. trends in percent involvement for each category of employee. Use the most important indicator(s) of effective employee involvement for each category.

Note: Different involvement goals and indicators may be set for different categories of employees, depending on company needs and on the types of responsibilities of each employee category.

4.3 Employee Education and Training (40 points)

Describe how the company determines what quality and related education and training is needed by employees and how the company utilizes the knowledge and skills acquired; summarize the types of quality and related education and training received by employees in all categories.

Areas to Address

a. (1) how the company determines needs for the types and amounts of quality and related education and training to be received by all categories and types of employees. Address (a) relevance of education and training to company plans; (b) needs of individual employees; and (c) all work units having access to skills in problem analysis, problem solving, and process simplification; (2) methods for the delivery of education and training; and (3) how the company ensures on-the-job use and reinforcement of knowledge and skills.

b. summary and trends in quality and related education and training received by employees. The summary and trends should address (1) quality orientation of new employees; (2) percent of employees receiving quality and related education and training per employee annually; (3) average hours of quality education and training per employee annually; (4) percent of current employees who have received quality and related education and training; and (5) percent of employees who have received education and training in specialized areas such as design quality, statistical, and other quantitative problem-solving methods.

c. key methods and key indicators the company uses to evaluate and improve the effectiveness of its quality and related education and training for all categories and types of employees. Describe how the indicators take into account (1) education and training delivery effectiveness; (2) on-the-job performance improvement; and (3) employee growth.

Note: Quality and related education and training address the knowledge and skills employees need to meet their objectives as part of the company's quality and performance plans. This may include quality awareness, leadership, problem solving, meeting customer requirements, process analysis, process simplification, waste reduction, cycle time reduction, and other training that affects employee effectiveness and efficiency.

4.4 Employee Performance and Recognition (25 points)

Describe how the company's employee performance, recognition, promotion, compensation, reward, and feedback processes support the attainment of the company's quality and performance objectives.

Areas to Address

a. how the company's performance, recognition, promotion, compensation, reward, and feedback approaches for individuals and groups, including managers, support the company's quality and performance objectives. Address (1) how the approaches ensure that quality is reinforced relative to short-term financial considerations; and (2) how employees contribute to the company's performance and recognition approaches.

b.   trends in reward and recognition, by employee category, for contributions to the company's quality and performance objectives.

c.   key methods and key indicators the company uses to evaluate and improve the performance and recognition processes. Describe how the evaluation takes into account cooperation, participation by all categories and types of employees, and employee satisfaction.

4.5 Employee Well–Being and Morale (25 points)

Describe how the company maintains a work environment conducive to the well-being and growth of all employees; summarize trends and levels in key indicators of well-being and morale.

Areas to Address

a.   how well-being and morale factors such as health, safety, satisfaction, and ergonomics are included in quality improvement activities. Summarize principal improvement goals, methods, and indicators for each factor relevant and important to the company's work environment. For accidents and work-related health problems, describe how root causes are determined and how adverse conditions are prevented.

b.   mobility, flexibility, and retraining in job assignments to support employee development and/or to accommodate changes in technology, improved productivity, changes in work processes, or company restructuring.

c.   special services, facilities, and opportunities the company makes available to employees. These might include one or more of the following: counseling, assistance, recreational or cultural, nonwork-related education, and outplacement.

d.   how and how often employee satisfaction is determined.

e.   trends in key indicators of well-being and morale. This should address the following, as appropriate: satisfaction, safety, absenteeism, turnover, attrition rate for customer-contact personnel, grievances, strikes, and worker compensation. Explain important adverse results, if any. For such adverse results, describe how root causes were determined and corrected, or give current status. Compare results on the most significant indicators with those of industry averages, industry leaders, and other key benchmarks.

5.0 MANAGEMENT OF PROCESS QUALITY (140 POINTS)

The Management of Process Quality Category examines the systematic processes the company uses to pursue ever-higher quality and company performance. Examined are the key elements of process management, including design, management of process quality for all work units and suppliers, systematic quality improvement, and quality assessment.

5.1 Design and Introduction of Quality Products and Services (40 points)

Describe how new and/or improved products and services are designed and introduced and how processes are designed to meet key product and service quality requirements and company performance requirements.

Areas to Address

a. how designs of products, services, and processes are developed so that (1) customer requirements are translated into design requirements; (2) all quality requirements are addressed early in the overall design process by appropriate company units; (3) designs are coordinated and integrated to include all phases of production and delivery; and (4) a process control plan that involves selecting, setting, and monitoring key process characteristics is developed.

b. how designs are reviewed and validated, taking into account key factors: (1) product and service performance; (2) process capability and future requirements; and (3) supplier capability and future requirements.

c. how the company evaluates and improves the effectiveness of its designs and design processes so that new product and service introductions progressively improve in quality and cycle time.

281

Notes: (1) Design and introduction may include modification and variance of existing products and services and/or new products and services emerging from
research and development.

(2) Applicant response should reflect the key requirements of the products and
services they deliver. Factors that may need to be considered in design include health, safety, long-term performance, environment, measurement
capability, process capability, maintainability, and supplier capability.

(3) Service and manufacturing businesses should interpret product and service requirements to include all product- and service-related requirements
at all stages of production, delivery, and use.

5.2 Process Management—Product and Service Production and Delivery Processes (35 points)

Describe how the company's product and service production and delivery
processes are managed so that current quality requirements are met and
quality and performance are continuously improved.

Areas to Address

a. how the company maintains the quality of processes in accord
with product and service design requirements. Describe (1) what
is measured and types and frequencies of measurements; and
(2) how out-of-control occurrences are handled, including root
cause determination, correction, and verification of corrections.

b. how processes are analyzed and improved to achieve better quality, performance, and cycle time. Describe how the following
are considered: (1) process simplification; (2) waste reduction;
(3) process research and testing; (4) use of alternative technologies; and (5) benchmark information.

c. how overall product and service performance data are analyzed,
root causes determined, and results translated into process improvements.

d. how the company integrates process improvement with day-to-
day process management: (1) resetting process characteristics to
reflect the improvements; (2) verification of improvements; and
(3) ensuring effective use by all appropriate company units.

Notes: (1) For manufacturing and service companies that have specialized measurement requirements, a description of the method for measurement quality

assurance should be given. For physical, chemical, and engineering measurements, describe briefly how measurements are made traceable to national standards.

(2) The distinction between 5.2b and 5.2c is as follows: 5.2b addresses ongoing improvement activities of the company; 5.2c addresses performance information related to the use of products and services ("performance in the field"), including customer problems and complaints. Analysis in 5.2c focuses on the process level—root causes and process improvement.

5.3 Process Management—Business Processes and Support Services (30 points)

Describe how the company's business processes and support services are managed so that current requirements are met and quality and performance are continuously improved.

Areas to Address

a. how the company maintains the quality of the business processes and support services. Describe (1) how key processes are defined based upon customer and/or company quality performance requirements; (2) principal indicators used to measure quality and/or performance; (3) how day-to-day quality and performance are determined, including types and frequencies of measurements used; and (4) how out-of-control occurrences are handled, including root cause determination, correction, and verification of corrections.

b. how processes are improved to achieve better quality, performance, and cycle time. Describe how the following are used or considered: (1) process performance data; (2) process and organizational simplification and/or redefinition; (3) use of alternative technologies; (4) benchmark information; (5) information from customers of the business processes and support services—inside and outside the company; and (6) challenge goals.

Notes: (1) Business processes and support services might include activities and operations involving finance and accounting, software services, sales, marketing, information services, purchasing, personnel, legal services, plant and facilities management, basic research and development, and secretarial and other administrative services.

(2) The purpose of this item is to permit applicants to highlight separately the quality activities for functions that support the product and service

production and delivery processes the applicant addressed in item 5.2. The support services and business processes included in item 5.3 depend on the applicant's type of business and quality system. Thus, this selection should be made by the applicant. Together, items 5.1, 5.2, 5.3, 5.4, and 5.5 should cover all operations, processes, and activities of all work units.

5.4 Supplier Quality (20 points)

Describe how the quality of materials, components, and services furnished by other businesses is assured and continuously improved.

Areas to Address

a. approaches used to define and communicate the company's quality requirements to suppliers: (1) the principal quality requirements for key suppliers; and (2) the principal indicators the company uses to communicate and monitor supplier quality.

b. methods used to assure that the company's quality requirements are met by suppliers. Describe how the company's overall performance data are analyzed and relevant information fed back to suppliers.

c. current strategies and actions to improve the quality and responsiveness (delivery time) of suppliers. These may include partnerships, training, incentives and recognition, and supplier selection.

Notes: (1) The term "supplier" as used here refers to other-company providers of goods and services. The use of these goods and services may occur at any stage in the production, delivery, and use of the company's products and services. Thus, suppliers include businesses such as distributors, dealers, and franchises as well as those that provide materials and components.

(2) Methods may include audits, process reviews, receiving inspection, certification, testing, and rating systems.

5.5 Quality Assessment (15 points)

Describe how the company assesses the quality and performance of its systems, processes, and practices and the quality of its products and services.

Areas to Address

a. approaches the company uses to assess (1) systems, processes, and practices; and (2) products and services. For (1) and (2), describe (a) what is assessed; (b) how often assessments are made and by whom; and (c) how measurement quality and adequacy of documentation of processes and practices are assured.

b. how assessment findings are used to improve products and services, systems, processes, practices, and supplier requirements. Describe how the company verifies that assessment findings are acted on and that actions are effective.

Notes: (1) The systems, processes, practices, products, and services addressed in this item pertain to all company unit activities covered in items 5.1, 5.2, 5.3, and 5.4. If the approaches and frequency of assessments differ appreciably for different company activities, this should be described in this item.

(2) Adequacy of documentation should take into account legal, regulatory, and contractual requirements as well as knowledge preservation and transfer to help support all quality-related efforts.

6.0 QUALITY AND OPERATIONAL RESULTS (180 POINTS)

The Quality and Operational Results Category examines the company's quality levels and improvement trends in quality, company operational performance, and supplier quality. Also examined are current quality and performance levels relative to those of competitors.

6.1 Product and Service Quality Results (75 points)

Summarize trends in quality and current quality levels for key product and service features; compare the company's current quality levels with those of competitors.

Areas to Address

a. trends and current levels for all key measures of product and service quality

b. current quality level comparisons with principal competitors in the company's key markets, industry averages, industry leaders, and others as appropriate. Briefly explain bases for comparison such as (1) independent surveys, studies, or laboratory testing; (2) benchmarks; and (3) company evaluations and testing. Describe how objectivity and validity of comparisons are assured.

Notes: (1) Key product and service measures are measures relative to the set of all important features of the company's product and services. These measures, taken together, best represent the most important factors that predict customer satisfaction and quality in customer use. Examples include measures of accuracy, reliability, timeliness, performance, behavior, delivery, after-sales services, documentation, and appearance.

(2) Results reported in item 6.1 should reflect the key product and service features described in the Overview.

(3) Data reported in item 6.1 are intended to be results of company ("internal") measurements—not customer satisfaction or other customer data, reported in Items 7.4 and 7.5. If the quality of some key product or service features cannot be determined effectively through internal measures, external data may be used. Examples include data collected by the company, as in item 7.1c, data collected by third-party organizations on behalf of the company, and data collected by independent organizations. Such data should provide information on the company's performance relative to specific product and service features, not on levels of overall satisfaction. These data, collected regularly, are then part of a system for measuring quality, monitoring trends, and improving processes.

6.2 Company Operational Results (45 points)

Summarize trends and levels in overall company operational performance, and provide a comparison of this performance with competitors and appropriate benchmarks.

Areas to Address

a. trends and current levels for key measures of company operational performance

b. comparison of performance with that of competitors, industry averages, industry leaders, and key benchmarks. Give and briefly explain basis for comparison.

Note: Key measures of company operational performance include those that address productivity, efficiency, and effectiveness. Examples should include generic indicators such as use of manpower, materials, energy, capital, and assets. Trends and levels could address productivity indices, waste reduction, energy efficiency, cycle time reduction, environmental improvement, and other measures of improved overall company performance. Also include company-specific indicators the company uses to monitor its progress in improving operational performance. Such company-specific indicators should be defined in tables or charts where trends are presented. Trends in financial indicators, properly labeled, may be included in this item. If such financial indicators are used, there should be a clear connection to the quality and performance improvement activities of the company.

6.3 Business Process and Support Service Results (25 points)

Summarize trends and current levels in quality and performance improvement for business processes and support services.

Areas to Address

a. trends and current levels for key measures of quality and performance of business processes and support services

b. comparison of performance with appropriately selected companies and benchmarks. Give and briefly explain basis for comparison.

Note: Business processes and support services are those as covered in item 5.3. Key measures of performance should reflect the principal quality, productivity, cycle time, cost, and other effectiveness requirements for business processes and support services. Responses should reflect relevance to the company's principal quality and company performance objectives addressed in company plans, contributing to the results reported in items 6.1 and 6.2. They should also demonstrate broad coverage of company business processes, support services, and work units and reflect the most important objectives of each process, service, or work unit.

6.4 Supplier Quality Results (35 points)

Summarize trends in quality and current quality levels of suppliers; compare the company's supplier quality with that of competitors and with key benchmarks.

Areas to Address

a. trends and current levels for the most important indicators of supplier quality.

b. comparison of the company's supplier quality levels with those of competitors and/or with benchmarks. Such comparisons could be industry averages, industry leaders, principal competitors in the company's key markets, and appropriate benchmarks. Describe the basis for comparisons.

Note: The results reported in item 6.4 derive from quality improvement activities described in item 5.4. Results should be broken down by major groupings of suppliers and reported using the principal quality indicators described in item 5.4.

7.0 CUSTOMER FOCUS AND SATISFACTION (300 POINTS)

The Customer Focus and Satisfaction Category examines the company's relationships with customers and its knowledge of customer requirements and of the key quality factors that determine marketplace competitiveness. Also examined are the company's methods to determine customer satisfaction, current trends and levels of satisfaction, and these results relative to competitors.

7.1 Customer Relationship Management (65 points)

Describe how the company provides effective management of its relationships with its customers and uses information gained from customers to improve customer relationship management strategies and practices.

Areas to Address

a. how the company determines the most important factors in maintaining and building relationships with customers and develops strategies and plans to address them. Describe these factors and how the strategies take into account fulfillment of basic customer needs in the relationship; opportunities to enhance the relationships; provision of information to customers to ensure the proper setting of expectations regarding products, services, and relationships; and roles of all customer-contact employees, their technology needs, and their logistics support.

b. how the company provides information and easy access to enable customers to seek assistance, to comment, and to complain. Describe types of contact and how easy access is maintained for each type.

c. follow-up with customers on products, services, and recent transactions to help build relationships and to seek feedback for improvement.

d. how service standards that define reliability, responsiveness, and effectiveness of customer-contact employees' interactions with customers are set. Describe how standards requirements are deployed to other company units that support customer-contact employees, how the overall performance of the service standards system is monitored, and how it is improved using customer information.

e. how the company ensures that formal and informal complaints and feedback received by all company units are aggregated for overall evaluation and use throughout the company. Describe how the company ensures that complaints and problems are resolved promptly and effectively.

f. how the following are addressed for customer-contact employees: (1) selection factors; (2) career path; (3) special training to include knowledge of products and services; listening to customers; soliciting comments from customers; how to anticipate and handle problems or failures ("recovery"); skills in customer retention; and how to manage expectations; (4) empowerment and decision making; (5) attitude and morale determination; (6) recognition and reward; and (7) attrition.

g. how the company evaluates and improves its customer relationship management practices. Describe key indicators used in evaluations and how evaluations lead to improvements, such as in strategy, training, technology, and service standards.

Notes: (1) Information on trends and levels in indicators of complaint response time and trends in percent of complaints resolved on first contact should be reported in item 6.3.

(2) In addressing empowerment and decision making in 7.1f, indicate how the company ensures that there is a common vision or basis guiding customer-contact employee action.

7.2 Commitment to Customers (15 points)

Describe the company's explicit and implicit commitments to customers regarding its products and services.

Areas to Address

a.   types of commitments the company makes to promote trust and confidence in its products, services, and relationships. Describe how these commitments (1) address the principal concerns of customers; and (2) are free from conditions that might weaken customer confidence.

b.   how improvements in the quality of the company's products and services over the past three years have been translated into stronger commitments. Compare commitments with those of competitors.

c.   how the company evaluates and improves its commitments, and the customers' understanding of them, to avoid gaps between expectations and delivery.

Note: Commitments may include product and service guarantees, product warranties, and other understandings with the customer, expressed or implied.

7.3 Customer Satisfaction Determination (35 points)

Describe the company's methods for determining customer satisfaction and customer satisfaction relative to competitors; describe how these methods are evaluated and improved.

Areas to Address

a.   how the company determines customer satisfaction. Include (1) a brief description of market segments and customer groups and the key customer satisfaction requirements for each segment or group; (2) how customer satisfaction measurements capture key information that reflects customers' likely market behavior; and (3) a brief description of the methods, processes, and scales used; frequency of determination; and how objectivity and validity are assured.

b.   how customer satisfaction relative to that for competitors is determined. Describe (1) company-based comparative studies; and

(2) comparative studies or evaluations made by independent organizations, including customers. For (1) and (2) describe how objectivity and validity are assured.

c. how the company evaluates and improves its overall processes and measurement scales for determining customer satisfaction and customer satisfaction relative to that for competitors. Describe how other indicators (such as gains and losses of customers) and customer dissatisfaction indicators (such as complaints) are used in this improvement process.

Notes: (1) Customer satisfaction measurement may include both a numerical rating scale and descriptors assigned to each unit in the scale. An effective customer satisfaction measurement system is one that provides the company with reliable information about customer views of specific product and service features and the relationship between these views or ratings and the customer's likely market behaviors.

(2) Indicators of customer dissatisfaction include complaints, claims, refunds, recalls, returns, repeat services, litigation, replacements, downgrades, repairs, warranty work, and warranty costs. If the company has received any sanctions under regulation or contract during the past three years, include such information in the item. Briefly summarize how sanctions were resolved or give current status.

(3) Company-based or independent organization comparative studies in 7.3b may take into account one or more indicators of customer dissatisfaction.

7.4 Customer Satisfaction Results (75 points)

Summarize trends in the company's customer satisfaction and trends in key indicators of dissatisfaction.

Areas to Address

a. trends and current levels in indicators of customer satisfaction, segmented as appropriate

b. trends and current levels in indicators of customer dissatisfaction. Address all indicators relevant to the company's products and services.

Notes: (1) Results reported in this item derive from methods described in item 7.3 and 7.1c and e.

(2) Indicators of customer dissatisfaction are listed in item 7.3, note 2.

7.5 Customer Satisfaction Comparison (75 points)

Compare the company's customer satisfaction results with those of competitors.

Areas to Address

a.   trends and current levels in indicators of customer satisfaction relative to that for competitors, based upon methods described in item 7.3. Segment by customer group, as appropriate.

b.   trends in gaining or losing customers, or customer accounts, to competitors

c.   trends in gaining or losing market share to competitors

Note: Competitors include domestic and international ones in the company's markets, both domestic and international.

7.6 Future Requirements and Expectations of Customers (35 points)

Describe how the company determines future requirements and expectations of customers.

Areas to Address

a.   how the company addresses future requirements and expectations of customers. Describe (1) the time horizon for the determination; (2) how data from current customers are projected; (3) how customers of competitors and other potential customers are considered; and (4) how important technological, competitive, societal, economic, and demographic factors and trends that may bear upon customer requirements and expectations are considered.

b.   how the company projects key product and service features and the relative importance of these features to customers and potential customers. Describe how potential market segments and customer groups are considered. Include considerations that address new product/service lines as well as current products and services.

c. how the company evaluates and improves its processes for determining future requirements and expectations of customers. Describe how the improvement process considers new market opportunities and extension of the time horizon for the determination of customer requirements and expectations.

APPENDIX B

Resources

Malcolm Baldrige National Quality Award
National Institute of Standards and Technology (NIST)
Route 270 and Quince Orchard Road
Administration Building, Room A537
Gaithersburg, MD 20899
Telephone: 301-975-2036
Fax: 301-948-3716

American Society for Quality Control
P.O. Box 3005
Milwaukee, WI 53201-3005
Telephone: 800-952-6587

BALDRIGE AWARD WINNERS

1991

Solectron Corporation
Bill Barley
Vice-President, Business Development
2001 Fortune Drive
San Jose, CA 95131
Telephone: 408-942-2939
Fax: 408-262-3311

Zytec Corporation
Karen Scheldroup
Baldrige Office
7575 Market Place Drive
Eden Prairie, MN 55344
Telephone: 612-941-1100, ext.104
Fax: 612-829-1837

Marlow Industries
Raymond Marlow
President & CEO
10451 Vista Park Road
Dallas, TX 75238-1645
Telephone: 214-340-4900
Fax: 214-341-5212

1990

Federal Express Corporation
John West
Manager, Corporate Quality Improvement
2605 Nonconnah Blvd.
Memphis, TN 38132
Telephone: 901-922-5454
Fax: 901-922-4451

Wallace Co., Inc.
John H. Wallace
Chief Executive Officer
P.O. Box 2597
Houston, TX 77252-2597
Telephone: 713-672-5803
Fax: 713-672-5815

Cadillac Motor Car Company
Jeff Clark
Manager, Baldrige Communications
2860 Clark Street
Detroit, MI 48232
Telephone: 313-554-7029
Fax: 313-554-7128

IBM Rochester
Center of Excellence
3605 Highway 52 North
Rochester, MN 55901-7829
Telephone: 507-253-9000
Fax: 507-253-4567

1989

Milliken & Company
Greg Easterlin
Vice-President, Quality
P.O. Box 1926, M-181
Spartanburg, SC 29304
Telephone: 803-573-2003
Fax: 803-573-2505

Xerox Corporation
Business Products and Systems
John F. Cooney
Manager, National Quality Award
Communications & Promotion Office
1387 Fairport Road
Building 810-01A
Fairport, NY 14450
Telephone: 716-383-7506
Fax: 716-383-7517

1988

Globe Metallurgical, Inc.
Public Relations/Quality
P.O. Box 157
Beverly, OH 45715
Telephone: 614-984-2361
Fax: 614-984-8695

Motorola, Inc.
Richard Buetow
Senior Vice-President and Director of Quality
1303 East Algonquin Road
Schaumburg, IL 60196
Telephone: 708-576-5516
Fax: 708-538-2663

Westinghouse Electric Corporation
Commercial Nuclear Fuel
Division
Michelle DeWitt
Manager, Total Quality
P.O. Box 355
Pittsburgh, PA 15230-0355
Telephone: 412-374-2274
Fax: 412-374-2624

APPENDIX C

After the Win

A fter Cadillac had its site visit, but before the Secretary of Commerce called to tell them they won, William Lesner put together a list of what would have to be done if Cadillac won the Baldrige Award. Work on the items marked with an "*" had to be in progress or completed before the phone rang.

1. Award Announcement*
   Communication to employees
   — Timing so employees hear from management, not media
   — Location
   Press conference
   Press kits
   Banners

2. Award Ceremony*
   Press kits
   Satellite broadcasting
   — Who will be watching?
   — Format?
   — Lead-in interviews?
   — Informational videos?
   Interviews (TV, radio, print, ad hoc, video)
   Selection of who to attend
   Other logistical details in Washington, DC
   Acceptance speech
   Luncheon speech
   Trophy handling

3. Standard Presentation Development
   Speeches (various versions)
   — Long and short "outside" versions
   — "Internal" version

— Specific emphasis (i.e., engineering, sales/zones, market-
ing, personnel, etc.)
Media (slides, videos, overheads, video disk, etc.)
Handout material (see standard information package)
Carrying case
Process for obtaining feedback from audiences

4. Standard Information Package Development*
    Overview of company's processes
    Section by section summary
    Key Baldrige information
    Company information (i.e., advertising)

5. Special Presentation Development
    Washington, DC "Quest for Excellence" conference
    — Six speeches, two workshops, company display, videos
    Three Baldrige regional conferences
    One-time requests
    Category presentations

6. Process for Dealing with Speaking Requests*
    What to accept? (how to deal with those denied)
    Who will speak?
    What will be presented?
    Who will approve?

7. Process for Dealing with Information Requests*
    Telephone call questions
    Standard information package
    Specific information requests
    Benchmarking requests
    Press release packages
    Responses to congratulations letters

8. Advertising Interface*
    Internal divisional guidelines
    Corporate interface
    Clearinghouse for approval
    Information for zones and dealerships

9. Facilities Tours*
    Who will schedule?
    What facilities?

Who will perform tours?
Who will make presentations?

10. "Quality Day" or Quality Forum?
    Frequency (if at all)
    Agenda
    Presentations
    Logistics
    Etc.

11. Baldrige Trophy Logistics
    Tour route
    Traveling and permanent cases
    Security
    Cleaning

Index